Edwin Abbott Abbott

How to Parse

an attempt to apply the principles of scholarship to English grammar - with

appendixes on analysis, spelling, and punctuation

Edwin Abbott Abbott

How to Parse

an attempt to apply the principles of scholarship to English grammar - with appendixes on analysis, spelling, and punctuation

ISBN/EAN: 9783337313142

Printed in Europe, USA, Canada, Australia, Japan

Cover: Foto ©Paul-Georg Meister /pixelio.de

More available books at **www.hansebooks.com**

HOW TO PARSE.

An Attempt to Apply the Principles of Scholarship

TO

ENGLISH GRAMMAR.

WITH APPENDIXES

ON

ANALYSIS, SPELLING, AND PUNCTUATION.

BY THE

REV. EDWIN A. ABBOTT, D.D.,

Head Master of the City of London School.

FIFTEENTH THOUSAND.

SEELEY, JACKSON, & HALLIDAY, FLEET STREET,
LONDON. MDCCCLXXXIII.

LONDON:
R. CLAY, SONS, AND TAYLOR, PRINTERS,
BREAD STREET HILL.

PREFACE.

THE First Part of this book is intended for pupils so far advanced as to be able to distinguish the *Parts of Speech*. The author's object has been to teach elementary English Grammar as simply as is consistent with the honest recognition of difficulties, and not to accumulate masses of information that might be of use to foreigners, but must be useless to English boys.

I have been accused, by a very friendly and favourable reviewer, of " unkindness " in completely ignoring the " Article " in my introductory treatise *How to Tell the Parts of Speech*. It has occurred to me, in consequence, to prefix to this work a *Glossary of Grammatical Terms*—many of them, let us hope, obsolete or obsolescent. Here the pupil may now and then refresh his memory as to the meaning of *Article, Genitive, Nominative, Accusative, Case, Proper Noun, Conjugation, Decline*, and the like ; and by this means he will be able to satisfy himself that many of these terms, when applied to the Grammar of his native tongue, are absolutely superfluous or erroneous. It is also probable that ready access to a Glossary, explaining etymologically *Cardinal, Inflection, Apostrophe, Climax, Bathos, Verse*, &c., may in many cases be of positive as well as negative benefit.

The Exercises are specially written to illustrate the rules. This has involved some labour ; but I am convinced that the labour was well spent. A pupil cannot be regarded as thoroughly tested in his knowledge of grammatical rules till he has applied them to *connected* narrative. As long as he is tested in nothing but short sentences, you can never feel sure that his accuracy is not merely mechanical.

Paragraphs 1—82 are of a much simpler character than those that follow; and the pupil should be well drilled in them before passing onward. The grammar-lessons of three or four months may be very well spent in teaching boys how to select the Subjects and Objects of the different Verbs in a Sentence, and a month or two more may well be given to Relative Sentences. Indeed, if the majority of a class of boys, between 11 and 12 years old, can, after six months' training in grammar, parse "jay" in:—

"The jay that robbed the other birds of their feathers was afterwards punished for robbing them"—

I should, myself, think the six months spent to very good purpose.

Paragraphs 82—162 are decidedly more difficult, and constitute work for a higher class. The chapter on the Subjunctive Mood is put last, out of its place, owing to the extreme difficulty of the subject.

The chapter on Irregularities, Paragraphs 191—230, is of a different nature from the former part of the book. It is intended to prepare the pupil for Part II., and is an attempt to apply the principles of scholarship to the explanation of the irregularities of English Grammar. These principles are few, and capable of brief enunciation, viz., (1) that every *irregularity* is a deviation from a "*regula*" or rule; (2) that there must be some *attracting force* to produce this deviation; (3) that this attracting force is generally one of *three* causes, of which the "*confusion of two constructions*" is by far the most common. Simple and brief though they are, these principles require, as every teacher knows, careful and constant inculcation before the pupil is imbued with them. But when the pupil has once mastered them, he has the key to unlock any idiomatic irregularity, in any language—always provided that he is well acquainted with the particular language in its *regular* expressions.

Not much space is given to Analysis; but perhaps as much as the subject deserves. If this subject is to be taught at all—and there is much in it that constitutes a useful mental exercise—it ought, in the opinion of the author, to be disencumbered of its present technicalities, and to be taught more logically. For example, in most treatises on Analysis, it is assumed that, in such a sentence as :—

"Feeling the man's hand in my pocket I turned suddenly round,"

—the words "feeling the man's hand" are an Adjective Phrase, or "Enlargement of the Subject." But nothing surely ought to be more obvious than that (whatever the grammatical construction may be) "feeling" here *means* "*when*, or *because* I felt," and is nearly the same as "*on* feeling;" so that the words in question form *really* an Adverbial, and not an Adjectival Phrase. It is almost startling that this Adjectival error should have been gravely inculcated for a generation in the best, as in the worst, treatises on English Grammar. Possibly the servile imitation of Latin Grammar—the ruin of all good English teaching—has been at work here, as in so many other cases, assimilating the English to the Latin Active Participle, and ignoring the extent to which the English Participle has been merged in the English Verbal Noun.[1]

For these reasons, in the Chapter on Analysis, several changes have been introduced with the view of discarding technicalities: and the terms *Phrase*, *Clause* and *Sentence*, are rigidly used according to their definitions. (See Glossary and also Par. 239.)[2]

In the "Hints on Spelling," Paragraphs 266—291, an attempt has been made to give explanations, or

[1] See Paragraphs 585—595.
[2] I gladly acknowledge my obligation to Mr. Mason for his excellent method of indicating the Subordination of Sentences by underlining.

suggestions of possible explanations, of a few among the thousand anomalies that strew this wilderness and despair of teachers. The author has at least succeeded (Par. 283) in impressing upon himself, what he never could remember before, the right spelling of "succeed," "proceed," and "exceed." Whether others will derive the same benefit from the explanation is perhaps doubtful; but the mere fact that an explanation exists is a just cause for thanksgiving. Mr. Laurie's useful *Manual of Spelling* has been of great service in the composition of this chapter.

Part II. Chapter I., is explained by its title, "Difficulties and Irregularities in Modern English." It is intended for the higher (not for the highest) classes in our first-grade schools. Here I must acknowledge very large obligations to Mätzner's two volumes on English Syntax. Adopting his arrangement, I have selected from these two volumes every difficulty that appeared *likely to be a difficulty to an English boy*—I believe I may add, in many cases, to an English man—*as distinct from a foreigner*. A few examples from Campbell, Scott, and Byron have been quoted from Mätzner, unverified; but in such cases, the reader is always warned by a foot-note. The vast majority of the examples have been modified or re-written to illustrate the difficulty under consideration, or they are the fruits of my own reading.

In this part of the work it has been of course necessary to illustrate modern English by older English of different periods: and here, while again acknowledging my obligations to Mätzner, I must also add the name of Dr. Morris, whose elaborate *Historical Outlines of English Accidence*—a book that, the more you study it, impresses you the more with the feeling that much is left to study—have been laid under large contributions for this part of my work, and more especially for the Appendix on the "Growth of the English language." Here I have also to acknowledge the invaluable assistance of Mr. Skeat, who was kind enough to correct the proof-sheets of the Appendix, and from whose

PREFACE. ix

edition of the Gospel of St. Mark[1] I derived great help in obtaining an insight into the "Period of Confusion" in early English. I have had the less hesitation in occasionally referring to statements and examples about early English found in the *Shakespearian Grammar*, because all of these were supervised and many of them originated by Mr. Skeat, but for whose kindness and learning I should scarcely have ventured on ground of which it may be said, no less than of the field of criticism, that—

"Fools rush in where angels fear to tread."

The chapter on Poetical Constructions will, I hope, be found as useful as any in the book. It is an attempt to draw out in grammatical detail the principles of poetry as laid down by Professor Seeley and myself in *English Lessons for English People*, and to lead the pupil to see the reason and the beauty of "poetical irregularities."

In the Appendix on the "Growth of the English Language," I have ventured so far to differ from Dr. Morris, in his account of the "Periods of the English Language," as to assign a separate period to the sixteenth century, and also to give names to the several periods. I do not think boys will find it easy to remember the periods without epithets of a rather more picturesque nature than ordinal numbers. I have also added some remarks on the Elizabethan period.

A few tables of the Early Forms are added in the Appendix with the view of illustrating remarks scattered through the book. But no attempt has been made to give any complete system of *Accidence*. To try to do this completely, in the face of Dr. Morris's *Accidence*, would have been superfluous: and to do it imperfectly, in the way in which it has been done in many Grammars, under the title of "Etymology,"

[1] The Gospel according to St. Mark, in Anglo-Saxon and Northumbrian Versions, Synoptically Arranged. Edited for the Syndics of the University Press by the Rev. Walter W. Skeat, M.A. Cambridge: Deighton, Bell, & Co. 1871.

would have been worse than superfluous, mystifying English children by telling them *what*, when they know *what* well enough already, and need only to be told *why*. But to tell the *why* of English Accidence requires—and it is useless disguising the fact—a great deal of knowledge in the teacher and not a little in the pupil. If it is to be done at all, it should be done thoroughly, with the aid of such a book as Dr. Morris's, and by pupils old enough to appreciate it.

Consequently, though the pupil will find "strong" and "weak" verbs defined in the Glossary, he will see no lists of them in the book. Lists of irregular plurals will also be missing; the teacher will look in vain for *focus, foci; datum, data; nebula, nebulæ*. The only apparent sacrifice to the mania for "learning something by heart" is this, that the modern verb will be found "conjugated" in the Appendix to Part II. But this has been done, not to give the pupil something to learn by heart, but to enable him to compare the old verb with the new at a glance. Throughout the book, the author has endeavoured to keep in view the main object of a teacher teaching English grammar to English children, viz., to teach, not so much *what* as *why*.

The division of the book into parts, the first of which is differently arranged from the second, might cause some difficulty in referring, were it not that a full Alphabetical Index is inserted at the end—an appendage that, in the Author's opinion, may fairly claim to be accepted as a compensation, in a book of this kind, for many faults of non-arrangement or mis-arrangement.

In passing the book through the press I have derived most valuable assistance from the two gentlemen whose names I had occasion to mention in the preface to *How to Tell the Parts of Speech*, viz., Mr. G. S. Brockington, one of the Assistant Masters of King Edward's School, Birmingham, and Mr. T. W. Chambers, B.A., Scholar of Sidney Sussex College, Cambridge, one of the Assistant Masters of the City of London School, whose sound judgment and practical experience have frequently induced me to modify or even re-cast large portions of the First Part. I must also mention two others among my colleagues, Mr. T. Todd, and Mr. James Pirie, M.A., whose criticism and corrections have been of very great service.

Lastly, while expressing my obligations to the admirable "Shakespeare Lexicon," compiled by Dr. Schmidt, and published by Messrs. Williams & Norgate, I may be also permitted, coming nearer home, to say that I have gained much help and many apt examples from the inspection of the proof-sheets of a *Complete Concordance to the Poetical Works of Pope*, compiled by my father, and now in course of publication.

CONTENTS.[1]

PART I.

ETYMOLOGICAL GLOSSARY OF GRAMMATICAL TERMS . xvii
RULES AND DEFINITIONS xxviii

CHAPTER I.
SUBJECT AND OBJECT 1

CHAPTER II.
THE RELATIVE PRONOUN 17

CHAPTERS III. AND IV.
USES AND INFLECTIONS :
    I. Nouns, Pronouns, Adjectives, &c. 28
    II. Verbs 45

[1] For all detailed reference the reader is referred to the Alphabetical Index at the end of the book.

CHAPTER V.
THE INDIRECT OBJECT, &c. 88

CHAPTER VI.
THE SUBJUNCTIVE MOOD 112

CHAPTER VII.
IRREGULARITIES 127

APPENDIX I.
THE ANOMALIES OF THE SUBJUNCTIVE MOOD . . . 148

APPENDIX II.
THE ANALYSIS OF SENTENCES 153
SCHEME OF ANALYSIS 172

APPENDIX III.
HINTS ON SPELLING 174

APPENDIX IV.
HINTS ON PUNCTUATION 185

SCHEME OF PARSING 195

PART II.

DIFFICULTIES AND IRREGULARITIES IN MODERN ENGLISH.

CHAPTER I.
PROSE 199

CHAPTER II.
POETICAL CONSTRUCTIONS 281

APPENDIX.
ON THE GROWTH OF THE ENGLISH LANGUAGE . . 293

ALPHABETICAL INDEX. 327

ETYMOLOGICAL GLOSSARY

OF

GRAMMATICAL TERMS.

FEW of the terms explained below are used by the author, and many of them are misused or badly constructed, e.g. "article," "accusative." But, as they are used in many grammatical treatises, it has been thought desirable to explain them, especially as an explanation is sometimes the best means of proving them to be superfluous or erroneous, when applied to English Grammar.

The References, when not otherwise stated, are to the *Paragraphs* in *How to Parse*.

The meaning given opposite to each word is the *Etymological* meaning. For a fuller or more accurate definition the pupil is referred to the Paragraph mentioned in each case.

Ablative (Case) [L. *ab.*, "from;" *latus*, "carried"]. The name for a Latin case denoting, among other things, *ablation*, or *carrying away from.*

Absolute (Construction) [L. *ab*, "from;" *solut-*, "loosed"]. A construction in which a Noun, Participle, &c., is used apart, *i.e. loosed from*, its ordinary Grammatical adjuncts (Par. 135).

Abstract (Noun) [L. *abs*, "from;" *tract-*, "drawn"]. The name of an *abstraction*, *i.e.* of something considered by itself, apart from (*drawn away from*) the circumstances in which it exists.

Accent [L. *ad*, "to;" *cantus*, "song"]. Perhaps originally a sing-*song*, or modulation of the voice, added *to* a syllable. Now used of stress laid on a syllable.

Accidence [L. *accident*—"befall"]. That part of grammar which treats of the changes that *befall* words.[1]

Accusative (Case).[2] The Latin name for the Direct Objective Inflexion. Pos-

---

[1] Quintilian I. 5, 41 : "frequentissime in verbo, quia plurima huic *accidunt.*"

[2] Probably a Latin mistake. The Greek original meant (1) *cause*, (2) *accusation*. The Latins took it in sense (2) instead of (1).

sibly the Romans regarded the object as being in front of the agent, like an *accused* person confronted with the prosecutor.

Active (Voice). The form of a Verb that usually denotes *acting* or doing.

Adjective [L. *ad*, "to;" *jact*, "cast or put"]. A word *put to* a Noun.

Aphæresis [Gr. *ap*, "from;" *hairesis*, "taking"]. Taking a letter or syllable *from* the beginning of a word.

Adjunct [L. *ad*, "to;" *junct*, "joined"]. A word grammatically *joined to* another word.

Adverb [L. *ad*, "to;" *verb*, "word" or "Verb"]. A word generally joined *to* a Verb (45).

Adversative [L. *adversus*, "opposite"]. An epithet applied to Conjunctions that (like "but") express *opposition*.

Affix [L. *ad*, "to;" *fix*, "fixed"]. A syllable or letter *fixed to* the end of a word.

Agreement. The change made in the inflections of words so that they may suit or *agree* with one another in a sentence. (78).

Alexandrine. A rhyming verse of twelve Iambic syllables, said to be so called from its being used in an old French Poem on *Alexander* the Great.

Alphabet [Gr. *alpha, beta;* "a," "b"]. The list of letters, so called from the names of the first two letters in Greek.

Anacolouthon [Gr. *a-*, "not;" *acolouthon*, "following"]. A break in the Grammatical sequence, or *following*.

Analysis [Gr. *ana*, "back;" *lusis*, "loosing"]. *Unloosing* anything (*e.g.* a Sentence) *back* into its constituent parts. Hence an *analytical* period in a language. See Par. 556.

Anomaly. A Greek-formed word meaning "unevenness," "irregularity."

Antecedent [L. *ante*, "before;" *cedent*, "going"]. (*a*) That part of a sentence which expresses a condition (167). So called because the condition must *go before* its consequence. See *consequent* (2). (*b*) Also used for the Noun that *goes before* a Relative Pronoun.

Anti-climax. The opposite of a *climax*. A sentence in which the meaning sinks in importance, instead of rising at the close.

Antithesis [Gr. *anti*, "against;" *thesis*, "placing"]. The *placing* of word *against* word, by way of contrast.[1]

Apodosis [Gr. *apodosis*, "a paying back"]. A Greek name for the "Consequent." The condition was regarded by the Greeks as demanding its consequence, as a sort of *debt*, to be *paid* in return for the fulfilment of the condition.

[1] See *How to Write Clearly*, Par. 41.

GRAMMATICAL TERMS.

Apostrophe [Gr. *apo*, "from;" *strophe*, "turning"]. A mark shewing a vowel is omitted, so called because it is *turned away* from the next consonant.[1]

Appellative [L. *appella*, "call to."] Another name for the *Vocative* or *calling* use of a noun. Paragraph 32.

Apposition [L. *ad*, "near;" *posit*, "placed"]. The *placing* of one noun or pronoun *near* another, for the purpose of explanation (137).

Archaism [Gr. *archaios*, "ancient"]. An *ancient* word or expression.

Article [L. *articulus*, "a little joint or limb"]. A name(*a*) correctly given by the Greeks to their "article" because it served as a *joint* uniting several words together: (*b*) then loosely used by the Latins (as was natural seeing they had no "article") of any short word whether Verb, Conjunction, or Pronoun; (*c*) foolishly introduced into English, and once used to denote "the" and "a."

Aspirate [L. *ad*, "to;" *spira-*, "breathe"]. The strongly *breathed* letter, *h*.

Asyndeton [Gr. *a*, "not;" *syndeton*, "bound together"]. The omission of Conjunctions, so that sentences are *not bound together*.

Attribute. A quality *attributed* to a person or thing.

Auxiliary (Verbs) [L. *auxilia-*, "to help"]. Verbs that are used as *helpers* or companions to other Verbs (95).

Bathos [Gr. *bathos*, "depth"]. A ludicrous fall to a depth, *i.e.* a descent from the elevated to the mean in writing or speech.[2]

Cardinal (Numbers) [L. *cardin-*, "hinge."]. That on which anything *hinges* or turns: hence, "important," "principal." A name given to those more *important* forms of Numeral Adjectives from which the Ordinal forms are derived.

Case [L. *Casus*, "falling"]. The Latin translation of the Greek term for the uses of a Noun. The Greeks regarded the subjective form as "erect" and the other forms as more or less *falling* away from it. Hence the terms "oblique," "decline" &c.

Clause [L. *claus-*, "shut"]. A number of words *shut* up within limits. In this book the word is used of a sentence preceded by a Conjunction, the *sentence and Conjunction together* being called a Clause (239).

Climax [Gr. *climax*, "lad-

---

[1] In Rhetoric, the *apostrophe* is the *turning away from* one's audience to address some *absent* person. The old name for the Grammatical *apostrophe* was *apostrophus;* and this would be useful to distinguish it from the Rhetorical term.

[2] See Par. 40, *How to Write Clearly.*

b 2

der"]. The arrangement of a sentence like a *ladder* so that the meaning rises in force to the last.[1]

Cognate (Object) [L. *Co-*, "together;" *nat-* "born"]. The name given to an object that denotes something *akin* to (*born together with*) the action denoted by the Verb (125).

Colon [Gr. *colon,* "limb"]. The stop marking off a *limb* or member of a sentence.

Comma [Gr. *comma,* a "section"]. The stop marking off a *section* of a sentence (294-308).

Common (Noun). A name that is *common* to a class and not *peculiar* or *proper* to an individual.

Comparative (Degree). The form of an Adjective denoting that a quality exists in a greater degree in some one thing than in some other with which it is *compared*.

Complementary [L.*comple-*, "fill up"]. That which completes or *fills up* (97, 106).

Complete (State). A name given to an action (whether Past, Present, or Future) that was, is, or will be *complete* (72).

Complex (Sentence) [L. *con-* "together;" *plic-,* "fold"]. A sentence that is *folded together*, or involved. Hence a sentence containing one or more Subordinate sentences (250).

Compound (Sentence) [L. *con,* or *com,* "together;" *pon-* "place"]. A sentence made up of a number of Co-ordinate sentences *placed together* (247).

Concord. The name given to syntactical *agreement* between words, *e.g.* between Verb and Subject.

Conjugation [*con,* "together;" *jugatio* "joining"]. A number of Verbs *joined together* in one class.[2]

Conjunction [L. *con,* "together;" *junct-,*"joined"]. A word that *joins* two sentences *together.*

Consequent. The name given to that part of a Sentence which expresses the *consequence* of the fulfilment of a condition. See *Antecedent,* and Paragraph 167.

Consonant [L. *con,* "together;" *sonant-,* "sounding"]. Letters (such as *p*) that can only be *sounded together with* a vowel.

Continuous (State). The name given to an action (whether Past, Present, or Future) that is, was, or will be *continuing* or incomplete (72).

Copula [L. *copula,* "bond"]. The word "is," so called because it *binds* or connects Subject and Predicate *in* Logic.

Correlatives. Words that are *related together* or mutually related, *e.g.*,

---

[1] See Par. 39, *How to Write Clearly.*
[2] Hence to *conjugate* a Verb is to repeat the inflections belonging to the class or *conjugation.* But the Romans used *decline* and not *conjugate* in this sense (Madvig).

"either," "or ;" "both," "and ;" "when," "then."
Dative [L. *dativ*,[1] "that which has arisen from giving"]. The Latin name for the Indirect Objective case used after Verbs of *giving* &c. (126).
Declension. The bending or *declension* of the Oblique (see *Oblique* below) cases from the Subjective form, which was regarded as "erect." Hence applied to the statement of the cases of a Noun.
Definite (Article). A name given to the Adjective "the" from the fact that "the" *defines* its Noun. See *Article.*
Definition [L. *de*, "from :" *finit-*, "marked out," "bounded"]. That which *marks out the boundaries* of anything so as to distinguish it from all other things. N.B. *Not* a mere "description."
Degree (of comparison) [L. *gradus*, Fr. *degré*, "step"]. The forms expressing the *steps* or *degrees* in which a quality can be expressed by an Adjective.
Dentals [L. *dent-*, "tooth"]. Consonants pronounced with the aid of the *teeth* ; *d, n, t.*
Dependent(Sentence). Sometimes used for Subordinate. But generally applied to *Subordinate* sentences that are the Subjects or Objects of Verbs.
Diæresis [Gr. *diairesis*, "separation"]. The mark placed over one of two vowels to shew that each is to be pronounced *separately e.g.* in "aërial."
Diphthong [Gr. *di*,"twice;" *phthongos*, "sound"]. Two vowel sounds pronounced as one.
Direct"(Object). The Noun that denotes what is regarded as the *direct object* of the action of a Verb.[2]
Ellipsis [Gr. *elleipsis*, "omission"]. The *omission* of words (said to be "understood" *i.e.* implied) in a Sentence.
Emphasis [Gr. *emphaino*, "I make clear"]. Stress of the voice laid on particular words or syllables in order to make the meaning *clear.*
Epigram [Gr. *epi*, "on ;" *gramma*, "writing"]. A *writing on* a monument. Hence a short poem. Hence a short *pointed* poem or saying.[3]
Epithet [Gr. *epithetos*, "placed to"]. An Adjective *placed to* a Noun to describe some quality of the person or thing denoted by the Noun.
Etymology [Gr. *etymon*, "true meaning ;" *logia*,

---

[1] Termination *-ivus* in Latin, when added to Participles, denotes *that which has arisen from*, *e.g.* "captivus," that which has arisen from "*capture.*"
[2] See Par. 14.
[3] The *point* will generally be at the *end*. Intentional "bathos sometimes borders on "epigram." See *How to Write Clearly*, Par. 42

"science "]. The *science* of the *true* meaning of words, according to their derivation.

Euphony [Gr. *eu*, "well;" *phone*, "sound"]. That which *sounds well*.

Flat (Consonants). *B, d, g.*

Foot. The metrical subdivision of a verse. A verse being supposed to *run*, its limbs or members might well be called *feet*.

Frequentative (Verb). A Verb that expresses a *frequently* repeated action, *e.g.* "pat-t-*er*."

Gender [L. *genus*, Fr. *genre*, "breed," or "class"]. Forms to denote *class*ification according to sex. There are no inflexions for Genders in English (37).

Genitive (Case) [L. *genitiv-*, "generating"]. The name for the Latin case denoting *generation*, origination, possession. Sometimes applied to the English Possessive Inflection.[1]

Gerund [L. *gero*, "I carry on"]. Part of a Latin Verb denoting the *carrying on* of the action of the Verb. There was once a gerundive form in English (551).

Grammar [Gr. *gramma*, a "letter;" Fr. "*grammaire*"]. The science of *letters;* hence the science of using words correctly.

Gutturals [L. *guttur*,

"throat"]. *Throat* letters, *k*, and hard *g*.

Heterogeneous (Sentence) [Gr. *hetero*, "different;" *genos*, "kind"]. A Sentence combining a number of Sentences of so *different* a *kind* from each other that they ought not to be combined.[2]

Iambus [Gr. *iambos*]. In English, a foot of two syllables, the first unaccented, the second accented.

Idiom [Gr. *idioma*, "peculiarity"]. A mode of expression *peculiar* to a language.

Imperative (Mood). [L. *impera-*, "command"]. The *commanding* Mood (70).

Impersonal (Verbs). Verbs not used in the first or second *Person* (328).

Incomplete (State). The forms of the Verb denoting an action in an *Incomplete State* (72).

Indefinite (Article). A name given to "an," "a," because the Adjective leaves its Noun undefined, or *indefinite*. See *Article;* also *Definite*.

Indefinite (State). The forms of the Verb denoting an action of which the *State* is *not defined* (72).

Indicative (Mood), [L. *indica-*, "point out"]. The Mood that *points out* or *indicates* an action, &c.,

---

[1] The Latin "genitivus" is a mistranslation of the Greek *genike*, which meant the *generic* case *i.e.* the case, that denoted the *genus* or class. For example, "life," "What *class* of life?" "*Man's* life."

[2] See Par. 43, *How to Write Clearly*.

GRAMMATICAL TERMS. xxiii

as a past, present, or future existence (70).

Indirect (Object). The Noun or Pronoun denoting the person or thing regarded as not directly but only *indirectly* influenced by the action of the Verb. But see Paragraph 118 for a more satisfactory test.

Infinitive (Mood) [L. *in*, "not;" *finit-*, "limited"]. A Mood *not limited* by any definition of Person or Number (70).

Inflection [L. *inflecto*, "I bend"]. The *bending* of a word from the simple form, by means of varying the termination. See *Oblique* below.

Interjection [L. *inter-ject-*, "thrown between"]. An utterance *thrown* in *between* words, to express emotion. Not a Part of Speech.

Intransitive (Verb). [L. *in*, "not"; *transitiv-*, "passing across"]. A Verb whose action is not supposed to *pass across* to any Object. But see *Transitive* below.

Labials [L. *labium*, "lip"]. *Lip*-letters: *f, v, p, b, m, hw* (the real sound in *which*) and *w*.

Language [L. *lingua*, Fr. *langue;* "tongue"]. The expression of meaning by the *tongue*.

Linguals [Latin *lingua*, "the tongue"]. Letters whose sounds are produced by the *tongue: sh, s* in pleasure.

Liquids. Letters of a flowing, *liquid* sound, as *l, r*.

Metaphor [Gr. *meta*, "from one to another"; *phora*, "carrying"]. The *carrying* of a relation from one set of objects to another *e.g.* of the relation of ploughing from "plough" and "land," to "ship" and "sea." [1]

Metre [Gr. *metron*, "measure"]. The *measuring* of language out into verses.

Monosyllable [Gr. *mono*, "only"]. A word of *only one* syllable.

Mood [L. *mod-*, "manner".] The form of a Verb expressing the *manner* of action (70).

Mutes [L. *mut-*, "dumb"]. Letters that are *dumb* without the aid of a vowel: *k, g, t, d, n, p, b, m*.

Nasal [L. *nas-*, "nose"]. Consonants sounded through the *nose; n, m*.

Nominative (Case) [L. *nomina-*, "to name"]. An old Latin term for the Subject, used because the Subject was regarded as a person or thing *named*.

Noun [L. *nomen*, Fr. *nom*, "name"]. The *name* of anything.

Object. The word, or group of words, denoting that which is regarded as the object or mark aimed at by the action of a Verb or the motion of the Preposition. [2] (13). But see Definition in Paragraph 14.

[1] *English Lessons for English People*, page 78.
[2] This Definition, though in accordance with Etymology, is often Grammatically inapplicable.

xxiv ETYMOLOGICAL GLOSSARY OF

Oblique (Case). A name given to all Cases but the Subjective. By the Greeks the Subjective form of a Noun was regarded as *erect*, and all the other forms as *fallings* or *oblique* deviations from the Subjective.

Ordinal (Adjective) [L. *ordin-*, ' order ']. An Adjective, that answers to the question "in what order."

Orthography [Gr. *ortho*, "correct"; *grapho*, " I write"]. The *correct writing* of words, *i.e.* correct spelling. N.B. *Not* "calligraphy," "pretty writing."

Parenthesis [Gr. *para*, "aside"; *enthesis*, "insertion"]. A word, phrase, or sentence, *inserted aside*, or by the way, in a sentence complete without it.

Participle [L. *particip-*, "participating"]. A form of a Verb *participating* of the nature of a Verb, and of the nature of an Adjective.

Partitive [L. *part-*, "part"]. Denoting *partition*.

Passive (Voice) [L. *pass-*, "suffering"]. The form of a Verb in which the Subject is supposed to *suffer* an action[1] (60).

Palatals. Letters whose sounds are produced by the *palate: ch, j.*

Perfect (Tense) [L. *perfect-*, "complete"]. The Name for the Latin Tense that has to represent (owing to paucity of their Tenses) Indef. Past and Complete Present.

Period [Gr. *peri*, ("round"; *od-*, "path"]. (1) The full, *rounded path* of a complex sentence, (2) a mark at the end of a sentence.

Person [L. *per*, "through"; *son-*, "sound;" hence, *persona* "a mask *through* which an actor *sounds;*" "an actor's *part* in a play."]. The *part played* in conversation, whether (1) speaking; (2) spoken to; (3) spoken of (79).

Personification. Endowing what is impersonal with a Personal Character.[2]

Phrase [Gr. *phrasis*, a "saying"]. A group of words not expressing a statement, question, or command (239).

Pluperfect (Tense) [L. *plu-*, "more;" *perfect-*, "complete"]. A *more than complete* Tense. A Latin way of expressing the Complete Past.

Plural (Number) [L. *plu-*, "more"]. The form of a Noun that denotes *more* than one (34—36).

Poetry [Gr. *poietes*, a "maker"]. Language that is artistically *made*, as distinguished from that which is ordinarily written or spoken.

Polysyllable [Gr. *poly*, "many"]. A word of *many* syllables.

Positive. The simple form of an Adjective; so called

---

[1] This definition is unsatisfactory, see Par. 60.
[2] *English Lessons for English People*, page 131.

because it expresses a quality not comparatively, but *positively* (42).

Possessive (Use) [L. *poss-*, "possessed".] The name given to the use or case of a Noun denoting *possession* (37).

Potential (Mood) [L. *potent-* "powerful"]. An old name for a supposed Mood, which is really either the Mood of Purpose, or else simply the Indic. of an *Auxiliary* Verb. So called, because it involves the meaning of *power* or possibility.

Predicate [L. "*prœdica-*," "proclaim," "state"]. A word or group of words making a *statement* about a Subject (263).

Prefix [L. *præ*, "before;" *fix-*, "fixed"]. A letter, syllable, or word *fixed before* another word.

Preposition [L. *præ* "before;" *posit-*, "placed"]. A Word (not a Verb) *placed before* a Noun or Pronoun as its object.

Preterite (Tense) [L. *præterit-*, "past"]. A pedantical expression for "the *Past* Tense."

Protasis [Gr. *pro*, "before;" *tasis*, "stretching,"]. Literally, *stretching before*. Hence, in a sentence, the Antecedent or Condition. See *Apodosis*

Pronoun [L. *pro*, "for;" L. *nomen*, "noun"]. A word used *for* a *Noun*.

Proper (Noun). [L. *propri-*, F. *propre;* "peculiar"]. A name that is *peculiar* or *proper* to the individual, not common to a class. See *Common.*

Prose [L. *prosa*, for *prorsa*, for *pro-versa*,[1] *i.e.* "turned forward"]. Writing that does not *turn* like *verses* (see *Verse* below) but runs *straight on.* Hence, the *straight forward* arrangement of prose.

Prosody [Gr. *prosodia*, a "song"]. Hence, that part of Grammar which treats of verse, whether intended to be sung or not.

Punctuation [L. *punctum*, "point"]. Dividing a sentence by means of *points* representing the pauses.

Quantity. The *quantity* of time necessary to pronounce a syllable.

Redundant [Latin *re(d)*, "back;" *undant-* "flowing"]. *Flowing back* or over, *i.e.* superfluous. N.B. This word is often lazily used to appear to get rid of a difficulty. But few words are, strictly speaking, *redundant;* they serve some purpose, although the purpose may not be easy to detect.

Reflexive (Verb) L. [*reflect-*, "bend back"]. A Verb in which the action of the Subject is as it were *bent back* on the Subject, so that the Subject and Object denote the same person or thing.

Relative (Pronoun) [L. *re*, "back;" *lat-*, "carried"].

Compare our *e'er, o'er* for *ever, over.*

A name given to *who*, *which*, &c. when they do not carry one forward (as they do when used Interrogatively) but *carry* one *back* to the Antecedent.[1]

Retained (Object). The name given to one of the Objects of a Transitive Verb when *retained* as the Object of the same Verb in the Passive (123).

Rhyme [A.S. *rim*, "number"], identity of sound (from the vowel to the end) between two syllables at the end of two lines.[2] The Anglo-Saxon Poetry was not based on rhyme but on alliteration.

Rhythm [Gr. *rhythmos*, "flowing motion"], the *flowing* regular motion of verse and of periodic prose.

Root. That form from which another word springs, as a tree springs from its *root*.

Semicolon [L. *semi*, half; Gr. *colon*, "limb"]. Half of the *colon*, i.e. of the stop that marks off a separate *limb* or member of a sentence.

"Sensuous" [L. *sensu-*, "sense"]. Appealing to the senses. Milton says that Poetry should be "simple, *sensuous*, and passionate."

Sentence [L. *Sententia*, a "meaning"]. A group of words of a *meaning* so far complete as to express a statement, question, command (239).

Sharp (consonants): *k, p, t,* so called from their sharp sound.

Sibilant L. [*sibila-*, hiss]. *Hissing* letters : *s, z, sh.*

Simile. A sentence expressing the *similarity* of relations *e. g.* between "plough" and "land," "ship" and "sea."[3]

Solecism [Gr. *soloikismos*; "speaking like the men of Soloi"[4]]. Inaccuracy of expression.

Spirants [L. *spira-*, "breathe"]. Letters in the pronunciation of whose sounds the *breath* is not wholly stopped, as it is in the pronunciation of "mutes."

Stanza [It. *stanza*, a "stop"]. A division of a poem containing every variation of measure in the poem, and generally furnishing a *stopping place* at its termination.

Strong (Verbs). Verbs that make their Past Tenses and Passive Participles not by adding *-ed, -t,* but by vowel changes.

Style [L. *stilus*, "an instrument for writing"]. A manner of expressing thought in language.

Subject [L. *subject-*, "placed under"]. That which is *placed under* one's thoughts, as the material or topic for

---

[1] See *How to Tell the Parts of Speech*, p. 124.
[2] Syllables altogether identical do not rhyme.
[3] See *English Lessons for English People*, page 126.
[4] The derivation usually given, but probably inaccurate.

GRAMMATICAL TERMS. xxvii

speech. Hence, the Subject of a Verb is said to be that about which the Verb makes a statement. But see Par. 1, note.

Subjunctive (Mood) [L. *subjunct-*, "subjoined"]. A Mood expressing a purpose, condition, &c., *subjoined* to some statement, question, or answer (163).

Subordinate (sentence) [L. *sub*, "beneath;" *ordin-*, "rank"]. A sentence that *ranks beneath* another sentence. See Par. 249.

Substantive (Noun) [L. *substantia*, "substance"]. A useless name given to Nouns denoting things said to have *substantial* existence.

Suffix [L. *sub*, "beneath," *fix-*, "fixed"]. Same as *Affix*.

Superlative (degree) [L. *super*, "above;" *lat-*, "carried"]. An Adjectival form denoting the expression of a quality in a degree *carried above* other degrees (42).

Supplement [L. *sub*, "up;" *ple-*. "fill"]. That which *fills up*, or supplies what is wanting in a Verb (148).

Syllable [Gr. *syn*, "together;" *lab-*, "take"]. A group of letters *taken together* so as to form one sound.

Syncope [Gr. *syn*, "altogether" or "quite;" *cope*, "cutting"], A considerable curtailment[1] or *cutting* of a word, by omitting letters in the middle, e.g. *ne'er* for *never*.

Syntax [Gr. *syn*, "together;" *taxis*, "arranging"]. The *arrangement* of words *together* in a sentence.

Synthesis [Gr. *syn*, "together;" *thesis*, "placing"]. *Placing together* parts so as to form a whole. The opposite of *analysis*. Hence a *synthetical* period in language. See Par. 551.

Tense [L. *tempus*, Fr. *temps*, "time"]. The forms of a Verb indicating the *time* of an action (71).

Transitive [L. *trans*, "across;" *it-*, "going"]. A Verb that has an Object, so called because the action of the Verb is regarded as passing or *going across* to the Object (55).

Trochee [Gr. *trochos*, "a running"]. In English, a foot of two syllables consisting of an accented, followed by an unaccented syllable. So called from its brisk, or *running* nature.

Verb [L. *verb-*, "word"]. The chief *word* in a sentence.

Verse [L. *vert*, "turn"]. A line of poetry at the end of which one *turns* to a new line.

Vocative [L. *voca-*, "call"]. The use or case of a Noun when the person or thing is *called to* (32).

Vowels [L. *vocalis* "having voice"]. The letters that have a *voice* or are sounded (not as the "consonants

---

[1] Perhaps "a *cutting* in the middle so as to pull the extremes *together*."

xxviii *RULES AND DEFINITIONS.*

but) by themselves: *a, e, i, o, u.*
Weak (Verbs). Verbs that form their Past Tenses and Passive participles by adding *d* or *t*, and not by changed Vowel.

RULES AND DEFINITIONS.

It is assumed that the ten following Definitions are known to the pupil :—

1. A *Noun* is a name of any kind (page 19[1]).
2. A *Pronoun* is a word used for a Noun (page 21[1]).
3. An *Adjective* is a word that can be put before a Noun either to distinguish it, or to point out its number or amount (page 32[1]).
4. A *Verb* is a word that can make a statement (page 39[1]).
5. An *Adverb* is a word that answers to the question "how?" "when?" "where?" or "how far is this true?" (page 54[1]).
6. A *Preposition* is a word that can be placed before a Noun or a Pronoun, so that the Preposition and Noun or Pronoun together are equivalent to an Adjective or Adverb (page 76[1]).
7.[2] A *Sentence* is a collection of words expressing a statement, question, or command (page 45[1]).
8.[2] Any other collection of words, having a meaning, is called a *Phrase* (page 45[1]), or *Clause*. See Glossary.
9. A *Conjunction* is a word that joins two sentences together (page 85[1]).
10. A *Relative Pronoun* is a Conjunctive Pronoun used so as to refer to a preceding Noun or Pronoun called the *Antecedent* (page 125[1]).

---

1. The *Subject* of a Verb making a statement is the word or words answering to the question "who?" or "what?" before the Verb (Par. 1).
2. The *Object* of a Verb or Preposition is the word or words

---

[1] The figures denote the pages of *How to Tell the Parts of Speech* on which the first ten Definitions will severally be found.
[2] A Sentence preceded by a Conjunction ceases to *state, command,* or *question;* it therefore becomes a Phrase, *e.g.* "When I saw John." Such a Phrase may conveniently be called a *Clause*. See Par. 239.

answering to the question "*whom?*" or "*what?*" after the Verb or Preposition (14 [1]).

3. When the Relative is followed by a Conjunction introducing a new Sentence, leave out this sentence in parsing the Relative (24).

4. The *Antecedent* must sometimes be *supplied* from the sentence (25).

5. The *Relative* is sometimes *omitted* (26).

6. Some Pronouns are used *Interrogatively, Conjunctively,* and *Relatively* (28).

7. The *Uses* or *Cases* of a Noun are four, viz. *Subject, Object,*[2] *Possessive,* and *Vocative* (32).

8. The Plural of a Noun is formed by adding *-s* to the Singular (34).

9. The Possessive Use or Case, in the Singular and Plural, is formed by adding *'s* to the Singular or Plural form (37).

10. An Adjective has three Degrees of Comparison, viz. *Positive, Comparative,* and *Superlative* (42).

11. To form the Comparative and Superlative, add *-er, -est* to Positives of one Syllable. "More" and "most" are used in other cases (43).

12. A Verb that can have an Object is called *Transitive;* a Verb that cannot, is called *Intransitive.*[3]

13. The *Passive Voice* of a Transitive Verb is the form assumed by the Verb when its Object is made the Subject (60).

14. The *Active Voice* of a Transitive Verb is the form that can be used with an Object (61).

15. A *Participle* can be distinguished by the fact that it can be, in part, replaced by a Conjunctive word (66).

16. Each Voice has four *Moods: Infinitive, Indicative, Imperative,* and *Subjunctive* (70).

17. The *Infinitive* Mood speaks of an action without defining the doer (70).

18. The *Indicative* Mood definitely points out an action (70).

19. The *Imperative* Mood commands an action (70).

20. The *Subjunctive* Mood expresses condition, purpose, wish, &c. (70).

21. Verbs have three *Tenses: Past, Present,* and *Future* (71).

22. Each Tense has four "*States*" of Action: the *Indefinite,*

---

[1] These and the following References are to the *Paragraphs* in *How to Parse.*

[2] If the Indirect Object is called a separate use, there will be five Uses of a Noun.

[3] The usual Definitions are given in Par. 55; but they are very unsatisfactory.

the *Complete*, the *Incomplete*, and the *Complete Post-Continuous* (73, 74).

23. A Verb *agrees* with its Subject in *Person* and *Number* (78).

24. "May," "can," "must," "will," "shall," "let," &c. are called *Auxiliary* Verbs (95).

25. "*To*" is *omitted* in the Infinitive after the Auxiliary Verbs, and after "see," "hear," "feel" (96).

26. An Infinitive may be used (1) as a Noun; (2) as an Adverb; (3) as an Adjective.

27. The *Indirect Object* of a Verb is the word or phrase answering to the question "For, or, to, whom?" "For, or, to, what?" when used after the Verb and the Direct Object (118).

28. When an Active Verb taking two Objects is changed into the Passive Voice, one Object becomes the Subject of the Passive Verb, but the other is *retained as Object* (122).

29. Some Verbs, generally Intransitive, can take an Object of a nature *akin* or *cognate* to the Verb, called the *Cognate Object* (125).

30. The *Object* is sometimes used *Adverbially* to denote *extension, price, point of time* (127--131).

31. The *Subject*, generally with a Participle, is sometimes used *Adverbially* (135).

32. A Noun or Pronoun, not Subject or Object of a Verb, but so connected with another Noun or Pronoun that we can understand between them the words "I mean," "that is to say," &c., is said to be in *Apposition* to the latter (137).

33. Nouns and Pronouns are used *Subjectively* when in Apposition to *Subjects*, and *Objectively* when in Apposition to *Objects* (138).

34. The (1) Intransitive Verbs "is," "looks," "seems," "appears," &c., and (2) the Transitive Verbs "make," "create," "appoint," "deem," "esteem," being used to express identity, and, as it were, to place one Noun or Pronoun in apposition with another, may be called *Verbs of Identity*, or *Appositional Verbs* (147).

35. Verbs of Identity, when Intransitive and Passive, take a *Subjective Supplement;* when Transitive, take an *Objective Supplement* (150).

36. "It" and "there" are sometimes irregularly used to prepare the way for the Subject or Object (151).

37. In a Conditional Sentence, (1) the Clause expressing the condition is called the *Antecedent*; (2) the Clause expressing the consequence of the fulfilment of the condition is called the *Consequent* (167).

38. Auxiliary Verbs (when not following "if" or any other Conjunction expressing Condition) are used Indicatively, *whenever they can be altered into the Indicatives of other Verbs* (181).

RULES AND DEFINITIONS. xxxi

39. Whenever language is irregular, there is some *cause* for the irregularity (192).

40. The three principal *causes* of irregularity are I. *Desire of brevity;* II. *Confusion of two constructions;* III. *Desire to avoid harshness of sound or of construction* (198).

41. A *Simple Sentence* is a sentence that has only one Subject and only one Stating, Questioning, or Commanding Verb (245).

42. When several Simple Sentences are connected by "and," "but," "so," "then," &c., so that each sentence is, as it were, independent, and of the same rank as the rest, each is called a *co-ordinate Sentence*[1] (246).

43. A *Compound Sentence* is a Sentence made up of Coordinate Sentences (247).

44. When a number of Sentences are connected by Conjunctions that are not Co-ordinate, the Sentence that is not introduced by a Conjunction is called the *Principal Sentence* (248).

45. Sentences connected with a Principal Sentence by Conjunctions that are not Co-ordinate are called *Sub-ordinate*[1] (249).

46. A *Complex Sentence* is the whole Sentence formed by the combination of the Principal and Subordinate Sentences (250).

47. When a word passes from one form to another, a letter is often changed or doubled in order to *preserve the original sound* (266).

48. Final *-e* is dropped before an affix beginning with a vowel, but retained before an affix beginning with a consonant (270).

49. A monosyllable ending in *-ll*, when followed by an affix beginning with a consonant, or when itself used as an affix, generally drops one *-l* (275).

50. If the termination of a word is a consonant preceded by a vowel, then, on receiving an affix beginning with a vowel, the final consonant in the word is doubled, provided that the word is a monosyllable, or accented on the last syllable (277).

51. When a word is separated from its grammatical adjunct by any intervening Phrase, the Phrase should be preceded and followed by a comma[2] (224).

---

[1] The *mark* of a Subordinate Sentence is that when preceded by its Conjunction, it *cannot* generally stand as a Sentence by itself. A Coordinate Sentence *can* thus stand by itself.

[2] For words, idioms, &c., the pupil is referred to the Alphabetical Index at the end of the book.

HOW TO PARSE.

CHAPTER I.

SUBJECT AND OBJECT.

The Subject in a Stating Sentence.

ALL Verbs that make a statement must be accompanied by some Noun, or equivalent of a Noun, about which the statement is made :—

(1) "*Thomas* failed."
(2) "*He* failed."
(3) "*The attempt to take the city* failed."
(4) "*That he failed* is certain."

In each of the three examples above, if you ask the question "Who or what failed?" the answer, being the *subject* of our statement, is called the *Subject* of the Verb.

This leads us to a Definition :

The Subject of a Verb in a stating sentence is the word or collection of words answering to the question asked by putting "Who?" or "What?" before the Verb.[1]

[1] It is not enough to say that the Subject is "that about which the statement is made." For, in "A tempest wrecked our ship," the statement is just as much about "ship" as about "tempest"; but "ship" is not the "Subject."

2 *Caution* I. If the Verb is accompanied by an Adverb, as—

   (1) "He *seldom* sleeps."
   (2) "She does *not* sleep."

—the Adverb should be repeated in the question:

   (1) "Who *seldom* sleeps?"   Answer: "He," Subject.
   (2) "Who does *not* sleep?"   Answer: "She," Subject.

3 *Caution* II. If the Verb is accompanied by words necessary to give the meaning, as—

   (1) "John is *a mere boy*."
   (2) "Thomas was made *happy*."

—these words may be repeated in the question:

   (1) "Who is *a mere boy*?"   Answer: "John," Subject.
   (2) "Who *was made happy*?"   Answer: "Thomas," Subject.

4   **The Subject in a Questioning Sentence.**

In a Questioning Sentence, *e.g.*—

   (1) "Did John come?"

—ask, "Did *who* come?"   Answer: "Did *John* come?" Therefore "John" is the Subject.

5 *Caution.* If the Sentence only answers our question by repeating " Who ? " " What ? " " Which ? " &c. as—

    (1) " *What* made you so foolish ? "
    (2) " *Who* saw him die ? "

—then, " Who ? " " What ? " " Which ? " are themselves the Subjects.

6   **The Subject in a Commanding Sentence.**[1]

The Subject in a Commanding Sentence is almost always " you " ; or, in Poetry, " thou " or " ye." It is generally not expressed :

    (1) " Stay (*you*) where you are : the rest may go."
    (2) " Follow (*thou*) me."

7 *Caution.* Where a Verb follows a Conjunction, as—

    (1) ". . . *that* the attempt may prosper."
    (2) ". . . *if* Thomas *helps* me."

—it is useful sometimes to repeat the Conjunction before " Who ? " or " What ? " :—

    (1) " *That* what may prosper ? "   Answer : " The attempt," Subject.
    (2) " *If* who helps me ? "   Answer : " Thomas," Subject.

[1] In these sentences, the name "Subject" is usually given to the Pronoun denoting the person *to whom* the command is addressed.

The Conjunctions "and," "but," "for," "then," "so," "therefore," &c. need not be repeated.

Exercise I. (Specimen).

Find out the Subjects of the italicized Verbs in the following Exercise :[1]—

Once upon a time there* *lived*[2] a mighty king whose* name was Xerxes, and he reigned over Persia. *Does* every boy *know* where Persia is? If you *do* not *know*, *look* it out in the Map. Though he was king of the Persians, and *reigned* over almost all the nations of the East, yet he was not satisfied with this; nothing but the whole world *could satisfy* him. So, learning that a little nation lived not far from him, on the other side of the Ægean sea, and *had* not yet *submitted* to him, the king determined to conquer it. This nation, which consisted of several independent cities—Athens, Sparta, Thebes, and many others—*was called* altogether by the name of "Greeks." All the Greeks together, when they mustered all their fighting men, *did* not *amount* to a hundred thousand, while Xerxes *was obeyed* by more* than a million of soldiers. Besides, the Greeks *were* often *divided* against themselves, one city fighting against another, so that they *seemed* to have no chance against the Great King—for this was the name by which the King of Persia *was known*.

Xerxes *did* not *believe* for a moment that the Greeks, few and divided as* they were, *would resist* him. So before he *collected* an army, he determined to try peaceable means. Accordingly he sent heralds to all the principal

[1] In this Exercise, and in those that follow, the Pupil may be asked to point out Nouns, Verbs, Adverbs, &c. But in that case, words marked thus * should be omitted.

[2] The term "Subject" includes not merely the Noun that answers to the question "Who?" or "What?" before the Verb, but also all Adjectives or Adjective Phrases put to the Noun; *e.g.* "a mighty king" is the Subject of "lived." "King" may be called the "Noun part of the Subject," or the "Noun Subject."

cities in Greece, and *bade* them demand from each city "earth and water." What *made* him ask for that? Why, you must know this was the Persian way of demanding obedience and subjection; for, among them, giving earth *was* the sign of surrendering their land to the Great King, and giving water meant that they surrendered their sea and navy to him. The heralds therefore, with this message from Xerxes, *went* forth on their several journeys.

"Who lived?" "A mighty king," Subject.

"Does every boy know?" "Does who know?" "Every boy," Subject.

"If who do not know?" "You," Subject.

"Look it out." A command: Subject "you," *implied*.

"Though who reigned?" "He," Subject. (Note that *reigned* is joined by the Conjunction "and" to the Verb *was*, and both these Verbs follow the Conjunction "though." We therefore repeat "though," in asking the question to find the Subject. Note, also, that the answer is "he," not "Xerxes." The answer must always be a word *in the sentence*.)

"Who or what could satisfy him?" "Nothing but the whole world," Subject.

"Who or what had (not yet) submitted?" "A little nation," Subject. These words are also the Subject of *lived*, which is joined to *had submitted* by "and."

"Who or what was called?" "This nation," Subject.

"Who or what did (not) amount?" "All the Greeks," Subject.

"Who was obeyed?" "Xerxes," Subject.

"Who were often divided?" "The Greeks," Subject.

"Who seemed?" "They," Subject.

"What made him ask?" Here the answer is the same as the question, viz. "What;" and "What" is the Subject of "made."

"What was (the sign of surrendering)?" "Giving earth," Subject.

8   **Position of the Subject.**

The Subject of a Verb expressing a statement generally (*a*) comes before the Verb; but it (*b*) sometimes comes after the Verb, *e.g.* when "there" or an emphatic Adverb, or some other emphatic word, comes at the beginning of the sentence :—

    (*a*) (1) "*He* reigned in Persia."
    (*b*) (1) "There is *no doubt* about it."
        (2) "Next came *my brother*."
        (3) "'Stop,' cried *the soldier*."

9   In Poetry, the Subject often comes after the Verb (See Pars. 513—4) :—

    (1) "Loud blew *the blast*."

10   In Questions, the Subject is generally (1) in the middle of the Verb, but sometimes (2) after the Verb—

    (1) "What did *the man* say?"
    (2) "What said *the man*?"

—unless the Subject happens to be "Who" or "What"—

    (1) "*Who* saw him die?"

Exercise II.

Write down the Subjects of the italicized Verbs in the following Exercise :—

When the heralds *had arrived* at the cities of Greece, and *delivered* their message, they were received differently in different places. Some cities *gave* earth and water, because they *were* afraid of the Great King; others, because they were jealous of their neighbours, and *hoped* the Great King would help them and destroy their enemies. But the men of Athens and of Sparta *would give* neither earth nor water. Indeed the Athenians were so angry at the message, that they threw one of the heralds into a pit, and *bade* him take his earth thence; another they *threw* into a well, telling him that he *could find* water there.

Xerxes, when he heard how his heralds *had been treated*, and how the men of Athens and Sparta *had refused* earth and water, *determined* at once to levy an army and to conquer Greece. Never before *was* so vast a host *collected*. They drank whole rivers dry.* The Hellespont, across which they had to pass into Greece, *was bridged* with boats: a promontory (its name was Mount Athos) *was cut through* to give a passage to their fleet. And now this monstrous army, amounting to a million at least, *had penetrated* Greece, and was marching southward. Still no one *ventured* to oppose them, and in a few days the hosts of Xerxes, with undimiuished numbers, had reached a pass called Thermopylæ.

11   **Different forms of the Subject.**

The Subject may be—

1. **A Noun, Pronoun, or Adjective put for Noun:—**
 "*John* runs," "*He* runs," "*Who* runs?" "*That* is a mistake."

2. **A group of Nouns connected by "and":—**
 "*Two and three* make five." "*You and I* are cousins."

3 **A Noun-Phrase, or Noun-Clause:—**

(1) "*To write an exercise without a fault* requires much care."

(2) "*That he was guilty* was not proved."[1]

Exercise III.

Write down the Subjects of the italicized Verbs in the following Exercise :—

"What *is* a pass?" perhaps you ask. A narrow path with steep mountains on both sides *is called* a pass. In this case there* *were* mountains on one side, and, on the other side, *was* a marshy place stretching down to the sea, so that there* *was* only room for a cart or two to pass. In such a place, to resist a host *was* an easy matter for a few* brave men. But, just then, the Greeks were terrified. To remain at Thermopylæ *seemed* to them certain death ; so they determined to retreat. Then Leonidas, who was king of the Spartans, when he *found* that he could not persuade the other Greeks to remain, *determined* to remain by himself with a few* brave Spartans, to resist Xerxes, and to gain time for his countrymen. With him *remained* about three hundred men, and the* rest* *departed*.
When Xerxes, after arriving at Thermopylæ, *saw* the handful of Spartans prepared to resist him, he laughed at them, and *bade* his soldiers bring them to him in chains. But the Persian soldiers, on advancing to the charge, *found* that their master was mistaken in his laughter. Charge after charge *was made* by the Persians, but to no purpose. The Persians *were slain* in hundreds, but the Greeks *were* neither *taken* nor *driven back*. That the Persians *were*

---

[1] The Noun-Clause in (2) may be called a *Noun-Sentence*, for convenience ; but it must always be borne in mind that a Sentence preceded by a Conjunction, so that it no longer *states, questions,* or *commands—* ceases, strictly speaking, to be a *Sentence*, and becomes a Clause. See the Definitions, p. xxviii. The word *Phrase* includes *Clause*.

no match for the Greeks *was made evident* even to the proud King Xerxes; and, when the sun set, he retired to his tent in great sorrow.

12 The Object.

Supply what is wanting to complete the sense after the following Verbs and Prepositions :—

1. The grey-hound killed —. 2. I am travelling towards —. 3. The woodman felled —. 4. The soldier shot —. 5. We wish for —. 6. We desire —. 7. I look for —. 8. John is seeking —. 9. I come to —. 10. They reach —. 11. The cart-wheel ran over —. 12. I am thinking about —. 13. I am living in —.

The best way to supply what is wanting is to repeat the Verb or Preposition, and ask *whom?* or *what?* (not before the Verb, as when you were finding the Subject, but) *after* the Verb.

For example, "Killed what?" Answer: "A hare." "Towards what?" Answer: "Paris."

Now "hare" is called the *Object* of the Verb "killed," and "Paris" the *Object* of the Preposition "towards."

13 "Object" means "put in the way." Just as a target is *put in the way of* the marksman, and is called the *object* at which he shoots, so the word or group of words answering to the question *whom?* or *what?* after a Verb or Preposition, often denotes the *object* of the action of the Verb, or of the motion implied by the Preposition. For example, "the hare" is the *object* of the action of "killing": "Paris" is the *object* of the motion implied in "towards."

10   OBJECT.   [Par. 14, 15

Hence the name "Object" is given to the words answering the question *whom?* or *what?* after the Verb or Preposition, even in some cases where the name may seem misapplied.

For example, in "He is travelling from *Paris,*" you can hardly say that Paris is the *object* of motion. Nevertheless, in conformity with the general rule, "Paris" is called the "Object" of the Preposition "from."

14 *The word or collection of words answering to the question whom? or what? after a Verb or Preposition is called the Object.*[1]

15   Different forms of the Object.

The Object, like the Subject, must be a Noun, or the equivalent of a Noun :—

1. **A Noun or Pronoun :—**
"I like *playing, John, nothing.*"

2. **A group of Nouns connected by "and" :—**
"He is sitting between *you and me*" : "This railway connects *Paris and Brussels.*"

3. **A Noun-Phrase, or Noun-Clause :—**
(1) "I like *to play, to hear music, hearing music, a rascal to be punished.*"
(2) "I know *that he was not guilty.*" "I asked *whether he had arrived.*"

[1] As in finding the Subject, so here, if the Verb is modified by "not." or any other Adverb, the Adverb may be repeated with the Verb in asking the question.

16   **Position of the Object.**

The Object generally follows the Verb or Preposition, but not always. For example :—

I. When the Object is an Interrogative or Relative Pronoun :—

    (1) " *Whom* did you see ? "
    (2) "The house *that* I live *in.*"

17   II. When the Object is emphatic :—

    (1) "*Silver and gold* have I none."
    (2) "*Not one word* did he say."
    (3) "*Some* he killed, *others* he took alive."

18   III. In Poetry (514) :—

    "*A monarch's sword* when mad vain-glory draws."

19   **Some Verbs have no Object.**

Some Verbs denote (1) *states, e.g.*, "be," "remain," "seem," "appear," and generally all forms of "be" followed by the Verbal forms in *-ed, -en*, &c.; others denote (2) actions *not regarded as having an external object, e.g.*, "run," "walk," &c.

These two classes of Verbs do not take a Grammatical Object. The former class suggests the question "who?" not "whom?" *e.g.*, "He seems —"; "seems *who* or *what* ?" Answer, "He seems *a rascal.*" Here "rascal" answers to the question "who?" (not "whom?") and is not called the Object of "seems." See Par. 147.

Exercise IV. (Specimen).

Find out the Objects of the italicized Verbs and Prepositions in the following Exercise :—

Next day the Persians *attacked* the Greeks again, but to no purpose. Not the slightest impression *did* they *make* on the little Greek phalanx. Their gold and silver armour was no match *for* the steel spears *of* the brave Greeks. Besides, the Greeks were fighting *for* their country, while the Persians *did* not *want* to fight, and were driven to the battle *with* the lash. So the sun set again, and Xerxes *found* that he was again defeated. But, that night, while the King *was* angrily *thinking* that he should have to retreat, a traitor came *to* his tent and *offered* to show him a path over the mountains, by which the Persians might come down *behind* the Greeks, and thus (might) *attack* them *in* the rear as well as in front. At once, a Persian battalion set out *under* the guidance *of* the traitor, and *by* sunrise next morning, the Persians, *with* two vast hosts, *had shut in*[1] the little band of Greeks *between* the sea, the mountains, and their enemies.

"Attacked whom?"   "The Greeks," Object.
"They did (not) make what?"[2]   "The slightest impression," Object.

---

[1] "Shut in" is one Compound Verb. See *How to Tell the Parts of Speech*, p. 77.
[2] See Note on page 10.
The term "Object" includes, not merely the Noun, but the *whole of the answer* to the question "whom?" or "what?" after the Verb. The Noun-part of the Object, may, for convenience, be called the Noun-Object, and may be stated separately, if desired. *e.g.*, "the slightest impression" is the "Object," but "impression" is the "Noun-Object" of ' did make."

"For what?" "The steel swords of the brave Greeks," Object.
"For what?" "Their country," Object.
"Did (not) want what?" "To fight," Object.
"With what?" "The lash," Object.
"Found what?" "That he was again defeated," Object.
"Was (angrily) thinking what?" "That he should have to retreat," Object.
"To what?" "His tent," Object.
"Offered what?" "To show him a path over the mountains," Object.
The rest you can answer for yourself.

20 Many parts of the Verb that take no Subject may take an Object.

For example, you cannot ask "Who or what *killing?*" but you can ask "*killing* whom or what?" Consequently "killing" can have no Subject, but may have an "Object." And so may "to kill."

Exercise V.

Find out the Objects of the italicized Verbs and Prepositions in the following Exercise :[1]—

Leonidas *saw* at once that he and his men *had* no chance of escape. But *instead of* lamenting, he seemed delighted *at* the thought of dying honourably. He told his men *to clean* their armour and weapons, and *to prepare* themselves as if for a feast. Then, when the sun was sinking, "*Take* your suppers," said he, "and *remember* that you

[1] The Subjects of the italicized Verbs may also be found both in this and in the preceding Exercise.

will *take* your breakfast elsewhere." But *in* that little band there was not one man that *feared* to die; for a soldier's death was counted an honourable, and not a terrible thing, among the Greeks. When night came, out marched the Greeks *against* the army of Xerxes. Wherever they went, they *carried* death and terror with them; they *overturned* the tent of Xerxes and *slew* his guards. The proud king was forced to flee for his life; and, if the night could have lasted *for* a night and a day, perhaps they might have destroyed the whole of that vast host. But, when day *began* to dawn, the enemy *discovered* the small number of the Greeks, and took courage. The Greeks were weary *with* slaying their thousands, the Persians were fresh; the Greeks were three hundred men, the Persians were more than three hundred thousand. So the Persians gathered *round* the Greeks, *attacking* them *with* slings and darts and spears, because they *did* not *dare* to attack them in close fight. When the Greeks charged, the Persians fled *from* them; when the Greeks retired, the Persians *approached* them. First one and then another of the Greeks fell *beneath* the shower of darts, others were wounded and could scarcely stand; but none would surrender. Before sunset, every Greek was slain, and the Persian army *had gained* the victory. But, *from* that day *to* the present (day), all men *have honoured* the names of Leonidas and his brave Greeks, who *have left* for us and for all men an example teaching us not to be afraid *of* dying honourably.

Exercise VI.

Write or repeat the Subjects of the italicized Verbs, and the Objects of the italicized Verbs and Prepositions, in the following Exercise :—

Tommy *had heard from* Mr. Barlow many stories *about* the tam*ing of* wild animals; so he thought *to* himself he sh*ould* like *to tame*¹ a pig. He *had heard* that the youngest animals *are* most easily *tamed*¹; so he *chose out* the youngest pig *in* the farm-yard, and *approached* it *with* some bread in his hand. "Come here, little pig," said he; but the pig *ran away.* "Then I must fetch you," cried Tommy, and, so say*ing,* he caught it by the leg. The little pig squeaked, and the old sow, com*ing* up, *ran between* Tommy's legs, and *knocked* him *down* in the mud. "Who *did* all this mischief?" said Mr. Barlow, coming out that moment from the house. "That foolish pig," said poor Tommy. "Oh! no," replied Mr. Barlow, "that foolish boy."

In doing the above Exercise, make three columns, thus :—

WORD.	Answer to the question *who?* or *what?* before the Verb, *i.e.* SUBJECT.	Answer to the question *whom?* or *what?* after the Verb or Preposition, *i.e.* OBJECT.
had heard	Tommy	many stories about the taming of wild animals
from	—	Mr. Barlow
to tame	—	a pig

¹ Some of these Verbs, *e.g. to tame*, have no Subjects; some, *e.g. are tamed*, have no Objects.

Exercise VII.

Write or repeat the Subjects of the italicized Verbs, and the Objects of the italicized Verbs and Prepositions, in the following Exercise:—

A lion, while* quietly sleeping, *was surrounded by* some mice. They *began* dancing *round* him, and at last[1] one young mouse, bolder than* the rest,* *jumped* up *on* his body and *scampered* across his face. The lion *awoke* with a roar, and the mice *ran* away: but the young mouse *was stopped by* the lion's* paw. "Spare me!" cried she, "and I *will* never *disturb* you again." The lion good-humouredly *took* his paw *off* her, and *lay* down again. Some days afterwards, the lion *was caught* in a net spread by some huntsmen. In vain[1] he roared and *struggled:* he found that his struggles only *entangled* him more in the net, and he cried in despair, "I *have* no chance *of* escaping." Just then, up *came* the little mouse *with* a thousand brothers and sisters. To work they fell, gnawing the net, and *in* ten minutes the lion *was released by* the mice.

[1] An Adverbial Phrase. See *How to Tell, &c.*, page 79.

CHAPTER II.

THE RELATIVE PRONOUN.

21 **How to Find whether the Relative is Subject or Object.**

In the sentence "Bring the book that pleases you best," what is the Subject of "pleases?" Perhaps you may ask the question in the usual way, "What pleases?" Answer, "the book." But this is not right. "Book" is the Object of "bring." "Bring what?" Answer, "the book."

Now the same word is never both Object and Subject; so "book" cannot be the Subject of "pleases;" and the real Subject of "pleases" is the Relative Pronoun "that."

You will generally answer questions of this kind rightly if you remember that the Relative Pronoun[1] is in some sense a *Conjunction*, so that it joins together two sentences, one of which states, commands, &c., and may be called (Par. 248) the *Principal Sentence;* while the other—as it is introduced by the Relative Pronoun—may be called a *Relative Sentence*. If these Sentences are kept quite distinct—*the Principal Sentence being first repeated*

[1] *How to Tell*, &c., page 125.

and parsed by itself, and afterwards the Relative Sentence—the pupil will have no difficulty.

22 In parsing the Relative Sentence, the Noun or Pronoun for which the Relative Pronoun is used—that is, its Antecedent [1]—should be written in brackets by the side of the Relative Pronoun. Thus, in parsing the Sentences of the next Exercise, write down the Principal and Relative Sentences as follows:—

Principal Sentence . . . . (1) "The jay was very soon punished for her robbery."

Relative   ,,   (2) "*That* (jay) robbed the peacocks of their feathers."

If the Sentence contains two or three Relative Sentences, they may be taken separately, *e.g.* in the seventh Sentence of the following Exercise:—

{ Principal Sentence   (*a*) (1) "The girl that I told you of was taught a lesson that she never forgot."
{ Relative   ,,   (*a*) (2) "*Who* (the girl) counted her chickens before they were hatched."

{ Principal   ,,   (*b*) (1) "The girl was taught a lesson that she never forgot."
{ Relative   ,,   (*b*) (2) "I told you of *that* (girl.)"

{ Principal   ,,   (*c*) (1) "The girl was taught a lesson."
{ Relative   ,,   (*c*) (2) "She never forgot *that* (lesson)."

[1] *How to Tell*, &c., page 125.

Par. 22] *THE RELATIVE PRONOUN.* 19

The form *who*, or *whom*, will of itself tell you at once whether it is Subject or Object.

In parsing a Relative Pronoun, state—
1. *Antecedent.*
2. *Subject of what Verb*, or,
3. *Object of what Verb or Preposition.*

Exercise VIII.

Parse the Relative Pronouns in the following sentences :—

1. The jay that robbed the peacocks of their feathers was very soon punished for her robbery. 2. The ass that frightened the beasts of the forest was laughed at when he began to bray. 3. The crow dropped the cheese, which the fox immediately snapped up. 4. The lion that spared the mouse was afterwards released by the mouse. 5. The travellers, all of whom had seen the chameleon, could not agree about its colour. 6. Shakespeare tells us that the man that does not love music is fit for murders and conspiracies. 7. The girl that I told you of, who counted her chickens before they were hatched, was taught a lesson that she never forgot. 8. Have you ever heard of Horatius Cocles, who defended the bridge against a host of enemies, and whom the Romans honoured by erecting a statue to his memory?

Write these down as follows :—

Word.	Antecedent.	Subject of	Object of
that	jay	robbed	—
which	cheese	—	snapped up

Find out the Subjects and Objects of all the Verbs in the foregoing sentences.

23   **The Position of the Relative.**

Note that the Relative Pronoun, when used as Object, precedes both the Subject and the Verb. The reason is that the Pronoun, *serving the purpose of a Conjunction, has to precede the sentence* that it joins to the Principal Sentence.

24   When a Parenthetical Sentence intervenes between the Relative Pronoun and its Verb, that sentence must be carefully separated from the Relative Sentence.

A Parenthetical sentence is a sentence inserted in the midst of another sentence, the latter being complete without the former.

The following are examples of sentences containing Relative Pronouns followed by Parenthetical sentences :—

    (1) "Yesterday I met Robert, *who*—you will hardly believe it—has grown to be six feet high, with a beard reaching to his watch-chain."

    (2) "Yesterday I met Robert, *whom* (though I had not seen him for ten years) I recognized at once."

In the following Exercise, the Conjunctional sentences are inserted between parenthetical marks;

Par. 24] *THE RELATIVE PRONOUN.* 21

but the pupil must be prepared to parse the Relative hereafter without the aid of these marks. The following will be found a useful Rule :—

When the Relative is followed by a Conjunction (e.g. *"though" above in* (2)) *introducing a new sentence, leave out this sentence in parsing the Relative.*

EXERCISE IX.

Parse the Relative Pronouns in the following Exercise, stating the Antecedent, and the Verb or Preposition of which each is Subject or Object :—

Once there *was* a quarrel between the eyes and the nose about the ownership of the spectacles, *which* (so *said* the nose) were undoubtedly intended for him and not for his two neighbours the eyes ; *who*, on their part (although they admitted that the nose had a share in the spectacles), yet claimed the largest share for themselves. The two ears, *whom* both parties accepted as judges, *called* on the tongue, *who* was counsel for both, to plead first the cause of the eyes, and then that of the nose. So the tongue began by saying that spectacles *that* had no eyes to look through them, *were* of no use ; the word "spectacle," *which* the Latins used to denote a "place for seeing," *proved*, of itself, that the instrument was meant for seeing and not for smelling. The judges, *who* (though they became rather inattentive while Latin was being quoted) had listened with great patience to the arguments *that* the tongue brought forward, now *desired* to hear what the nose *had* to say. So the tongue, taking that side of the question, *which* he pleaded remarkably well, *called* attention to the saddle *that* was between the two glasses, *which*, said he, was clearly intended for the nose. He added, with great force, that, if the eyes were closed or even altogether removed, the spectacles would still remain faithfully in their place, but a man *that* suddenly lost his nose *would* certainly *lose* his spectacles as well— "*which*,"[1] said he, "clearly proves that the nose is the owner of the spectacles. If a dog were placed between two claimants, *should* we not readily *admit* that the claimant to *whom* the dog went would be the rightful owner? My lords, the spectacles, *which* (because they have no power of motion) sit patiently there between my two clients, *would* clearly *shew* you, if they could move, to which claimant they adhered. *Cut* out the eye, the spectacles will sit unmoved : cast down the nose, the trusty spectacles will immediately follow their fallen master."

Here the judges, declaring that *what*[2] they had heard was enough to enable them to arrive at a decision, *stopped* the counsel, and at once decided in favour of the nose.

Exercise X.

Write or repeat the Subjects and Objects of the Verbs italicized in the last Exercise.

25 Omission of the Antecedent.

Tell me the Antecedent of *which* in the following sentence:—

"The ass in the lion's skin frightened all the beasts in the forest till he began to bray :* *which* at once changed their fear into laughter."

[1] See "Omission of the Antecedent," Par. 25.
[2] *What* should be parsed here thus: "*what* is put for *that which*; *that* is the Subject of *was*; *which* is the Object of *had heard*." The sentence, fully expressed, would run thus: "declaring that *that* (Subj.) *which* (Obj.) they had heard was enough," &c.

There is no Noun or Pronoun here that can be called the Antecedent of *which*. *Which* stands for "the ass's beginning to bray," or "the braying of the ass," or some other words *to be supplied* from the previous sentence. In parsing *which* you must say, "*which* stands for an Antecedent *to be supplied*, viz. 'the braying of the ass.'"

26   **The Omission of the Relative.**

When the Relative would be the *Object*, it is often omitted :—

    (1) "The book (*that*) you sent me is not mine."
    (2) "Where is the parcel (*that*) I left here yesterday?"
    (3) "The message (*that*) I was sent with was to this effect."

In Poetry it (Par. 520) is sometimes omitted, even where, if inserted, it would be the *Subject :*—

    (1) "'Tis distance (that) lends enchantment to the view."

EXERCISE XI.

Write down the Subjects and Objects of the italicized Verbs, and parse the Relatives, as in the last Exercise :—

The sun had nearly set when Harry, having delivered the message *he had brought, began* to turn his steps homewards. There was no moon, *which*[1] (together with his ignorance of the neighbourhood) made him quicken his pace across the common. For some time he managed to keep the path, *which* was nothing but two cart ruts leading from one farm to another. Presently, however, a track *that* turned off to a gravel-pit, led him astray. When he had once gone wrong, he found that he could not find the path he *had lost*. Through brambles, over furze-bushes, he scrambled onward, till, at last, he fell into a deep pit *which*, having been left by the peat-cutters, had been filled with water oozing from the bog around, and *would have drowned* him, if he had not been able to swim. Suddenly, to his great joy, he saw a light, *which*[2] he wondered that he had not noticed before. He ran towards it, supposing it came from some cottage belonging to a shepherd *he had seen* in the morning keeping his sheep near the middle of the common. Just when he was close on the light, he fell into another deep pool, *which* was so broad that he had great difficulty in swimming across it. Scrambling out, he looked round for the light *he was seeking;* but to his surprise, it seemed to be behind him. Just at this moment another light appeared, straight before him, *which*, when he approached it, retired from him. Thinking it was the torch of some traveller *that*, like himself, had lost his way, he shouted to the man to stop, and ran towards him ; but, instead of stopping, the light ran away faster than before, seeming to choose the most miry and boggy spots it *could find*, so that poor Harry soon fell a third time into the water.

[1] See Paragraph 25.
[2] *Which* is not the Object of *wondered.*

27   Uses of "Who," "What," &c.

The Pronouns "who," "what," "which," were once always used Interrogatively :—

    A. (1) "*Who* has a good conscience?"

In time, questions of this kind were used with their answers, thus :—

    (2) "*Who* has a good conscience? He is prepared to die."

Afterwards, for shortness, the two sentences were blended in one. Then, sometimes the whole of the Interrogative sentence was treated as a Noun—

    (3) "(*Who*, or *whoever*, has a good conscience) is prepared to die."

But, more commonly, the Interrogative force of the first sentence was quite forgotten, and, "who" being treated like "that," the two sentences became—

    B. "(4) "He *who* has a good conscience is prepared to die."

28   Again, when Sentence A was made the Object of a Verb in a preceding sentence, *e.g.* "I *asked*," the second sentence lost its Interrogative force; and "who," instead of being Interrogatively used, was used Conjunctively, so as to join the sentence "I asked" with the following words :—

    C. (5) "I asked *who* had a good conscience."

Carefully distinguish the three uses :—

(A) "*What* say you?" (Interrogative.)
(B) "*What* you say is true." (Relative.)
(C) "I asked *what* you said." (Conjunctive.)

If you are asked where are the Antecedents of the Relatives "what" and "whoever," you can often supply the Antecedents, thus :—

(1) "What you say, (*that*) is true."
(2) "Whoever said that, (*he*) was mistaken."

29 Sometimes, as in the fourth line of the next exercise, "what" may be parsed either as (1) Conjunctively, or as (2) Relatively used :—

(1) "*What* should he do? Harry did not know."
(2) "Harry did not know *what*, i.e., *that which* he should do."

Exercise XII.

Parse the italicized words, stating the Subjects and Objects of Verbs and Prepositions :—

Harry's* efforts had almost exhausted him. Wet, weary, and almost in despair, he stood shivering on the pool's* brink, looking at the waters from *which* he had escaped, not knowing *what* he should do. Another light began to dance before him, but the chase *he had had* after the light already, made him decide not to pursue it. "I have had enough of following you, Mr. Traveller,"* said he; "yet *what* shall I do? If I stand here much longer, the little strength I *have* will be exhausted; yet I do not know *which* way to turn, and *what* I have seen of this common convinces me that a man *that* does not know the road well, *may go* on walking round and round for hours and only come back to the place he started *from.*" Just then the clouds, *which*, while he had been wandering about, had hitherto covered the sky, now parted and shewed a few stars. Among them was a constellation he *knew* very well, called the Great Bear. Then, all at once, *what* Mr. Barlow had told him *occurred* to his mind, that two of the Great Bear's* stars always point to the Pole-star, *which* is always in the North. Now he knew that the farm he *had* lately *left was* six miles to the south of his home, so that the path he ought *to take*, *lay* to the north. Off he started at once, keeping his eyes on the Pole-star, *which*, though it led him through more brambles and furze and pools, yet at last brought him out of the common. When he came home, he told his father about the moving lights, *which*, his father informed him, were called Will o' the Wisps, or Jack o' Lanterns. Those lights came from the marshes, and it* was* the wind* that* made* them shake and dance about—*which* poor Harry mistook for the motion of a traveller.

Words marked * are not to be parsed for the present.

CHAPTER III.

USES AND INFLECTIONS OF WORDS.

30   **Inflections.**

THE different forms of the same words, as, (1) "like," "likes," "liked;" (2) "man," "man's," "men;" (3) "quick," "quicker," "quickest," are called **Inflections**.

The word "Inflection" means a "bending," or slight alteration.

31   Some words in a sentence are inflected to suit or *agree with* other words with which they are put.

For example, we say "He *likes* me;" but, if "he" is altered into "they," "likes" must be altered into "like" to *agree with* "they."

The rules for the "putting together" or arrangement of words so as to agree with one another, are called Rules of **Syntax** (*syn-*, together; *taxis*, putting).

32   **Uses of the Noun.**

I. A Noun may be used in the

(1) *Singular Number.*

     Apple, man, mouse, ox.

(2) *Plural Number.*

Apples, men, mice, oxen.

Singular is nearly the same word as "single." *Plural* means "*more* (than one)."

II. Again, a Noun in a sentence may be used as—

(1) *Subject.*
"*John* strikes."

(2) *Object.*
"I strike *John.*"

(3) *Possessively* (*i.e.* to denote the Possessor).
"*John's* book," "*men's* thoughts."

(4) *Vocatively* (*i.e.* "calling by").
"Come here, *John.*"

33 These *Uses,* inasmuch as they represent the *condition* or *case* in which the Noun stands relatively to other words in the Sentence, are sometimes called "Cases."

<small>The word *case*, in its original Greek use, πτῶσις, meant "falling." By the Greeks the Subject was regarded as *erect*, while the action, and those affected by the action, were regarded as subordinate, bent, or *falling*. Hence the Greeks would not have used such an expression as the *Subjective case* at all : to them it would have been as absurd as to speak of "an *erect falling.*" But the Latins, translating πτῶσις into *casus*, lost the Greek sense, and we have lost it also ; so that now *case* means little more than "use in connection with other words."</small>

34   Inflections of the Noun.

I. The Plural use of a Noun is denoted by an Inflection, which is generally formed according to the following Rule :—

The Plural of a Noun is formed by adding -s to the Singular ; as apple, apples.

35   To this rule there are some exceptions well known to all English children. The reason for the exceptions generally is, that the regular Plural would be harsh and hard to pronounce: hence for "churchs" we say "churches," and for "calfs," "calves."

36   Some of our irregular Plurals are remains of old Plural forms, and are made by—

     (1) Adding -*en* : *e.g.* "oxen."
     (2) Changing the vowel sound of the monosyllable : *e.g.* "mice," "men," "feet," "teeth."
     (3) Leaving the singular form untouched : *e. g.* "sheep," "deer."

In some cases the modern Plural is derived from an old disused Singular. For example, the old Singular forms, "flie," "citie," are retained in the modern Plurals, "flies," "cities."

In other cases words (1) early introduced into the language received (and retain) the old -*e*, while (2) words, with similar terminations, later introduced, are spelt without -*e* :—

     (1) Echoes, heroes, potatoes.
     (2) Grottos, tyros, dominos.

See Par. 283 ; also Morris's *Historical Outlines of English Accidence*, p. 95.

37 II. The Possessive Use or Case, in the Singular and Plural, is formed by adding 's to the Singular or Plural form, *e.g.* "sun," "sun's;" "children," "children's."

> The mark ('), called an Apostrophe (see Glossary), denotes that something is omitted. In Early English there was a vowel instead of the Apostrophe.
>
> The Apostrophe serves the purpose of distinguishing the Possessive, *e.g.* "sun's" from the Plural "suns."

When the Plural Noun ends in -*s*, the Possessive -*s* is omitted, and nothing is added but the Apostrophe: "*boys*' books." This is also the case in the Singular, where a Singular Noun of more than two syllables ends in -*s*, *e.g.* "*Lycurgus*' laws."

The other uses of Nouns have no Inflections to denote them.[1]

38   Uses and Inflections of Pronouns.

The uses of Pronouns are the same as those of Nouns, except that (1) some of the Pronouns, *e.g.* "I," "he," cannot be used Vocatively; (2) instead of being used Possessively, they have Possessive Adjectives formed from them.

> These Possessive Adjectives are really old Possessive Inflections or *Cases* of the Pronouns, which have now ceased to be recognized as Cases. See Par. 569.

---

[1] Some inflections were once used to denote gender, *e.g.* -*ster*, ('spinster,' meaning a female spinner) and -*ess*. But these inflections cannot now be used to denote the genders of all or even of many Nouns: consequently they are now *terminations*, and no longer to be called *inflections*.

Uses and Inflections of the Adjective.

41   I. USE.—The use of an Adjective is to point out, qualify, or "enumerate," a certain Noun.[1]

42   II. INFLECTIONS —There are three *degrees* (*degree* means *step*) in most Adjectives, *e.g.* "long."

(1) "Longer" of *two* things, *i.e.* long when *compared* with one other thing. This we call the *Comparative degree.*

(2) "Longest" of *more than two*. This is, as it were, *carried above* the Comparative degree, and we therefore call it the *Superlative degree* (*super-* above, *lat-* carried).

In poetry the Superlative inflection is sometimes used, without any notion of *comparison*, to mean "very."
   "A little ere the *mightiest* Julius died."

(3) "Long," without any thought of comparison at all, but simply and positively long. This is called the *Positive degree.*

43   To form the Comparative and Superlative, add—

(1) *-er, -est,* to Positives of one syllable.[2]

(2)   „   „   two syllables ending in *-y, -le, -ow, -er.*

---

[1] See *How to Tell,* &c., page 32.
"Enumerate" here means to answer the question *how many?* or *how much?* before a Noun.
[2] For changes in spelling, see Par. 268.

These forms *sound* as though they had only two syllables, e.g. "happier," "nobler." Hence the exceptional formation.

(3) *More* and *most* in other cases.

"More," "most," are not Inflections, but substitutes for Inflections. A few disyllabic Adjectives are occasionally found with -*er*, -*est*, e.g. "sublim*er*." But this license is best reserved for Poetry.

(4) Other formations are quite irregular, *e g.* not "good-er," but "bet-ter," from an old form "bet;" so "worse." "Every" has no Inflections.

Some few Adjectives (*e.g.* "*these*") have a Plural Inflection; but these are so few that they need not be considered. There was once a Definite form in -*e*, of which perhaps "olde*n*" retains a trace (MORRIS).

How to Parse an Adjective.

In parsing an Adjective, state—

I. *Degree of Comparison*.

II. *Function of Adjective*, *i.e.* whether it qualifies, defines, enumerates, &c.

This may be found by answering the question, "What does the Adjective tell me?"

III. *Noun or Pronoun*, qualified, defined, enumerated, &c.

Where the Noun is omitted, as in "I do not like these books; are they the *best* (*books*) that you have?"—you may say that "best" qualifies the Noun "books," *implied* or *understood*.

EXERCISE.

Parse the Adjectives in Exercise I., thus :—

Adjective.	Degree.	Function.	Noun or Pronoun.
Mighty	positive	tells you what sort, or "qualifies"	king.
Whose	—	tells you whose, or "defines"	name.
Every	—	tells you how many, or "enumerates"	boy.

The other Adjectives in this and other Exercises may be similarly parsed.

Uses and Inflections of the Adverb.

45 I. **Uses.** An Adverb may be used with—

1 (*a*). *A Verb:*

"He declared *positively* that he would not come."

1 (*b*). *An implied Verb* having for its Subject a Noun Clause made up of the Sentence : —

(1) "He will *positively* not come," *i.e.*, "That he will not come *is positively true*."[1]

(2) "*Perhaps* he made a mistake," *i.e.*, "That he made a mistake *is perhaps true*."[1]

2. *An Adjective:*

"He is *very, more, less, least*, successful."

[1] Adverbs thus used are sometimes said to *modify sentences*.

3. (a) *An Adverb*, or, (b) *Adverbial Phrase*:
(a) "*More, less, very,* often."
(b) "I laboured *altogether* in-vain."
"I came *merely* to-help-you."
"You live *far* from-me."

4. *A Noun* (rarely):
"*Even* Homer sometimes nods."

This is a short way of saying "Even (so *wakeful* a poet as) Homer;" so that, in reality, "even" modifies an implied Adjective.

Only requires care in such sentences as:
"*Only* a tyrant would act thus."

In early English "one" (ân) was used in many places where we should use "only," or "alone." (For the use of "one" as an *Adjective* to signify "only," cf. the Latin "Ego *unus* supersum.") Thus, instead of "not (this) *only* that," they wrote :—

(1) "Not that *one* (ân) that," &c.
(2) "God ône (*i.e.*, God *alone*, or *only* God) can do this."
(3) "He was king ône," *i.e.*, "He *alone*, or, *only* he."

In the earliest times "only" (*ônlich*) appears to have been used as an Adjective for "lonely," "solitary," and to have had a Superlative form (*ônlukest*). In this sense we still speak of "an *only* child." But the Adverbial termination *-ly* (cf. the *-y* in "many") (Par. 218) has encouraged the Adverbial, and discouraged the Adjectival, usage. Our modern Adverbial "only" is therefore a compromise between an Adjective and an Adverb. It is not exactly an Adjective in the sense of "an *only* tyrant"; nor yet is the "only" an ordinary Adverb modifying "would act." It is a confusion between "A tyrant is the *only* or *one* person that would act thus," and "A tyrant *by himself* (one-ly) would act thus."

"Only" should be parsed as "Adjectival Adverb irregularly modifying 'tyrant.'"

46 II. **Inflections.** Adverbs have their Degrees of Comparison expressed (rarely) by Inflections, *e.g.* "soon," "soon-*er*," "soon-*est*"; more commonly by the addition of "more," "most," *e.g.* "happily," "*more* happily," "*most* happily."

47 In parsing an Adverb, therefore, you may state—

I. With what Verb, Adjective, Adverb, or Noun it is connected.

Always ask yourself before parsing an Adverb, "What does this Adverb tell me?" The answer will contain the Verb, Adjective, or Noun with which the Adverb is used.

II. Whether it is in the Positive, Comparative, or Superlative degree.

48 *Caution.* Some Adverbs are used as Conjunctions:—

"You say you wish me well; will you help me *then?*"

Here "then" must be parsed as a Conjunction, or as an Adverb used Conjunctively.[1]

49 The Adverbs "where," "when," "whence," &c., are used (1) Interrogatively, (2) Conjunctively, (3) Relatively.[2]

(1) "*Where* is the book?"
(2) "I asked him *where* (in what place) the book was."
(3) "You will find the book *where* (in the place in which) you laid it."[2]

[1] See *How to Tell*, &c., page 101.
[2] In (3), as well as in (2), *where* is Conjunctively used; but it is also used Relatively, and is thus described, to distinguish it from the *merely Conjunctive* use.

Exercise.

Parse the Adverbs in Exercise I., thus :[1]—

Adverb.	Used with what Word.	What the Adverb does.[2]
Once	lived	Tells you *when* he lived.
There	see Par. 152	
Where	is	Asks *where* Persia is. Used Conjunctively. See *How to Tell, &c.* pages 101, 102.
Not	do know	See *How to Tell, &c.* page 55.
Out	part of "look out"	See *How to Tell, &c.* page 78.
Almost	all	See *How to Tell, &c.* page 60.
Far	"from him" (par. 45.)	Tells you *where* the nation lived.
Yet	had (not) submitted.	Tells you *when* the nation had not submitted.
Altogether	"taken" understood.	The meaning is (taken) altogether, the nation was called "Greeks"; or "altogether" may be connected with "was called" as "together" below.
Together	did (not) amount	Tells you *how* or in what circumstances "they did not amount."
Often	were divided	Tells you *when* they were divided.

The rest of this, and other Exercises, may be similarly parsed by the pupil.

[1] The Degree of Comparison is so unimportant that it need not be mentioned unless specially asked.
[2] This column should not be written ; nor need it be repeated, if the pupil has been well drilled in such work, while learning to distinguish an Adverb.

46 II. **Inflections.** Adverbs have their Degrees of Comparison expressed (rarely) by Inflections, *e.g.* "soon," "soon-*er*," "soon-*est*"; more commonly by the addition of "more," "most," *e.g.* "happily," "*more* happily," "*most* happily."

47 In parsing an Adverb, therefore, you may state—

I. With what Verb, Adjective, Adverb, or Noun it is connected.

Always ask yourself before parsing an Adverb, "What does this Adverb tell me?" The answer will contain the Verb, Adjective, or Noun with which the Adverb is used.

II. Whether it is in the Positive, Comparative, or Superlative degree.

48 *Caution.* Some Adverbs are used as Conjunctions :—

"You say you wish me well; will you help me *then?*"

Here "then" must be parsed as a Conjunction, or as an Adverb used Conjunctively.[1]

49 The Adverbs "where," "when," "whence," &c., are used (1) Interrogatively, (2) Conjunctively, (3) Relatively.[2]

  (1) "*Where* is the book?"
  (2) "I asked him *where* (in what place) the book was."
  (3) "You will find the book *where* (in the place in which) you laid it."[3]

[1] See *How to Tell,* &c., page 101.
[2] In (3), as well as in (2), *where* is Conjunctively used; but it is also used Relatively, and is thus described, to distinguish it from the *merely Conjunctive* use.

EXERCISE.

Parse the Adverbs in Exercise I., thus : [1]—

Adverb.	Used with what Word.	What the Adverb does. [2]
Once.	lived	Tells you *when* he lived.
There	see Par. 152	
Where	is	Asks *where* Persia is. Used Conjunctively. See *How to Tell, &c.* pages 101, 102.
Not	do know	See *How to Tell, &c.* page 55.
Out	part of "look out"	See *How to Tell, &c.* page 78.
Almost	all	See *How to Tell, &c.* page 60.
Far	"from him" (par. 45.)	Tells you *where* the nation lived.
Yet	had (not) submitted.	Tells you *when* the nation had not submitted.
Altogether	"taken" understood.	The meaning is (taken) altogether, the nation was called "Greeks"; or "altogether" may be connected with "was called" as "together" below.
Together	did (not) amount	Tells you *how* or in what circumstances "they did not amount."
Often	were divided	Tells you *when* they were divided.

The rest of this, and other Exercises, may be similarly parsed by the pupil.

[1] The Degree of Comparison is so unimportant that it need not be mentioned unless specially asked.
[2] This column should not be written; nor need it be repeated, if the pupil has been well drilled in such work, while learning to distinguish an Adverb.

50   **The Use of the Preposition.**

The Preposition has no Inflections; and, in order to parse it, there is no need to state anything but the Noun or Pronoun that is the Object of the Preposition.

> *Cautions:* 1. Some Prepositions are used as Adverbs, *e.g.*—
> "Come *in*," "Heave *to.*"
>
> 2. Some Prepositions or Prepositional Adverbs are parts of Compound Verbs, *e.g.*—
> "He was *run over* by a heavy waggon."
>
> **51** 3. When a Preposition has a Relative Pronoun for its Object, it often follows the Pronoun, *e.g.*—
> "The people that I am *with.*"
>
> In such cases the Relative Pronoun is often omitted—
> "The boy you spoke *to* was my brother."

Exercise.

Parse the Prepositions in Exercise I., thus :[1]—

    Upon : Object, "a time."
    Over :   ,,   "Persia."
    In :   ,,   "the map."
    Of :   ,,   "the Persians."
    Over :   ,,   "almost all the nations of the East."
    Of :   ,,   "the East."

[1] All this ought to have been done by the Pupil in learning to distinguish Prepositions. See *How to Tell*, &c., pp. 71, 80.

The other Prepositions in this and other Exercises may be similarly parsed.

52   **The Use of the Conjunction.**

The Conjunction has no Inflections, and therefore, in order to parse it, nothing is needed except to state what it does, *i.e.* what are the two sentences joined together by it. (See pages 104 and 105 of "*How to Tell,*" &c.)

53   *Caution.* Some Adverbs are used as Conjunctions :—

    (1) " I asked the man *where*[1] my brother was."
    (2) " It was useless to attempt to persuade him ; *so*[1] I took my leave."

In "as far as," "as soon as," &c., the first "as" is an Adverb modifying "far," "soon ;" the second "as" is a Conjunction. See *How to Tell,* &c., p. 99. These words are, however, sometimes parsed as *Compound Conjunctions.*

Exercise.

Parse the Conjunctions in Exercise I., thus :[2]—

"If" joins { (1) "You do not know."
           (2) "Look it out in the map."

"Where" joins { (1) "Does every boy know"
               (2) "Persia is."

"Though" joins { (1) "He was king — of the East"
                 (2) "He was not satisfied."

"Yet" joins the same sentences.

[1] See *How to Tell,* &c., pages 101, 102.
[2] "And," "than," and the second "as" in "as—as," may be simply called Conjunctions, without attempting to write down the Sentences joined by them : *ib.*, page 142.

The other Conjunctions in this, and in other Exercises may be similarly parsed.

54 **How to Parse a Verbal Noun.**

A Verbal Noun is a Noun formed from a Verb by adding *-ing* to it, *e.g.* "I like *walk-ing*."[1]

A Verbal Noun resembles other Nouns in being the Subject of some Verb, or Object of some Verb or Preposition; but it differs from other Nouns in often taking an Object of its own, *e.g.*—

"I like *eating* beef."

Here "eating" is the Object of "I like," but also has for its Object "beef."

Hence in a Verbal Noun you may state—

1. Whether it is used as Subject or Object.[2]

2. (*a*) Of what Verb it is Subject, or (*b*) of what Verb or Preposition it is Object.

3. What is its Object, if it has one.

EXERCISE XIII. (SPECIMEN).

Parse the Verbal Nouns in the following Exercise:—

On *reaching* the shore, Mr. Barlow pointed to a speck far off on the horizon, and asked Tommy what it was. After *observing* it attentively, Tommy replied that it must be a very small boat. "What can the boatmen be doing so far out at sea?" asked Mr. Barlow. "They must be

---

[1] Verbal *Noun Phrases* may also be formed, such as, "I do not like *being deceived*," "He does not like *having been deceived*," &c. As to spelling, see Par. 267—73.

[2] Verbal Nouns are generally in the Singular, so that the Number need not be stated.

engaged in *catching* fish," said Tommy. " Look again," said Mr. Barlow a few minutes* afterwards; "and, before *replying*, note whether the speck has changed." " Yes, indeed!" cried Tommy, "instead of *appearing* a boat,* it now seems to be a small vessel,* sailing this way." A half* an hour* afterwards, Mr. Barlow bade Tommy look* once more. "Why," said Tommy, "the vessel, by *coming* nearer, seems to have changed into a ship, and, on *looking* more closely, I see that it has three masts." "Then," replied Mr. Barlow, smiling, "I trust you will now believe, without *being* very much *surprised*, that the sun is really larger than the earth, and only appears to be smaller, because of its *being-so-far-off*. And when you hear people saying that '*seeing* is believing,' remember for the future, that, though you may see rightly, your *reasoning* may be wrong. You said you saw nothing but a speck at first, and there you were right; but you were wrong in *inferring* that the speck was a boat."

Verbal Noun	is the Object of	is the Subject of	has for its Object
reaching	on	—	the shore
observing	after	—	it
catching	in	—	fish
replying	before	—	—
appearing[1]	instead of	—	—
coming	by	—	—
looking	on	—	—
being surprised	without	—	—
being, &c.	of	—	—
seeing*	—	is	—
reasoning	—	may be	—[a boat
inferring	in	—	the speck was

[1] "Appearing" does not take an Object after it; for you cannot ask "appears *whom?*" See Par. 147.

For the same reason, "believing" is not the Noun-Object after "is," for "is" cannot be followed by "him." We say "it is *he*," not "is *him*."

Exercise XIV.

Parse the italicized Verbal Nouns in—

The Sun and the Wind were one day disputing which was the stronger. On *seeing* a traveller approaching, "Cease your *bawling*," said the Sun to the Wind, "and let us decide the question by *doing* and not by *talking*. Whoever can succeed in *taking* away that traveller's cloak shall be confessed to be the conqueror: what do you say to *deciding* thus?" "I agree," cried the Wind; "but would you mind my *trying* first?" "Not a bit," said the other; and straightway the Wind set to work. First he tried *blowing* quietly, then more furiously; and at last he blew so loud that you could not have heard yourself speak for his *howling*; but all his *blustering* was in vain. So far from *giving* up his cloak, the traveller only drew it closer round him. Now it was the Sun's turn to try. He began by *driving* away the clouds that the Wind had gathered; then he warmed the air with his bright face till the traveller was forced to loosen his cloak because of the heat. On *seeing* this, the Sun redoubled his efforts, till at last, fainting with the heat, the weary traveller flung himself on a bank to rest, after *stripping* himself of cloak and coat as well.

CHAPTER IV.

USES, FORMS, AND INFLECTIONS OF THE VERBS.

55   Transitive and Intransitive Verbs.

WHEN you hear a person say "I struck ——," you are led to ask "struck whom?" for the action *passes across*, as it were, from the Verb to the Object of the Verb. In "I walk," the action is confined to the walker, and you are not led to ask "walk whom or what?"

Hence "strike" is called a *Transitive* Verb (*trans*, across; *itive*, passing): "walk" is called an *Intransitive* Verb.

The following Definitions are usually given:—

I. *Transitive Verbs are those that denote an action not confined to the agent, but affecting something else.*

II. *Intransitive Verbs are those that denote* (1) "*being*" *or* (2) "*becoming*," *or* (3) *some action confined to the agent, and not affecting anything else.*

56   Most Transitive Verbs can take a Noun-Object or Pronoun-Object after them, *e.g.* "I love, hate, strike *Thomas, them :*" and, as a rough test, it may be said that *if a Verb cannot take "them" after it, it is not a Transitive Verb.*

57 But a few Transitive Verbs take a Noun-Phrase or a Noun-Clause as Object, and rarely or never a Noun or Pronoun, *e.g.* "I *think, hope,* that he will come." Here "that he will come" is the Object of the Transitive Verbs *think* or *hope*.

These Verbs are very seldom followed by a Noun-Object, *e.g.*—

(1) "Think not so foul a *thought.*"
(2) "I hope better *things.*"

58 *Caution.* Some Verbs *seem* to be (but *are not*) used Transitively. The apparent Object is really a kind of Adverb; it might be made the Object of an inserted Preposition, but it is not the Object of the Verb. See Par. 131.

(1) "He ran (for) a mile."
(2) "She waited (for) an hour."
(3) "We slept (during) the whole morning."

The Verbs *is, seem, appear, remain, become,* &c., are Intransitive Verbs (see Par. 147).

59 Active and Passive Forms.[1]

When the Object of a Transitive Verb, *e.g.* "John wounds *Thomas,*" is made the Subject, *e.g.* "*Thomas*

---

[1] These forms are usually called *Voices;* but the Latin term (Madvig) seems to have been "forma" or "genus."

is wounded by John," then the Verb in the second sentence tells us what *is done* to Thomas, or what Thomas *suffers*. Hence the form of the Verb, *is wounded*, is called the *Passive* (*i.e.* "suffering").

60 *The Passive Voice is the form assumed by the Verb when its Object is made the Subject.*

Hence only Transitive Verbs can have Passive Voices, for only Transitive Verbs have Objects.

> It is sometimes said that a Verb is in the Passive Voice when its Subject "denotes a person or thing acted on"; but this is not true. In "Goliath *fell*, or *perished*, by the hand of David." "Goliath" denotes "a person acted on": yet "fell" and "perished" are not Passive Forms.

The ordinary form of the Verb is often called the *Active* (*i.e.* "doing") Voice, because it generally tells us what the person or thing denoted by the Subject *does*, *e.g.* "John *wounds*."

> This is not always true. In "Goliath *fell* or *perished*," "fell" and "perished" tell you rather what Goliath *suffered* than what he *did*: yet they would be called Active.

The following definition seems truer :—

61 *The Active Voice of a Transitive Verb is the form that can be used with an Object.*

Intransitive Verbs are always in the Active Voice.

62 Verbs of Motion are exceptions to this rule. We still say (and once used to say more commonly) "I am arrived," "he *is come.*"

The agent is here considered as affected by his own act: cf. the French "s'en aller," "se promener."

63 *Participles.*

1. Most Verbs, Transitive or Intransitive, can have Verb-Adjectives formed from them by adding -*ing* (rejecting final -*e*), *e.g.* "dancing," "wandering."[1]

64 These words are used as—

(1.) *Adjectives:*

"A *dancing* bear," "a *wandering* gipsy."

(2.) *Verbs with Conjunctions or with Relative Pronouns:*

"A gipsy *wandering* (i e. *when, while,* or *because* he was wandering) across the heath, found the child."

(3.) *Parts of a Stating Verb:*

"A gipsy *was wandering* across the heath."

Consequently, as these words *participate* in the nature of Adjectives and also in the nature of Verbs, they are called *Participles.*

[1] For changes in spelling, see Par. 267—78.

When these words are used as Adjectives, they should be parsed as "Participles used as Adjectives."

65 2. A second Participle is formed from Transitive Verbs by adding -*ed* to the Verb, *e.g. wound, wounded.* See Par. 558.

This kind of Participle is often used with a Noun, to denote that the person or thing represented by the Noun *suffers* the action denoted by the Verb; *e.g.* in "a *wounded* man," "wounded" denotes that a "man" has *suffered* wounding. Hence the Participle in -*ed* is called the *Passive Participle*.

> The Passive Participle is also formed in other ways, *e.g.*, break, broken: bring, brought: sing, sung.

The Participle in -*ing* is called the *Active* Participle.

66 **How to Tell a Participle.**

A Participle can at once be distinguished (1) from an Adjective, (2) from part of a Stating Verb by the fact that it can be, in part, *replaced by a Conjunctive word,* i.e. by a Conjunctive or Relative Pronoun.

You must judge from the sense of the passage what Conjunction is (partly) to replace any Participle. For example, "walking" might be replaced by—

1. *While* or *when:* "*Walking* along the street one day, I saw Thomas."
2. *Because:* "*Walking* on the ice in spite of the park-keeper's warning, the boy fell in."
3. *Though* or *if:* "*Walking* with the greatest care you will scarcely keep yourself from slipping."
4. "I once saw a man *walking* on a rope," *i.e.*, "a man *that was walking.*"
5. "I saw him *walking* towards me," *i.e.* "*while* he was walking," or "*that* he was walking."

67 There is probably some confusion between (1) "I saw him *a-walking*," i.e. "*in*, or, *in the act of, walking* (Noun)"; (2) "I saw him *walking* (Participle)"; (3) "I saw him *walk* (Infinitive)," which Infinitive was once "walk-*en*," easily confused with the Verbal Noun and with the Active Participle.

Exercise XV. (Specimen).

Change the italicized Participles into Verbs and Conjunctions or Verbs and Relative Pronouns:—

A little boy *running* carelessly along the street, knocked against an old woman *carrying* a basket of eggs on her head. Down fell the basket *smashing* all the eggs. The thoughtless boy at first ran on; but, *looking* round and *seeing* the people *staring* and the old woman *beginning to cry*, he turned back, *saying*, "I am very sorry; I would not have knocked against you, if I had seen you." "Yes, master," replied the old woman, *looking* sadly at the fragments of her broken eggs *lying* about the dirty pavement, "but your sorrow will not mend my eggs, nor feed my grandchildren *waiting* for bread at home."

PARTICIPLES.

Participle.		Conjunction, or Relative Pronoun.	Verb.
running carrying smashing looking seeing staring beginning saying looking lying waiting	can be altered into	while who and when when that (Conj.) that (Conj.) and while which who	he was running was carrying it smashed he looked back he saw people were staring *she was* beginning he said she looked were lying are waiting

Passive, as well as Active, Participles can be changed into Verbs with Conjunctions or with Relative Pronouns.

EXERCISE XVI. (SPECIMEN).

Change the Participles in the following Exercise into Verbs and Conjunctions or Verbs and Relative Pronouns :—

A rich gouty man *troubled* with disease in his feet, went to a physician *distinguished* for his skill, *promising* to do exactly what the physician ordered, if only he would cure him. *Seeing* his patient *deprived* of the use of his feet and too lazy to use them, the physician took him up into a room *containing* no chair, couch, or seat of any kind, and *having* a floor *lined* with iron. There he left him and went out, *locking* the door behind him. Presently the rich man found his feet *growing* unpleasantly hot. *Irritated* at this he called out, but no one answered.

Hobbling to the door on his crutches, he found it *locked*. By this time his feet, *heated* by the hot iron floor, pained him so much that he began to raise them, *lifting* first one, then the other, at first slowly, then more and more quickly. In this way, *forced* to use his legs, he found the use of them grow more and more easy, and was cured against his will.

Participle.	Conjunction or Relative Pronoun.	Verb.
troubled	that	was troubled
distinguished	that	was distinguished
promising	and	promised
seeing	since	he saw
deprived	that (Conj.)	his patient was deprived
containing	that	contained
having	that	had
lined	that	was lined
locking	after	he had locked
growing	that	his feet grew
irritated	since	he was irritated
hobbling	after	he had hobbled
locked	that (Conj.)	it had been locked
heated	since	they were heated
lifting	and	he lifted
forced	because	he was forced

(can be changed into)

Participle after " see," " hear," &c.

You must be particularly careful after the Verbs of the senses, such as " see," " hear," and " find," (where " find " means " understand.") Thus, in " I saw my friend *shot* down," the meaning is "I saw my friend *being, i.e. when* he was *in the act of being*, shot down;" but in "I saw his body, *thrown* on one side and frightfully *mangled*," the meaning might be, either "*when* it *was being* thrown," or "*after* it *had been* thrown:" and you cannot tell which is meant without carefully looking at the whole of the passage.

In other words, a Passive Participle, *e.g.* "shot," may stand for "being shot," or, "having been shot."[1]

How to Parse a Participle.

A Participle, like an Adjective, (1) must always be connected with some Noun or Pronoun; (2) as being part of a Verb, it must be either Active or Passive; (3) if Active, it *may* have an Object. In parsing a Participle, therefore, you can state—

1. What Noun or Pronoun it is joined to.
2. Whether it is Active or Passive.
3. What is its Object, if it has one.

In order to answer (1), first replace the Participle by a Conjunction (or Rel. Pronoun) and Verb; then ask the question *who?* or *what?* before the Verb that replaces the Participle.

[1] See Par. 67. Possibly, in some cases, the Passive Participle represents the old Infinitive.
Compare :—
"That they would suffer these abominations
By our strong arms from forth her fair streets (*to be*) *chased*."
SHAKESPEARE, *Rape of Lucrece*, l. 1,634.
"Would swear him (*to have*) *dropped* out of the moon."—POPE.

The answer *given by the sentence to this question* is the Noun or Pronoun to which the Participle is joined.

For example, in the last Exercise, " troubled " is replaced by " that was troubled." " Who was troubled ? " The answer given by the story is " a rich gouty *man ;* " then " man " is the Noun to which " troubled " is joined. " Seeing " is replaced by " since he saw." " Who saw ? " Answer, " The physician ; " then " physician " is the Noun to which " seeing " is joined.

EXERCISE.

Parse fully Participles not marked * in previous Exercises.

70 Moods.

When we speak about an action or state, we may speak of it in several different *ways* or *Modes*.

I. We may *point out* the action definitely, as present, past, or future, *e.g.* " he comes, came, will come." This is called the *Pointing* or **Indicative Mode** or **Mood**. (*Indica-*, point out.)

II. We may speak of an action *without defining* the doer, *e.g.* " *to come* is easy." This is called the **Infinitive Mode** or **Mood** (*in*, not ; *finit-*, *marked out, defined*).

III. We may *command* an action. This is called the *Commanding* or **Imperative Mode** or **Mood** (*impera-,* command).

IV. We may speak of an action not as past, present, or future, but as (1) expressing a *condition,* *e.g.* "if *he should come;*" or (2) subject to a *condition, e.g.* "I *should see* him;" or (3) (*a*) *purpose, e.g.* "Come here that *I may see* you;" or (*b*) *purpose* approximating to a *wish, e.g.* "I pray that his life *may be spared.*"

In all these cases, except (2), the Verb is preceded by a *Conjunction—if, that,* &c.; and this *Mood* might therefore be called the *Conjunctive* Mood. But it is generally called the **Subjunctive Mood**.[1]

71 **Times or Tenses.**

For the present, in speaking of the Times or Tenses of a Verb, we shall confine ourselves to those of the Indicative Mood.

A Verb may tell you—

1. What any person or thing does at the *present* time:—

"He *catches* fish."

---

[1] In any sentence, the statement of *fact* is called the *principal* clause, and the part of the sentence describing the *purpose, condition,* &c., is called *sub*-ordinate, and is said to be *sub-joined* to the principal clause. Hence the Mood of the Verb in this *subjoined* clause is called *Subjunctive*.

2. What he did in *past* time :—
"He *caught* fish."

3. What he will do in *future* time :—
"He *will catch* fish."

A Verb, then, has three *times* of which it can speak—Past, Present, and Future.

Now the French for "time" is *temps;* and from this French word, slightly altered, we have made the word **Tense.**

A Verb has three Tenses—Past, Present, and Future.

72   States of Action.

Suppose you are speaking of a fisherman whom you saw some time ago, *i.e.* in *past* time, catching fish.

1. You may say simply—
"He *caught* a salmon."

Here you do *not define* the action further than by saying it is *past*. This Tense may therefore be called the "not-defined Past," or **Past Indefinite.**

2. You may say—
"He *was catching* a salmon just as I left him."

—that is, the action was in an *incomplete state*, still going on, or *continuing*. This Tense may therefore be called the **Past Incomplete**, or **Past Continuous**.

3. You may say—
   "He *had caught* a salmon just as I left him."

—that is, the action was in a *complete state*. This Tense may therefore be called the **Past Complete**.

The same three divisions may be found in the Future and Present:—

1. Future Indefinite:
  "I *shall catch* fish."

2. Future Incomplete:
  "I *shall be catching* fish."

3. Future Complete:
  "I *shall have caught* fish."

1. Present Indefinite:
  "I *catch* fish."

2. Present Incomplete:
  "I *am catching* a salmon, but have not yet landed it."

3. Present Complete
  "I *have caught* a salmon, and here it is in my basket."

73 In old English, it was more easy to see that "I *have caught*" was a present tense: for they used to arrange it thus, "I *have* the salmon *caught*," clearly showing that the Time of the Verb was Present (as is shown by "I have" *i.e.* "I possess") and that "caught" was only a Participle or Adjective telling you what had happened to the salmon. But it is not so easy to see this in Intransitive and Passive Verbs, *e.g.* "I *have run.*"

Each Tense has three States, the Indefinite, the Complete, and the Incomplete.

The Passive Tenses are formed by placing the Passive Participle after the different Tenses of the Verb " to be."

74 Some of the Passive Tenses are rarely or never used, owing to their lengthiness; and there is one "state" that is found in the Present, Past, and Future of the Active, but not of the Passive.

(1) "I *have been*
(2) "I *had been*   } *catching.*"
(3) "I *shall have been*

This "state" denotes an action *completed, after being continuous.* It may therefore be called the **Complete Post Continuous**.

Hence all the Tenses may be arranged as follows :—

75 Scheme of Tenses.[1]

STATE.	INDEFINITE	INCOMPLETE	COMPLETE	COMPLETE POST CONTINUOUS.
Time.		ACTIVE.		
Present...	(I) take	(I) am taking	(I) have taken	(I) have been taking
Past ...	(I) took	(I) was taking	(I) had taken	(I) had been taking
Future...	(I) shall take	(I) shall be taking	(I) shall have taken	(I) shall have been taking
		PASSIVE.		
Present...	(I) am taken	(I) am being taken	(I) have been taken	—
Past ...	(I) was taken	(I) was being taken	(I) had been taken	—
Future...	(I) shall be taken	(I)shallbebeing[2] taken	(I)shallhavebeen taken	—

[1] For a fuller scheme of the whole of the Active form, see Par. 584.   [2] Not used.

76 — Common Mistakes in Tenses.

The Tenses and Participles of Irregular Verbs will be best learned by practice. But the pupil may be cautioned against confusing :—

I. "Lay," "lie," "lie."

LAY (Transitive) = "to place or put down."

Present.	Past.	Passive Participle.
(I) **lay**	(I) **laid**	(I have) **laid**

LIE (Intransitive) = "to recline."

| (I) **lie** | (I) **lay** | (I have) **lain** |

LIE (Intransitive) = "to tell a falsehood."

| (I) **lie** | (I) **lied** | (I have) **lied** |

II. The Past Indefinite, and Passive Participle of "ring," "sing," &c. ; often confused by Milton and Pope, but to be kept distinct in Modern English :—

| (I) **sing** | (I) **sang** | (I have) **sung** |
| (I) **ring** | (I) **rang** | (I have) **rung** |

See Dr. Morris's *Historical Outlines, &c.* In E.E., *sang* was used in the Singular, *sung* in the Plural, of the Past Tense. "Lay" is the Causative form of "lie," as "raise" of "rise," "set" of "sit," "fell" of "fall," "drench" of "drink."

77 — The Negative, or Interrogative Form.

In questions and denials we prefer a different form of the Indefinite Present and Past. Instead of "I came not;" "Why speak you?" we say "I did not come;" "Why do you speak?" The advantage of this form of the Verb is, that it enables us to put the Verb at the end, while the *did* or *do* prepares the way for it. You may call this the Negative or Interrogative form of the Verb.

More rarely this form is used affirmatively, to emphasize the truth of a statement :—

"Who says I did not come? I *did come.*"

78   **Person and Number.**

If you alter the Subject of a Verb, you often have to alter the Verb *so as to agree with the Subject.*

1. If you alter "I" into "he," you must alter "catch" into "catches," *so as to agree with* "he."

2. Again, if you alter "he" into "they" you must alter "catches" to "catch," *so as to agree with* the alteration of the Subject from Singular to Plural.

This is expressed by saying that—

A Verb agrees with its Subject in Person and Number.

79   As an explanation of our distinction between *First, Second,* and *Third Persons,* it may be remembered that the Romans, whose grammar we have copied, thought it natural for a person speaking to think *first* of himself (*I*), *secondly* of the person to whom he was speaking (*you*), and *thirdly* of any one else about whom he was speaking (*him* or *her*).

    . The following Scheme shews how a Verb *agrees with* its Subject :—

	Subject	Verb agreeing with its Subject.	
1st Person Sing.	I	am	walk
2nd ,, ,,	thou[1]	art	walkest
3rd ,, ,,	he, she[2]	is	walks
1st Person Plural	we	are	walk
2nd ,, ,,	you[3]	are	walk
3rd ,, ,,	they	are	walk

The Verb "to be" is the only Verb in English that has a separate form of the Verb when the Subject is in the Plural. In other Verbs the Plural form is the same as that of the First Person Singular, *e.g.* "I have," "they have."

80   How to Parse a Verb.[4]

If asked to parse a Verb in the Indicative Mood fully, *e.g.* "has caught," in "He *has caught* a fish," you may state—

1. *The kind or nature of the Verb:* Transitive.
2. *The Voice:* Active.
3. *The Mood:* Indicative.
4. *The Tense:* Complete Present.

[1] Old Form.
[2] *It* is sometimes called a Personal Pronoun, for convenience; it does not stand for a Person (except in the curious idiom mentioned in Par. 158.) Not only *he* and *she*, but *it* and all Nouns *spoken of*, are said to be *in the Third Person.* A Noun denoting a Person *spoken to* is said to be *in the Second Person, e.g.* "come here, *John.*"
[3] There was once an old form of the Subject *ye*, still used in Poetry, and sometimes now used as Object.
[4] For the present, only the Indicative Mood is here spoken of.

5. *The Person :* in the Third Person.
6. *The Number :* Singular.
7. *It agrees with its Subject* "he."
8. *It has for its Object* "a fish."

Caution.—Note that the Present Indicative is often used where, logically, the Future should be used :—

(1) "He will come when he *is* able."
(2) "I shall wait till he *comes.*"

After "when," "till," &c., Shakespeare often uses the Future or Subjunctive, *e.g.* "When he *shall be* able." The modern Present may in these cases be parsed as "used for Future." For the Present after "if," see Par. 168.

81   The Noun-Subject, and Noun-Object.

It is usual, in parsing a Verb, and stating the Subject and Object, not to state the whole of the Subject or Object, but only the Noun or Pronoun, omitting any Adjectives or Adjective Phrases connected with the Noun. For example, in the sixth Verb parsed in the Exercise below, the Subject of "had seen" is "the keen eyes of the lion;" but you need only take the *Noun part* of the Subject, and may answer simply "eyes."

In the same way, when stating the Object of "didst thou leave," you need not write down "thy cruel master," but only the *Noun part*, "master."

82   EXERCISE XVII.[1]

Caxton *brought* the printing press to England from Bruges in 1476. In addition to the difficulties that *attended* the new art of printing, the language *had come* into such a state that an author needed much judgment to select his words and frame his style. A conflict *was raging* between the new-fangled French affectation and English pedantry, and Caxton *was* sorely *distracted* between the "honest and great clerks," who *advocated* the former, and the "gentlemen," who stood up for "old and homely terms." "Our language," says the printer, "*varieth* far from that which *was used* and *spoken* when I *was born*;" and he adds that "the English that is spoken in one shire varieth from the English spoken in another." He goes on to tell a tale how certain merchants on the Thames sailing to Zealand and compelled by contrary winds to remain on the Foreland, *went* into a farmhouse and asked for "eggs." The good-wife answered that she *spoke* no French. "Why *talkest* thou of French?" replied the merchant, angry at being taken for a Frenchman, "I speak no French, nor *understand* it, I ask for eggs." But the farmer's wife, in spite of all his anger, *could* none the better *understand* him, till one of his companions said he wanted "eyren," and the eggs *came* fast enough.

"Lo what shall a man in these days now write?" *adds* the puzzled printer. "Shall he write 'eggs' or 'eyren?' Certainly, it * is hard to please every man, by cause of diversity and change of language."

[1] This Exercise is modified from the admirable *Short History of the English People*, J. R. Green, M.A. (Macmillan, London). It may be parsed after the following Specimen Exercise.

Par. 82] VERBS. 65

EXERCISE XVIIa. (SPECIMEN).

State the Noun-Subjects, Noun-Objects, Kinds, Voices, and Tenses of the italicized Verbs :—

Many centuries ago, a slave, who *had made* his escape from a cruel master, *fled* to a forest where night surprised him, so that he *was forced* to take refuge in a cave. Scarcely *had* he *closed* his eyes in the attempt to sleep, when he heard the roar of a lion beside him. He started up, but it *was* too late ; the keen eyes of the lion *had seen* him, and *were* slowly *coming* nearer. Androcles— who *had* no arms of any kind—now gave himself up for lost. "What *shall* I *do?*" said he : "I have no spear or sword—no, not so much as a stick to defend myself with." And he *cried* aloud in agony, "O foolish Androcles, why *didst* thou *leave* thy cruel master, who at least would have spared thy life because thou *wast* useful to him, whereas now thou *wilt be* the meal of this hungry lion?" What was his surprise, however, to find that the lion, instead of springing on him, *was walking* quietly up to him, limping as though he were in pain. Gaining courage at this, Androcles made no attempt to run away. Presently the lion *held* out his paw, and on examining it Androcles *found* that it was inflamed [1] and swelled. Looking more closely, he perceives that a thorn *has pierced* the ball of the foot, and that it is from this that the lion *is suffering*.

[1] Notice that here "inflamed" and "swelled" are Adjectives describing the condition of the foot. But in the sentence "on hearing this, the king was inflamed with fury," *was inflamed* would be a Verb. You can say "an *inflamed* foot," but not "an *inflamed* king.

83

Verb	Kind and Voice.	Tense	State, or Division of Tense
had made	Trans. Act.	Past	Complete
fled	Intr. Act.	Past	Indefinite
was forced	Passive [1]	Past	Indefinite
had closed	Tr. Act.	Past	Complete
was [2]	—	Past	Indefinite
had seen	Tr. Act.	Past	Complete
were coming	Intr. Act.	Past	Incomplete
had [3]	Tr. Act.	Past	Indefinite
shall do	Tr. Act.	Future	Indefinite
cried	Tr. Act.	Past	Indefinite
didst leave	Tr. Act.	Past	Indefinite
wast	—	Past	Indefinite
wilt be	—	Future	Indefinite
was walking	Intr. Act.	Past	Incomplete
held	Tr. Act.	Past	Indefinite
found	Tr. Act.	Past	Indefinite
has pierced	Tr. Act.	Present	Complete
is suffering	Intr. Act.	Present	Incomplete

84   **"Governing" an Object.**

Where a word, e.g. *he*, has one form when used as a Subject, *he*, and another when used as an Object, *him*—the Verb is sometimes said to *govern* the Object, because the Verb, as it were, controls and alters the form of the Object.

---

[1] Passive Verbs are necessarily almost always Transitive in their Active Forms; this, therefore, may be taken for granted, and "Transitive" need not be repeated every time with "Passive."

[2] "Be," "was," &c., are not called either Active or Passive. See Par. 147.

[3] Carefully distinguish the Indefinite Past "had," when used by itself, from the Complete Past "*had* seen him."

Person	Number	Subject	Object
3rd	Sing.	who	escape
3rd	Sing.	slave	—
3rd	Sing.	he	—
3rd	Sing.	he	eyes
3rd	Sing.	it (*i.e.* his starting up)	
3rd	Plural	eyes	him
3rd	Plural	eyes	
3rd	Sing.	who	arms
1st	Sing.	I	what
3rd	Sing.	he	"O, foolish," &c.
2nd (old)	Sing.	thou	master
2nd (old)	Sing.	thou	—
2nd (old)	Sing.	thou	—
3rd	Sing.	lion	
3rd	Sing.	lion	paw
3rd	Sing.	Androcles	"that it was inflamed," &c.
3rd	Sing.	thorn	ball
3rd	Sing.	lion	—

Only in cases where the Objective differs from the Subjective form, can a Verb be said, with truth, to *govern* the Object.

Exercise XVIII.

85 Parse, as above :—

Gathering fresh courage from the behaviour of the lion, Androcles at last *ventures* to lay his hand on the extended paw; he *touches* and handles the swelling, and, in spite of the growing darkness, *succeeds* in drawing out a large thorny splinter, which *had run* deep into the foot. As soon as the thorn *was extracted*, the lion *showed* his joy by evident signs, and at first *lay* down by the side of his benefactor, as though to protect him; but presently he departed.¹ Next morning, however, before the sun *had risen*, back *comes* the lion to the cave with a deer in his jaws, which he *sets* down at the feet of Androcles; and, for several days, while Androcles *was hiding* in the cave, he *was protected* from all danger and¹ *supplied* with ample food by the grateful lion. But one day, just when the slave *was congratulating* himself that he *had escaped* his pursuers for ever, a party of soldiers, passing through the forest, *catch*² sight of him resting in the cave in the absence of the lion. At once they arrest him, and carry him back to the city whence he *had escaped*.³

86   Singular Nouns with Plural Verbs.

Some Nouns, though Singular, are sometimes treated as Plural, because they are Plural in *meaning*, e.g. "party" in "A *party* of friends are coming to dine with me to-day." Here, although "is coming" would not be absolutely wrong, yet "*are* coming" sounds more natural, because "party" means a number of persons coming from distinct quarters, and *regarded as distinct*. See Pars. 334—9.

87   Shall, Will.

Note that in the Indefinite Future, *shall* is used in the First Person, and *will* in the Second and Third Persons:—

1st Person	I shall	We shall.
2nd Person	Thou wilt	You will.
3rd Person	He will	They will.

¹ Repeat "was."
² Note "catch" not "catches." See next Paragraph.
³ Continued in Par. 102.

The reason is this: *shall*, like "must," implies compulsion. Now we do not mind using a word implying compulsion about ourselves; but it seems rather rude to use it about others. For this reason we dislike saying, except in anger, "you shall," "he shall," and prefer to say, "you will," "he will." "You will" once meant "you wish *or* are willing to;" but now it generally means no more than "you are going (to)."

When we are bestowing a favour that does not depend on the recipient but on our own will, we may use "shall" with the Second Person :—

(1) "You *shall* have a holiday to-morrow."

Here the context absolutely destroys the notion of compulsion, and therefore "shall" may be used without rudeness.

For a similar reason, there is no rudeness in—

(2) "*Shall* you see him to-morrow?"
(3) "He says he *shall* be out of town all the summer."

Imperative Mood.

You cannot *command* a man to do anything unless you speak *to him*; consequently the commanding or Imperative Mood is, strictly speaking, always in the Second Person, Singular or Plural, *e.g.* "come."

Sometimes we, as it were, exhort or command ourselves, *e.g.* "let me see," "let us run." But this is the same as "suffer me to see," "suffer us to run." Here, therefore, "suffer" and "let" are Imperatives, *addressed to some imaginary person;* but "see" and "run" are not Imperatives, but Infinitives, the "to" being left out. (See Par. 94).

89 Again, sometimes, when we are speaking *of* a Third Person, we seem to command him, *e.g.* "let him beware;" but this is explained in the same way, and is put for "let him (to) beware."

The Imperative is almost always in the Active.

The Passive, when used, is formed (like every other Mood and Tense of the Passive) from the Passive Participle preceded by "be":—

(1) "*Be pleased* to enter."
(2) "*Be pacified, be persuaded* that all is well."

90 In the Bible, the Subject of the Imperative is often expressed, *e.g.*, "come ye": but it is generally omitted in modern English.

As a command applies mostly to the present time, there are no *Tenses* in this Mood. A command relating to the future is sometimes expressed by the Future Indicative; either the compulsory form, "You *shall* bring the book to-morrow," or the courteous form, "You *will* have dinner ready by seven." We also say "*Have* done," Pres. Compl.

91 How to Parse the Imperative.

An Imperative has no Inflections, and therefore cannot with truth *agree with* its Subject. It is therefore wrong to use *agree* about the Imperative. The Imperative *has* a Subject.

In parsing an Imperative, use the form given in Par. 80, remembering that, though the Subject of an Imperative is seldom expressed, yet it is always implied.

92
Forms of the Infinitive.

The Tenses of the Infinitive Mood of a Verb, *e.g.* "send," are as follows:—

	Active.	Passive.
Indefinite	(to) **send**	(to) **be sent**
Incomplete	(to) **be sending**	(to) **be being sent**[1]
Complete	(to) **have sent**	(to) **have been sent**
Complete Post-Continuous	(to) **have been sending**	(to) **have been being sent**[1]

There is no Past Tense. The Future is expressed by different phrases, such as "to be on the point of sending," "to be about to be sending," "to be going to send," &c.

The "to" is inclosed in brackets, because it is sometimes omitted, *e.g.* "I saw him (to) *fall*," where "fall" is Infinitive. See next Paragraph.

93
"To" Omitted.

We can say indifferently—

(1) "He dares not *come.*"
(2) "He has not dared *to come.*"

Why is "to" inserted in the second, and omitted in the first, example?

[1] Rarely or never used.

Again, compare together—

I bade him	⎫	I ordered him	⎫
I let him	⎬ come	I permitted him	⎬ to come
I made him	⎭	I compelled him	⎭

I can	⎫	I am able	⎫
I dare	⎪	I venture	⎪
I may	⎪	I am allowed	⎪
I must	⎬ come	I am compelled	⎬ to come
I shall	⎪	I am certain	⎪
I should	⎪	I ought	⎪
I will	⎭	I am willing	⎭

To is also omitted after the Verbs *see, hear, need, feel*, e.g. "I saw him die," "I heard her sing." What is the reason for the omission of *to* after all these Verbs?

94 The reason is that our ancestors used not to put *to* before the Infinitive. Instead of "to walk" they used to say "walk-*en*." "To" was only used to denote *purpose*, with a special form of the Verb, "to walk-*ene*," *i.e.* "*in order to* walk." In time, the inflections -*en* and -*ene* became disused. So, to denote the Infinitive, they used "to" in all cases, not only in its proper sense of purpose, but also as the mere sign of the Infinitive, even where the Infinitive was nothing but a Noun. Thus, instead of saying "I like walk-*en*," they began to say "I like *to* walk."

95 But after some Verbs, such as *let, may, can*, &c., it was not found necessary to use *to*. These Verbs, because they are so often *companions* or *allies* to other Verbs, are called "allied" or **Auxiliary** Verbs. When these Verbs therefore were used, everybody knew that an Infinitive was pretty certain to follow, even though *to* was not put in: "let us (to) pray."

96 For a similar reason, *to* was not inserted after *see*, *hear*, &c., because they were Verbs of such common use that everybody understood that a Verb could be in the Infinitive after them, without the insertion of *to*.[1]

But remember, the Verbs after the Auxiliary Verbs, *e.g.* "let us *pray*," are Infinitives, just as much as after other Verbs where *to* is inserted, *e.g.* "permit us *to pray*."

"To" is omitted in the Infinitive after the Auxiliary Verbs "may," "can," "will,"[2] *"let," "must," &c., and also after "see," "hear," "feel," &c.*

97 **The Complementary Infinitive.**

The Infinitive is often used to *complete*, *i.e.* to be

---

[1] Partly also the *to* may have been omitted because these words *may, can, see, hear,* &c. are so common that the insertion of *to*, whenever we use them, would make our language lengthy and tedious. Occasionally in Shakespeare, *to* is found inserted where we should omit it, and omitted where we should insert it. People had not yet drawn a fixed line between Auxiliary Verbs and others. Even now, where the Verb "dare" is used like an ordinary Verb, *to* must be inserted after it. You may say, "He *dares* not come," but scarcely, "He *will* never *dare* come." *To* must be inserted in the last sentence. So, "they *made* him *sit* on the ground;" but "he *was made to sit*."

[2] The Infinitive, after "shall" or "will" denoting futurity, is generally connected with "shall" or "will" and treated as part of a Future Tense.

the *Complement* of, a preceding Noun or Pronoun. For example, in—

(1) "I like *a rascal to be punished.*"
(2) "*The prisoner* was ordered *to be executed.*"

Here (1) "a rascal" is not the Object of "like," for you do not like "a rascal," but "a rascal to be punished." Consequently, "rascal" is only the *Partial Object*, and it has for its *Complement* the Infinitive "to be punished."

In the same way (2) (though the Subjective Construction is less common than Objective), the "prisoner" was not "ordered" at all; what was ordered was *the execution of the prisoner*, or, in the words of the sentence, "the prisoner to be executed." Consequently, "prisoner" is only the *Partial Subject*, and it has for its *Complement* the Infinitive "to be executed."

Uses of the Infinitive.

The Infinitive is used—

I. (*a*) As a Noun:
    (1) "I like *to walk.*"
    (2) "*To walk* is healthy."

I. (*b*) As *part* of a Noun-Phrase used Objectively:—
    (1) "I like *a rascal to be punished.*"
    (2) "I know *him to be honest.*"

(3) "He reported *the experiment to have failed.*"
(4) "I perceived *him to have made* a mistake."
(5) "I saw *him (to) fall.*"

I. (c) Less frequently, as *part* of a Noun-Phrase used Subjectively :—

(1) "*He* is said *to be coming.*"
(2) "*The prisoner* was ordered *to be executed.*"

But these may also sometimes be parsed as Adverbial Infinitives. See Par. 105.

99 II. As an Adverb, or part of an Adverb, modifying a Verb or Adjective :—

(1) "I am come (for what purpose ?) *to see* you."
(2) "I am sorry (on account of what ?) *to hear* this."
(3) "He is slow (in what respect ?) *to forgive.*"
(4) "You are cruel (in what respect ?) *to frighten* her."

100 III. As an Adjective-Phrase :—

(1) "Water *to drink,*" i.e. "*drinking*-water."
(2) "Paper *to write with,*" i.e. "*writing*-paper."
(3) "Their importunity was not *to be resisted,*" i.e. "ir-*resistible.*"
(4) "Your mistake is *to be deplored,*" i.e. "*deplorable.*"

101 How to Parse an Infinitive.

Hence, in parsing an Infinitive, you may first state—

1. *Kind of Verb.* Transitive, or Intransitive.

2. *Voice.* Active or Passive.

3. *Mood.* Infinitive.

4. "*State*," or *Division of Tense, i.e.* whether Indefinite, Complete, or Incomplete.

5. *Object,* if it has any.

To these statements you may add whether it is used as a—

I. *Noun:* and, if so, (*a*) of what Verb it is the Subject or Object, Complementary or otherwise; and (*b*) to what Noun or Pronoun it is Complementary.

II. An *Adverb:* and, if so, by what Preposition and Verbal Noun it may be replaced.[1]

III. *Adjective:* and, if so, with what Noun it is connected.

Exercise XIX. (Specimen).

102 Parse the Infinitives in the following Exercise[2]:—

Having been brought before the judge, Androcles was at once condemned, and ordered *to be exposed to* wild beasts

[1] The pupil may also be asked to mention the word modified by the Adverbial Infinitive as in parsing an ordinary Adverb.
[2] For brevity, the Voice, Mood, and "State," are omitted, as also is the Object of the Infinitive, and the word modified by the Adverbial Infinitive.

in the amphitheatre, *to strike* terror into all other slaves that might wish *to run* away from their masters. Accordingly, on the appointed day, the wretched slave was made *to stand* in the presence of thousands of spectators, opposite the cage of a lion, which had not been suffered *to eat* anything for several days, *to increase* its natural savageness. The furious roaring of the famished lion struck terror into every heart, and made the poor slave *prepare* for the worst. Suddenly, the signal is given, and from the open cage forth bounds the lion. But, what was the astonishment of the spectators, *to see* the savage beast, on reaching its victim, at once *change* its nature. Instead of devouring Androcles, it began *to fawn* on and caress him. The spectators, indignant at the cowardice of the beast—for so they called it—bade the officers *let loose* a second lion to destroy the first. It was done, and forthwith a monster larger and more furious than the first, rushed with open jaws at the trembling slave. But the first lion, at once springing on the assailant, forced it *to turn* from Androcles, and after a terrible contest, left it disabled on the sand. The admiring spectators now shouted[1] applause,[1] declaring that the slave must *be asked to explain* the lion's extraordinary conduct. On hearing the story of his adventures, they begged the Governor *to pardon* Androcles, and not only to give him his freedom, but also to bestow on him his faithful lion. Their importunity was not *to be resisted*, and both requests were granted.

---

[1] See Par. 125.

103	Infinitive.	Of what class?	1. Subject or Object. 2. Adverbial. 3. Adjectival.
	to be exposed		Complementary Subject.
	to strike		Adverbial.
	to run away		Object.
	to stand		Complementary Subject.
	to eat		Complementary Subject.
	to increase		Adverbial.
	(to) prepare [1]		Complementary Object.
	to see		Adverbial.
	(to) change [1]		Complementary Object.
	to fawn		Object.
	(to) let loose		Complementary Object.
	to turn		Complementary Object.
	(to) be asked [1]		Complementary Subject.
	to explain		Adverbial.[1]
	to pardon		Complementary Object.[1]
	to be resisted		Adjectival.

EXERCISE XX.

104 Parse the Infinitives in the following Exercise :—

Long ago, when people used [2] *to worship* many gods, a carter was striving [3] *to make* his way with a heavily-laden waggon through a miry lane. The horses did their best, but the waggoner, who did not wish *to take* more trouble than he could [4] *help*,[4] was content *to* [5] *sit*

---

[1] "To" omitted, see Par. 93. "To explain," see Par. 105
[2] 'Used' is a Transitive Verb, and can govern a Noun or an Infinitive as its Object, *e.g.* "we use steel *pens*," "we used *to walk*." The Object Infinitive now rarely occurs after *use*, except after the Indefinite Past, as here. 'Began' is also a Transitive Verb and can be followed by an Object.
[3] 'Strive' is not a Transitive Verb; therefore "to make" should be considered as an Adverbial Infinitive of purpose "striving for the

Subject or Object of what Verb.	1. If Complementary, state the Partial Subject or Object. 2. If Adverbial, replace by a Preposition and Verbal Noun. 3. If Adjectival, state Noun qualified.
was ordered ——— might wish was made had been suffered ——— made ——— see began bade forced must ——— begged ———	Androcles for the purpose of striking ——— the slave which for the purpose of increasing the slave at seeing the beast ——— the officers it the slave for the purpose of explaining the Governor qualifies "importunity"

upon the waggon and *let*[4] the horses *carry* him, while he cracked his whip and sang songs. Presently the road began[2] *to rise*, but still the waggoner kept his seat. Soon they came to a place where a torrent seemed *to have dashed* across the road, wearing a deep pit with its waters. The horses put forth all their strength *to pull* the waggon across, but in vain; all their efforts could[4] not even *move* the wheels, which began[1] *to sink* deeper and deeper into the pit. Now, when it was too late[5] *to do* anything, the good-for-nothing

purpose of making his way." On the other hand, "try" is a Transitive Verb, and therefore can take an Object after it.

[4] "Could" is the same as "was able." The following Infinitive may be regarded as the Object of "can" or "could;" "can" was once a Transitive Verb. "Let" is the same as "suffer;" "dare" is the same as "venture." "Help" meant 1st "to remedy," 2nd "get rid of," 3rd "avoid." "Than he could help." "Than he could avoid."

[5] "*To sit*" is the same as "with sitting." "Too late to do anything" is "too late for the purpose of doing anything."

carter got down from his waggon; but all that he did was *to curse* and swear at the horses. Finding that cursing did not move the waggon, he at last thought he would try what praying could[4] *do*. So, falling on his knees, he besought Hercules, the god of hard work, *to come* and help him in his troubles. In an instant Hercules was on the spot; but, instead of helping him, "You lazy fellow!" said he, "how dare[4] you *send* for me, till you have tried[3] *to do* without me? Learn that Hercules helps none but those that are willing *to help*[5] themselves."

105 *Caution.* After Verbs of asking, commanding, advising, compelling, it is not always easy to determine whether the Infinitive is Adverbial or Complementary. For example, in—

(1) "They besought him *to help* them."

—the meaning is the same as—

(2) "They besought him *that he would* help them."

Here there is a notion of *purpose*: and hence "to help" in (1) may be parsed as an Adverbial Infinitive meaning "for the purpose of helping."

---

[3] "Strive" is not a Transitive Verb; therefore "to make" should be considered as an Adverbial Infinitive of purpose, "striving for the purpose of making his way." On the other hand, "try" is a Transitive Verb, and therefore can take an Object after it.

[4] "Could" is the same as "was able." The following Infinitive may be regarded as the Object of "can" or "could;" "can" was once a Transitive Verb. "Let" is the same as "suffer;" "dare" is the same as "venture."

[5] You might be disposed to say here that "are willing" is the same as "wish," and that "to help" is the Object of "wish," which is implied in "are willing." But, if you bear in mind how often *to* is used in such sentences, *e.g.* "I am sorry, glad, willing, able, *to do* this," it will seem better to take "to help" as an Adverbial Infinitive, meaning 'as regards doing," "in the matter of helping."

But "him to help" might also be treated as meaning "his helping," and regarded as the Object of "they besought."

Either parsing may therefore be allowed, Adverbial or Complementary.

When the pupil has once grasped the notion that *could*, *would*, &c., are followed by Infinitives, it will be no longer necessary to separate the Auxiliary from the Infinitive. The whole may be parsed together as a Compound Verb. For example, in the last exercise, "could do," may be treated as a Compound Verb.

106   **The Complementary Subject Infinitive.**

Note that the Complementary Object Infinitive cannot always be converted into a Complementary Subject Infinitive. You can say—

(1) "I like *a rascal to be punished.*"

But not—

(2) "*A rascal* is liked *to be punished.*"

The reason is this, that in (2) the Noun "rascal" is separated and disconnected in meaning from the Infinitive "to be punished;" and therefore "rascal" would be in danger of being regarded as the complete Subject of "is liked."

107   Consequently the Complementary Subject Infinitive is seldom used except where the Noun-Subject and the Verb are so related that the former

G

might be made the Complete Subject of the latter, without making utter nonsense. For example, "he" *might* be made the Complete Subject of "is known," "was heard," "was asked"; although in a very different sense from that of the following examples, in which "he" is Partial Subject :—

(1) "*He* is known *to be* honest."
(2) "*He* was heard *to say,* seen *to do*," &c.
(3) "*He* was asked *to do,* ordered *to come,*" &c.

In all these cases it is better to parse the Infinitive as Complementary; but it may be parsed, though not so well, Adverbially, *e.g.* "he is known *as regards being* honest," "he was heard *in the act of* saying," &c.

108   The Infinitive after Adjectives.

I. As an Adjective can be modified by an Adverb, so can it by an Adverbial Infinitive :—

(1) "Pleasant *to see,*" *i.e.*, "*in* seeing," or, "*for the purpose of* seeing."
(2) "This is hard *to bear,*" *i.e.*, "*in*" or "*for* bearing."
(3) "I am content *to be poor,*" *i.e.*, "*with* being poor."
(4) "He is quick *to detect* imposition," *i.e.*, "*at* detecting."
(5) "This apple is fit *to eat,*" *i.e.*, "*for the purpose of* eating."

109   The Adjectival Infinitive Explained.

An Adjectival Phrase may be made up by the Preposition *to* and the Infinitive, as easily as by a Preposition and Noun. There is no difference, in principle, between "a monkey *with a long tail;*" "apples *for eating;*" "paper *for writing;*" "water *for drinking,*" and—

(1) "Apples *to eat;*" "paper *to write with;*" "a house *to let.*"
(2) "Duties *to perform;*" "debts *to pay;*" "work *to do.*"
(3) "A time *to work,* and a time *to play;*" "nothing *to do.*"

(1) "This is not *to be believed;*" "it is not *to be denied.*"
(2) "It is to be *deplored,* to be *remembered,*" &c.

The Adjectival force of the Infinitive may be seen by the ease with which, in many cases, "to" may be replaced by *-ing* or *-able,* so as to convert the Adjective-Phrase into an Adjective: "writ*ing*-paper," "play*ing*-time," "deplor*able,*" "undeni*able,*" &c.

110   The Parenthetical Infinitive.

The Adverbial Infinitive of Purpose is often briefly used in a Parenthesis :—

(1) "I came by a circuitous path, or rather—*to* tell the truth—I completely lost my way."

This seems to be a short way of saying "(In order) to tell the truth (I must say that), I completely lost my way."

(2) "Will you come then?" "*To be sure,* I will."

This seems to be a condensation of "(In order for you) to be sure, (I say distinctly) I will come."

111 The Exclamatory Infinitive.

The Infinitive is sometimes used absolutely in exclamations:—

(1) "*To think* that he should be so foolish!"
(2) "Simpleton! *To dream* that he could succeed without effort!"

In (1) "to think" appears to be the Subject of some Verb understood, *e.g.* "astonishes me;" in (2) "to dream" is probably an Adverbial Infinitive modifying "simpleton" repeated. "Simpleton *to dream*" is the same as "foolish *to dream*," or "*for* dreaming."

112 EXERCISE XXI.

Parse the italicized words in the following Exercise:—

A lean hungry wolf one day met a mastiff, who had lost himself in the forest, and asked the wolf *to shew* him the way home.* For a moment the wolf thought of springing at the dog's throat; he was so plump and sleek and seemed so good *to eat*. But the mastiff was too strong *to be overpowered;* so the wolf replied, "Show you the way, Sir? *To be sure* I will": and away they trotted together.
Presently the mastiff looked askance at the wolf. "You seem to me," said he, "*to be* in good condition for the chase, but you are not shapely *to look at:* one can count your ribs." "I am content *to be* poor," replied the wolf: "here in these woods there is not much *to eat*. But what makes you so fat¹ and sleek?¹ I would give anything *to be* in such condition." "Then I advise you *to*

come with me," replied the mastiff, "and you will be sure *to get* what you want. You will have nothing *to do*, but *to bark* at beggars and vagrants, and then you may *eat* as much as you like of good beef and mutton. Will you come?" At the mention of mutton, the wolf could not *contain* himself; his mouth watered and he began *to weep* for joy. "*To think* of your doubting whether I would come," he cried: "most gladly will I accept your offer: my life is no longer *to be endured*. Indeed, *to tell* you the truth, I have not tasted food for the last four days." So on they went at a quickened pace.

113 As they walked and talked, the wolf could not forbear every now and then turning *to admire* his companion. While* doing* so, he noticed a mark round the dog's neck where the hair appeared *to be worn* away. "What's that?" asked the wolf. "Nothing." "Nothing?" "Nothing *to speak* of," answered the mastiff in a rather confused way. "But what is it?" asked the wolf again: for he began *to be* suspicious. "Well then, if you are determined *to know*—it is only the mark of the collar round my neck. Sometimes I am ordered *to be* tied up *to prevent* my losing my way, as I have done to-day. It is of no consequence." "It is of so much consequence," interrupted the wolf, "that I must wish you* good-bye,* and bid you *go* home by yourself. *To lose* one's freedom is a loss not *to be endured*. I prefer *to starve* free[1] rather than *to be* a plump slave."

114   **The Tenses of Participles.**

Participles, like Adjectives, have no Tenses of their own, but borrow the time they express from

---

[1] Cf. "to live happy," "die rich," &c. This use of the Adjective is a sort of compromise between (1) an Adverb, and (2) the Supplementary use in Par. 149.

some other Verb in the sentence. Thus "walking" or "supported" may be Past, Present, or Future :—

1. *Past :—*

    (1) "*Walking* on, I soon *reached* Windsor," *i.e.*, "after I *walked on*."

    (2) "*Supported* by this scanty food, he lived for ten days longer," *i.e.*, "since he *was supported*."

2. *Present :—*

    (1) "I see an old man *walking* towards me," *i.e.*, "who *is walking*," or, "and he *is walking*."

    (2) "I see an old man coming this way, *supported* by his son," *i.e.*, "who," or, "and he, *is being supported*."

3. *Future :—*

    (1) "*Walking* on, you will soon *reach* Windsor," *i.e.*, "if you (*will*) *walk* on."

    (2) "*Supported* by his son's daily labour, he will live for the rest of his life in comfort," *i.e.*, "since he *will be supported*."

115 The Participial forms might be arranged as follows, according to their forms :—

	ACTIVE.	PASSIVE.
INCOMPLETE	supporting	(being) supported
COMPLETE	having supported	having been supported

But the Incomplete form may sometimes denote an action in the Indefinite Past, as in the first example of Paragraph 114.

Note that the Complete as well as the Incomplete form of the Participle can be used either for Present, Past, or Future. For example, "*Having walked* on, I came to Windsor" means not "when I have walked on," but "when I *had walked* on," so that the Participle is here put for the Complete Past.

A future action is expressed in a Participle by a Phrase with "being," *e.g.* "being *on the point of death*," "being *about to die*" (where "to die" must be regarded as the Object of "about").

116 The confusion in the uses of the Participle is, perhaps, in part explained by its having been confused with the abbreviated Adverbial use of the Verbal. For example, "*in*," or, "*on* walking" could naturally mean either "engaged in walking," or "*upon*," i.e. "*after* walking." When this Adverbial Phrase was contracted to "a-walking," or simply "walking," it was easily confused with the Participle.

Originally the Participle ended in *-nd*, and the Verbal in *-ng;* but very early, the Particle assumed *-ng*. See Par. 554—8.

CHAPTER V.[1]

THE INDIRECT OBJECT.

117 FIND the Object of the Verb in the first of the following sentences:—

(1) "John brought Thomas a book."
(2) "I will forgive them their fault."
(3) "The father allowed his son two hundred pound, a year."
(4) "I envy her her good health."
(5) "This conduct will lose you your friends."
(6) "Fill me the cup."
(7) "My mother taught my brother French."
(8) "I will ask your sister this question."

Ask the question in the usual way, "Brought whom or what?" Answer, "Brought a book;" therefore "book" is the Object of "brought."

If any one were to say, "No, the sentence gives the answer 'brought Thomas,'" you would reply, "John did not bring Thomas, he brought the book *for* or *to* Thomas; and 'brought Thomas' is only a short way of saying 'brought *for* or *to* Thomas.'"

---

[1] The Subjunctive Mood, which would naturally follow here, is deferred to Par. 163, owing to its difficulty.

118 Nevertheless, as "Thomas" does (in a certain sense) answer to the question "whom?" after the Verb, it is called an Object. But "book" is called the **Direct Object**, as it is the first and *direct* object of the action; and Thomas is called the **Indirect Object**, as being the second object *indirectly* affected by the action.

Rule.

The Indirect Object of a Verb is the word or phrase that answers to the question " For, or, to whom ? " " For, or, to what ? " when asked after the Verb and its Direct Object.

119 There are a few exceptions to this rule. In "he *played* me a trick," "on," not "for," would be supplied before "me." Also, after "ask," "of" or "from" has to be supplied: "he asked (*of*) his sister a question."[1]

120 *N.B.* The Indirect Object can easily be detected as follows: it always comes *before the Direct Object*, and cannot be placed after the Direct Object without the insertion of a Preposition, in which case it ceases to be the Indirect Object of the Verb, and becomes the Object of the Preposition:—

(1) "John brought a book *for* Thomas."

---

[1] Probably in (8), after "ask," the word "sister" may be regarded as the Direct Object, and "ask-a-question" as a Compound Verb having as its Object, "sister."

(2) "I will forgive their fault *to* them."[1]
(3) "The father allowed two hundred pounds a year *to* his son."

Exercise XXII.

121 Which are the Direct and which the Indirect Objects of the italicized Verbs?—

1. John *fetched* me a book. 2. He *forgave* me my fault. 3. My mother *taught* me French. 4. The judge *asked* him a question. 5. He *refused* me this slight favour. 6. My cousin *did* me a good turn. 7. The thief *gave* me a sudden blow. 8. My uncle *left* me a small sum of money. 9. She will *tell* me what she wants. 10. You shall *send* me some more soldiers at once. 11. He *lent* me a thousand pounds. 12. I *will shew* your friend everything that is to be seen. 13. This man *owed* me money. 14. He *played* me a trick. 15. This conduct will *lose* you the esteem of your friends. 16. He *promises* us much, but does little. 17. He *answered* me nothing. 18. I *envy* you your good health. 19. A little forethought *will save* us a great deal of trouble. 20. His father *allowed* him two hundred pounds a year.

122   **The Object after a Passive Verb.**

When an Active Verb, taking two Objects, is changed into the Passive Voice, one Object becomes the Subject of the Passive Verb, but the other is *retained as Object*. This Object may be—

[1] This and other similar constructions, *e.g* "I envy your good health to you," are extremely harsh, and not to be imitated.

I. *The former Indirect Object of the Active :—*
   (1) "Their lives were offered *them* by the conqueror, if they would surrender."
   (2) "His fault was forgiven *him* by his master upon his promise of amendment."
   (3) "This favour was refused *me* by my friend."
   (4) "Much trouble was saved *me* by his kindness."
   (5) "Three questions were asked *me* by the examiners."
   (6) "Writing was taught *me* by my mother."

II. *The former Direct Object of the Active :—*
   (1) "They were offered *their lives* by the conqueror."
   (2) "He was forgiven *his fault*."
   (3) "I was refused *this favour*."
   (4) "I was saved *much trouble* by his kindness."
   (5) "I was asked *three questions* by the examiners."
   (6) "I was taught *writing* by my mother."

123 If a distinction is needed between the two kinds of Objects used after a Passive Verb, the terms *Direct* and *Indirect Object of the Active* may be used. But unless such a distinction is asked, it will be enough to say that it is the *Object retained after a Passive Verb*, or, for shortness, the *retained Object*.

124 *Caution.* Carefully distinguish the *Retained Object* from the Supplement (Par. 148) of a Verb in itself incomplete. For example, "to make king," is a Compound Verb, equivalent to "to *king*," or "to *be-king*." Consequently, "king" is not the *Retained Object*, but the Supplement of an incomplete Verb in :—

"They *made* him *king*," i.e., "they *made-king*" or "*be-kinged* him."

125   The Cognate Object.

Some Verbs, though generally Intransitive, take occasionally after them an Object whose meaning is *akin* to the Verb. Such Objects are called **Cognate** (*co-*, together; *nate*, born: hence "born together," "related," "akin").

This usage is more common in Poetry and in elevated language than in ordinary Prose :—

(1) "They have slept their *sleep*."
(2) "He has fought a good *fight*;" "They shouted *applause*."
(3) "We have walked a long *walk* to-day."

126   The Early English Dative.

In the earliest English there was a special Inflection to denote the Indirect Object. Being mostly used after such Verbs as "give," "lend," "send," "forgive," "refuse," &c. —all of which imply "giving" or "not giving"—this Use or Case of the Noun or Pronoun was called the **Dative** (*i.e.*, giving) **Case**.

In the earliest English, this Inflection would make it perfectly clear which was the Direct and which the Indirect Object. Compare together (1) the modern English, and (2) the earliest English, in the following examples :—

(1) "This king gave (to) the minsters large gifts."
(2) "This king gave large gifts mynstr-*um*."

In (2), but not in (1), we see distinctly by the Inflection -*um* (which is the sign of the Dative use), that "mynstrum" is the Indirect Object.

If the old Dative case had to be specified, wherever it is found in Modern English, we should have to call the Objects in the following examples, *Datives* :—

(1) "Trust *me* and believe no *one* else."
(2) "A calamity has befallen *us.*"
(3) "Obey *me* and disobey *him*." [1]
(4) "It displeased the *king*, though it pleased the *people*." [1]

But in modern English the Object after "trust," "befall," &c. must now be called the Direct Object.

The Adverbial Object.

127 An Adverbial Phrase is sometimes contracted into a Noun with a Prepositional Prefix, *e.g.*, "a-board," "a-foot," "a-field;" and sometimes still further contracted into a Noun without Prefix of any kind:

(1) "I am going *fishing*" (this is a contraction for "go *on fishing*," or, "go *a-fishing*").

Home (E.E. ham) is repeatedly used as an Adverb in "Layamon," and also as an Inflected Noun.

128 Again, in the earliest periods of the language, an Adverbial Phrase was sometimes represented by an *Inflected Noun*, the Inflection representing a modern Preposition (*see* last paragraph):

(2) "He that was dead came forth, bound hand-*um* and fôt-*um*," i.e., "*as regards*," or, *in*, "hands and feet."
(3) (Modern English), "— bound *hand* and *foot*."

[1] In (3) and (4) the Verbs are derived from French, and were followed (generally) by the Preposition "à."

129 Hence, even where no Preposition was ever inserted, the Objective form is sometimes used in answer to the questions "How far?" "How much?" "When?" "Where?" *e.g.*—

(1) "He is worth *you* and *me* put together."
(2) "He walked *a mile*."
(3) "He is *ten years* old."

The Objective form *me* in the first sentence shews that all these Nouns and Pronouns must be regarded as Objectively used.

130 These Adverbial Objects are sometimes, as it were, compromises between Adverbs and Direct Objects. For example, "is worth" *implies* the Transitive Verb "equals," and may therefore, naturally be followed by a Direct Object. On the other hand, it is in form Intransitive, so as to require an Adverb rather than an Object.

131 In some of these cases a Preposition may be inserted before the Object, as—

(1) "We waited (for) *an hour.*"
(2) "He is (by) *a trifle* taller than I."
(3) "We will come (in) *three days* from this time."
(4) "(At) *that moment*, Thomas appeared."
(5) "He came (by) *the shortest way.*"
(6) "He stood (on) *this side* of me."

But it is not to be supposed that a Preposition was thus inserted in early English.

Exercise XXIII. (Specimen).

132 Parse the italicized Nouns and Pronouns in the following Exercise :—

The Romans had given *Lars Porsena offence* by banishing their king Tarquin the Proud. So Porsena sent *them* an *ambassador* bidding them take back their king or prepare for war. But the Romans knew well that they would never be forgiven their *rebellion* by king Tarquin ; and, although pardon was offered *them* if they would submit, they knew they could not trust his *promises*. So they gave the *ambassador* an *answer* of defiance, and sent him away. Then king Porsena, after waiting some *days* to see whether they would submit, determined to teach the *Romans* a *lesson* and to humble their pride. So, two *months* after the banishment of Tarquin, the Tuscan king set out for Rome.

133 Great was the fear *that* the Tuscan army caused the *Romans*, when it suddenly appeared on the other side of the Tiber. The senate was just then taking counsel ; but on hearing of the enemy's approach, all rushed that *instant* toward the wall. Messenger after messenger had arrived bringing the *consuls word* that this town had been taken or that village burned ; but still the Romans had not expected that the army could reach Rome that *day*. Forcing his way through crowds that pressed round asking *him* anxious *questions* about their friends and relations, the consul mounted the wall and at once cried out : "If yonder bridge is not broken down, the enemy will be upon us this *moment*." Then out spoke Horatius and said : "I and two others will keep the bridge for you : hew it down at once." So Horatius and two other brave Romans, took their stand on the bridge, to fight their *battle* against the whole Tuscan army, while the rest of the Romans, Senators and Commons together, worked hard at the bridge, loosening the props and tearing down the planks.

134 An Object may be parsed as follows :—

Object.	After Active Verb. } 1. Direct. 2. Indirect. After Passive } 3. "Retained." 4. Adverbial.	1. } 2. } After what Verb. 3. } 4. Answering what question.
Lars Porsena Them Rebellion Them Days Romans Lesson	Indirect Indirect Retained Retained Adverbial Indirect Direct	had given. sent. would be forgiven. was offered. "How long?" to teach. to teach.

Answer the rest for yourself.

135   **Adverbial Subject**

I. The Subject is sometimes used with the Participle (without any Verb of which it can be called the Subject) so as to make an Adverbial Phrase :—

(1) "They dragged my friend away, *I* in vain *resisting* and *protesting*," *i.e.* "while I,?" &c.
(2) "Up we climbed, *he remaining* below."
(3) "*This done*, they departed."
(4) "*Breakfast ended*, they went out for a walk."

Examples (1) and (2) shew us that in this construction the Noun is used *Subjectively*, and not

Objectively; for the Subjective forms "I" and "he" are used, not "me" and "him."

The Subject may be explained as Subject of the Verb *implied* in the Participle ; *e.g.* in (1) "*I* resisting" is the same as " while, or, though, *I resisted.*"

The Subject in this construction being free from or *loosed from* its usual connection with the Verb, is sometimes called the **Subject Absolute** (*ab,* from ; *solut-,* loosed).

136 II. Sometimes the Participle is omitted :—
(1) "*Sword* in hand, the captain led on his men."
(2) "I was lying on the grass, an unopened *book* by my side."
(3) "*Breakfast* over, we prepared for our journey."

In all these cases some Participle, such as "being," can be easily supplied.

137   Apposition.

Sometimes a Noun or Pronoun is used not as the ordinary Subject or Object of a Verb, but as a sort of repetition and explanation of the Subject or Object.

In such cases, "I mean," or "that is to say," or some similar expression, may be supplied between the two Nouns :—

(1) "Next came } Thomas, (that is to say) *the boy*
    Then we saw }   that cleans the boots."

H

Here "the boy," being in close connection with "Thomas," is said to be in **Apposition** (*ad*, near; *position*, position) to "Thomas."

138 For "the boy," write the Third Personal Pronoun. Then the sentence becomes—

(2) "Next came Thomas, *he* that cleans the boots."

(3) "Then we saw Thomas, *him* that cleans the boots."

In (2) "Thomas" is the Subject, and the Pronoun in Apposition has the Subject-Inflection; in (3) "Thomas" is the Object, and the Pronoun in Apposition has the Object-Inflection. Hence we get this Rule:—

Nouns and Pronouns are used Subjectively when in Apposition to Subjects, and Objectively when in Apposition to Objects.

139 By "used Subjectively" or "Objectively" is meant that—if the word has Subject and Object Inflections—the Subjective Inflection or Objective Inflection must be used.

140 In most cases it may be shewn that words "used (1) Subjectively" and (2) "Objectively" respectively, answer the question (1) "who?" or "what?" before the Verb, or (2) "whom?" or "what?" after the Verb—so that they are *logically entitled* to be described as being themselves Subjects or Objects. Thus "he," above, answers "who came?"

Nouns or Pronouns in Apposition may be therefore described as *Appositional Subjects* or *Objects* respectively.

Apposition with Indirect Object, &c.

141   The Indirect Object is not often emphatic enough to have another Indirect Object in Apposition to it. But such a construction may occur :

> "Will you give *him* your confidence—a rascal banished from all respectable society?"

142   The Noun when used Possessively, being almost an Adjective, is rarely or never followed by a Noun in Apposition. It would scarcely be English to say :

> "This picture was not mine but my *brother's*—an artist himself, and a great *connoisseur*."

Even were such an Appositional use allowable, the Possessive could not be tolerated in Apposition ; the Objective would have to be employed, *e.g.* "artist" above, and would have to be regarded as the Object of an *implied* "of."

In the following examples there is no Apposition ; the Noun that was once Appositional has now become part of a Compound Noun :—

> (1) "*William the Conqueror's* character;"   "*King Alfred's* reign."

The word "house" must be supplied after *each* of the Possessive Nouns in the following Example :

> (1) "Let us go to *Macmillan's* the *Publisher's*."

Apposition with an Implied Noun.

143   Sometimes a Noun is "in Apposition" not to another preceding Noun, but to *some Noun implied from the preceding words* :—

> (1) "He was said to have disobeyed his parents—*a fault* deemed unpardonable in those days."
>
> (2) "You were silent when accused—a clear *confession* of guilt."

100 INDIRECT AND ADVERBIAL [Par. 144

In some cases the Noun implied from the preceding sentence would, if expressed, be Objective. For example, the sentences might have run—

(1) "He was guilty of *disobedience*—a *fault*," &c.
(2) "You kept *silence*—a *confession*," &c.

But in other cases the implied Noun might be Subjective, *e.g.* :—

"If he were elected a Member of Parliament—not a very probable *event*," *i.e.* "if his *election* were to happen," &c.

Exercise XXIV.

Parse the italicized words in—

By this time the Tuscan army had come up, their *spears* advanced, and *trumpets* sounding in triumph. When they saw the three brave Romans on the bridge offering *them battle*, at first the sight caused *them laughter*, and three of the bravest chiefs spurred forth at Porsena's command to open *him* a *path*. But the next *moment*, their three bodies lay bleeding beneath the Roman spears. Then three more Tuscans rode forward ; but, *these* too being slain by the three Romans, fear and wrath fell on the whole army. So now, with levelled spears and closed ranks, they advanced all together against the champions, a *sight* to make the bravest shrink back. But the three stood their *ground:* and now they had gained their *countrymen time* enough to loosen the props of the bridge, which began to shiver under the force of the stream. "Back, Horatius, back," shouted the Consul ; and back rushed his two friends, just in time, the bridge *cracking* beneath their feet, and thundering downward,

Par. 145]   *OBJECT.*   101

as they touched the bank. But the brave Horatius, his *wound* retarding him (for he had been wounded in the last contest) could not run back in time, and so was left alone, the enemy *pressing on* him in front, and the *river* —which was fully fifty *yards* broad—surging and foaming behind.⁄⁄One *moment* he paused, and offered up a prayer ; then leaped into the stream. Romans and Tuscans, all alike, eagerly watched the brave swimmer, swimming a strong *stroke*, wounded though he was : and Porsena cried aloud that he was worth twelve ordinary *lives*, and prayed that he might live and fight many another *battle*. One *minute* he seemed to be sinking, but the *next* he rose, and at last, weary and faint, he reached the shore. From that time all the Romans paid *Horatius* due *respect*, and bestowed gifts upon him, and set up his statue in the market-place, an *honour* rarely bestowed on any Roman citizen.

Exercise XXV.

Parse the italicized words in—

145 A great battle was raging between the birds and the beasts : it had lasted all *day*, and was not yet decided. Not a bird or beast but* had taken one side or other in the battle—*all*¹ but the bat. She alone, the cowardly *creature*, would take no part with either side. In vain the eagle, the *general* of the birds, being hard pressed by his enemies the *beasts*, sent *her* his *commands* by the swallow to join the army of the birds. "How can you give *me* the *name* of bird ?" she replied ; "what bird has teeth as I have?" Soon afterwards the lion, the *king* of the beasts, finding the battle going against

---

¹ "All" is *in apposition* with a Subject understood. It is as though the sentence had run, "the birds and beasts had all taken sides in the battle, *all* but the bat ;" and "all" is an Adjective used as a Noun, and in apposition with "birds and beasts," implied from the preceding sentence.

146 him, sent to say that he would forgive *her* her past *cowardice* if she came at once to join his army. "What right has he to ask *me* such a *favour?*" replied the bat. "How can he take me for a beast? Even a mole can see that I have wings. Who ever saw a beast with wings?"

Saying these words, she flew to the birds, who seemed on the point of gaining a complete victory, and eagerly offered the *eagle* her *services*. But the eagle answered, "Just now you told *us* you were a beast. Go to your friends the *beasts:* they need your help more than we." The bat retired in confusion; but an *hour* afterwards, *fortune* inclining toward the beasts, she humbly approached the lion, offering him her help. "You would not de *us* a *kindness* when we were in trouble," roared the lion, "and now do you talk about giving *us* your *help?* Away with you! The *battle* once over, I will make short work with you."

Rejected by both parties—the natural *result* of her cowardice —the bat was forced to lead a solitary life. So she skulks in dark places, and prefers the night to the day —a *warning* to all men that they must not "trim."

147

Appositional Verbs, or Verbs of Identity

It has been shewn that two Nouns or Pronouns when "in Apposition" are both used Subjectively, or else both used Objectively. There are some Verbs whose nature it is thus to connect Nouns or Pronouns, placing them, as it were, in Apposition.

These Verbs sometimes express the *identity* between two persons or things. The Verb "is" is commonly used thus :—

(1) "The author of this book *is* my brother."

Here "is" expresses the *identity* between "my brother" and the Subject of "is," *i.e.* "the author."

Hence the name Object could not be given to "my brother." Indeed, if you alter the sentence by putting yourself in your brother's place, it becomes—

(2) "The author of this book is *I*."

Since, therefore, you are obliged to use the Subjective form "I" (not "me"), it follows that "brother" in (1) is Subjectively, not Objectively, used.

For a similar reason, the ordinary term "Object" cannot be given to the Noun following the Verb in—

(3) "He was made, appointed, created, *king*."
(4) "He was thought, deemed, believed, supposed, called, named, a *rascal*."
(5) "He seems, appears, looks a *rascal*."

In these sentences the Verb by itself is incomplete. "He was *made*" is not only not the complete meaning; it is even untrue. The Verb is, not "was *made*," but "was *made-king*." "To *make-king*" and "to *make-beautiful*" are, each, just as much one Verb, as "to *be-king*" and "to *beauti-fy*."

148 Since the words "rascal" and "general" *supplement* the preceding Verbs, they may be called the *Supplement of the Verb*; and, since they are here used Subjectively, they may be called the *Subjective Supplement of the Verb.*[1]

On the other hand, in—

(6) "They made, appointed, created, *him general.*"
(7) "We thought, deemed, supposed, believed, called, named, *him a rascal.*"

—since the identity is here between the *Object* "him" and the "rascal" or "general," we may call "rascal" and "general" *Objective Supplements of the Verb.*[1]

149 Adjectives are sometimes thus used as Supplements :—

(1) "We thought her *foolish.*"
(2) "I painted my house *white.*"

Here "thought-foolish" may be regarded as a Compound Verb.

Somewhat different is the Participial use of Adjectives in—

(1) "They found the man *dead.*"
(2) "I bought the house *new.*"
(3) "I ate my dinner *cold.*"

Caution. Distinguish carefully between :—

1. *The Complementary Infinitive,* which is the Complement of a Noun or Pronoun (see Par. 97).

3. *The Supplement,* which is the Supplement of a Verb.

[1] The term "Supplement," and not Complement, is used, for fear of confusion between the Supplement of the Verb, and the Complement of the Subject or Object mentioned in Par. 97.

150 N.B.—*The Intransitive Verbs "is," "looks," "seems," "appears," and the Transitive Verbs "make," "create," "appoint," "deem," "esteem," being often used to express identity, may be called "Verbs of Identity."*

Rule.—*Verbs of Identity, when Intransitive and Passive, take a Subjective Supplement; when Transitive, take an Objective Supplement.*

Preparatory 'it' and 'there.'

151 Instead of saying "To walk is healthy," "To steal is dishonest," we sometimes wish to put the Subject, *e.g.* "to walk," at the end. But we should not like to say "is healthy to walk;" we want to put in some little word as the Subject of *is*, as it were to *prepare* the way for the real Subject that is coming later on. So we say "*It* is healthy to walk," *i.e.* "it is healthy—I mean to walk is healthy."

This "it" may be called the *Preparatory Subject* of "is;" for it is like a servant sent on to *prepare* the way for his master and to secure room for him at an inn. "To walk" is the real Subject of "is."

152 The Adverb *there* is used in the same *preparatory way*, though of course it is not a Subject. For example, if you are beginning a story about a boy, it does not sound well to say "once a little boy was;" so we place "little boy" last, and put in the word "there," not to mean "in that place," but simply to make us feel that something is coming:—

"Once *there* was a little boy."

When *there* is thus used, you may say "it prepares the way for the Subject, and is a Preparatory Adverb."

Exercise XXVI. (Specimen).

State the Subjects and Objects of the italicized Verbs, and parse the italicized Nouns in the following Exercise :—

153 Once there *was* a stag in a forest. Looking one *day* at the reflection of his antlers in the water, he *thought* himself the most beautiful creature he had ever seen, till his eyes fell on the long, slim, shadows of his legs. "Why," cried he, "*has* not Providence *made* all my limbs ornaments to me? Why *has* not Heaven *given* me the legs of the horse, which, though they do not carry him quite so swiftly as I run, *are* nevertheless swift and beautiful at the same time? It is certain that then I *should*[1] *be* the king of the forest, and there *would*[1] *be* none to dispute the title with me. But alas! my legs *are* mere sticks, and *make* me the scarecrow of the forest. However, *complaints* being unavailing, I must submit."

154 Scarcely had he spoken, when there *was* a sound of the huntsman's horn. Away flew the stag, through the thick wood; but he was sadly hindered, his long *antlers* catch-

[1] You need not state the Mood of this Verb.

ing in the low branches, and checking his furious leaps. Before he had gone a *mile*, the hounds were close upon him ; but luckily he reached the open plain. Here his fine antlers, the *ornaments* of which he had been so proud, no longer hindered him ; and by the aid of his legs, the ugly *sticks* that he had been so contemptuously despising, he soon got safe away.

It *is* a mistake you see, sometimes, to despise *what* is ugly.

155

Verb.[1]	Subject.	Direct Object.	Supplement of the Verb. 1. Objective. 2. Subjective. 3. Adjective.	Indirect Object.
was	a stag (Prep Adverb, "there.")	—	—	—
thought	he	himself	"the, &c. seen" (Obj.)	—
has made	Providence	limbs	ornaments (Obj.)	—
has given	Heaven	legs, &c.	—	me
are	which	—	swift, &c. (Adj.)	—
is	that then I should, &c. (Prep. Pronoun, "it.")	—	certain (Adj.)	—
should be	I	—	king of the forest (Subj.)	—
would be	none (Prep. Adverb, "there.")	—	—	—
are	my legs	—	sticks (Subj.)	—
make	(my legs)	me	scarecrow (Obj.)	—
was	a sound, &c. (Prep. Adverb, "there.")	—	—	—

[1] It will be convenient, for the sake of uniformity, to parse Verbs first, and then other words.

Noun.	Use or Case.	Reason for Use or Case.
day	Object	Adverbial (Ans. *when?*)
complaints	Subject	Absolute with Participle, "being unavailing"
antlers	Subject	Absolute with Participle, "catching"
a mile	Object	Adverbial (Ans. *how far?*)
ornaments	Subject	In apposition to "antlers"
sticks	Object	In apposition to "legs"
what	Subject	"is ugly"
(that) Par. 28	(Implied Object)	Object of "despise."

EXERCISE XXVII.

State the Subjects and Objects of the italicized Verbs, and parse the other italicized words in the following Exercise:—

156 In a crack near a cupboard, filled with good things, there once *lived* a young mouse with her mother. One *day* the little mouse, who had been wandering about by herself—a common *custom* with her—came running hastily back: her *face* and tail proclaiming unusual delight. "Dear mother," cried she, "it *seems* certain that the people here are very fond of us, for they *have built us* a house that *will give* us everything we *need*. They *have made* it square, and just of the right size: the floor *is* wooden, and so are the sides; but *there* are windows to let in the light, and bars to keep out those monstrous striped animals that you *call cats*. Besides, just inside the cottage, close to the door, *there is* a piece of toasted cheese. As soon as I perceived it, the delicious *smell* attracting me, I was on the point of rushing in to taste it; but I thought *it* my duty to come and bring *you word* first."

157 "My dear daughter," replied the old mouse, "*it* is most fortunate that you did not enter that trap (for it was a trap) which you thought a cottage. If you had entered, you would have been taught by your death a *lesson* that you have now learned very cheaply. When young mice grow *old*, they find that many things that seemed *made* for them were made for quite a different purpose—a *truth* that, I trust, you will never forget."

"It" as Antecedent.

158 I. "It" is still clearly used for the Antecedent of the Relative Pronoun in questions :—

(1) "Who was *it* (*i.e.*, the person) that you saw ?"

It is also thus used in the Bible, where we could hardly use "it" :—

(2) "Art thou not *it* that hath cut Rahab and wounded the dragon ?"

Similarly in Shakespeare :—

(3) "There was *it* for which my sinews shall be stretched upon him," *i.e.*, "*the thing* for which I will attack him."

159 II. We do not now like to put "it" in an emphatic position. The word seems too light to bear, as it were, the weight that would sometimes fall on it, if placed in the usual position of the

Antecedent. For example, in answer to (1) above, we do not like to say, though it would be logically correct—

(4) "*It* that I saw was John."

Instead of this, we prefer to take some of the emphasis from "it" by shifting the place of "that." In this way, "it" becomes almost as unemphatic as the preparatory "it" in Par. 151 :—

(5) "*It* was John that I saw."

160 By a similar transposition, instead of saying, "It that says so is you," we ought to say, strictly speaking—

(6) "*It* is you that *says* so."

But this sounds harsh. We feel that what we want to express is "You *say* so." Hence "*You that says* so" seems ungrammatical. Consequently, by a mistake of confusion (confusing (6) with "you say so"), we have fallen into the habit of writing the sentence thus :—

(7) "*It* is you that *say* so."

161 But, in parsing (7), the only right method is 1st, to state that "say" is, by confusion, used for "says ;" 2nd, that the sentence is transposed from "it that says so is you ;" 3rd, that "it" is the Antecedent of "that," and Subject of "is."

The same parsing applies to—

(8) "*It* was you that I laughed at," *i.e.*, "it that I laughed at was you."

162 It would appear also to apply to—

(9) "*It* was at you that I laughed."

(10) "*It* was from you that I received this insult."

These sentences would appear to be for "It that I laughed at was you," "It that I received this insult from was you."

It has been suggested that "it" is here the "Preparatory *it*," and "that" a Conjunction, the meaning being "The fact that I received this insult was owing to, or, from you.' But this does not seem to hold good for (9) "The fact that I laughed was at you."

Of course however "it" is the Preparatory "it," and "that" is a Conjunction in :

(11) "*It* was in the time of Julius Cæsar *that* the Romans first invaded Britain."

CHAPTER VI.

SUBJUNCTIVE MOOD.

BESIDES expressing *facts*, a Verb may express—

163   I. **Purpose:**[1]—
    (1) "Give him some water that he *may drink*."
    (2) "We hid the water lest he *should drink* it all."

164   II. **Condition:**[1]—
    (1) "If you *were to give* him some water..."
    (2) "*Should* you *see* him to-morrow..."

165   III. **The Consequence of the fulfilment of Condition:**[1]—
    (1) "... he *would drink*."
    (2) "... you *would find* him much changed."

Every ordinary Verb has a *manner*, *mode*, or **Mood** of expressing Purpose, Condition, and Conditional Consequence.

166   Subjunctive of Purpose.

Present.	Past.
(that he) **may** drink	(that he) **might** drink
(lest he) drink [2]	(lest he) **should** drink

[1] Since purpose is not generally so important as statement of fact, and is generally *subjoined* to statement of fact, the Mood of purpose is called the "Subjoined" or **Subjunctive**.
The name also includes (less properly) the Conditional Mood.

[2] This is rarely used; more commonly, the Past Subjunctive, "should drink," is used in its stead.

Par. 167] *SUBJUNCTIVE MOOD.* 113

"Would" (apparently of purpose) is used in "We begged, besought, that he *would* come." See Par. 173.

The distinction between "might" and "should" appears to be, that "might" (expressing *possibility*) is a more modest word wherewith to represent one's object, than "should," which expresses *futurity*, and necessity.

> (1) "I gave him water (in the hope) that (possibly) he *might* drink."
>
> (2) "I took away the water (for fear) lest (which would certainly have happened) he *should* drink."

In other words, since we do not like to express our hopes so strongly as our fears, we use "might" of what we *hope*, and "should" of what we *fear*.

Subjunctive of Condition.

The following is an important division of a Conditional sentence :—

167 *In a Conditional sentence,* (1) *the clause expressing the condition is called the* Antecedent *("going-before")*; (2) *the clause expressing the consequence of the fulfilment of the condition is called the* Consequent.[1]

The forms in the Antecedent differ from the corresponding forms in the Consequent, and three out of five are identical with the Indicative, as will be seen from the following scheme :—

---

[1] These are also called (1) Protasis; (2) Apodosis. See *Glossary of Grammatical Terms*.

I

168   Conditional Mood.

Antecedent.	Consequent.
(If he) { *sees*[1] / **were to** see / **should** see / *saw* / *had seen* } (me).	(he) { *will know* / — / **would** know / — / **would have** known } me.

169   The Conditional Mood of Auxiliary Verbs.

The Auxiliary Verbs have only the Indicative form of the Subjunctive; they do not use the "shall-form." For example, we do not say, "If I *should can* (be able to) come, I *should will* (wish to) do so," but "If I *could* come, I *would* do so." Remembering that "could," "might," and "would" are the Past Tenses of "can," "may," and "will," and also bearing in mind the meanings of "can," "will," &c., viz. "to be able," "to be willing," we shall be able to express their Indicative Subjunctive forms in the ordinary Subjunctive forms, as follows:—

---

[1] The form "if he *see*" is now nearly extinct in good modern English. But a remnant of it remains in "if it *were*," which is the only correct modern form for the Past Conditional. "If I *was* you" is ungrammatical, though found (as well as "*you was*") in the eighteenth century. "If it *be*," "though it *be*," are also still used, though falling into disuse. "Were" generally implies a Condition not fulfilled.

For an explanation of the curious anomalies of this Scheme, see Appendix I., Par. 231.

Par. 170] **CONDITIONAL MOOD.**

170 Conditional Mood.

Can = "to be able."

TENSE	ANTECEDENT	CONSEQUENT
Present	If I { *can* (am able)	I { *can* (shall be able)
Past	If I { *could* were to be able / should be able	I { *could* (should be able)
Compl. Past	{ *could have* (had been able)	{ *could have* (should have been able)

May ¹ = "to be allowed."

Present	If I { *may* (am allowed)	I { *may* (shall be allowed)
Past	If I { *might* were to be allowed / should be allowed	I { *might* (should be allowed)
Compl. Past	{ *might have* (had been allowed)	{ *might have* (should have been allowed)

May ¹ = "to be possible.²"

Present	If I { *may* (it is possible for me)³	I { *may* (it will be possible for me)
Past	If I { *might* it were to be possible for me / should be possible for me	I { *might* (it would be possible for me)
Compl. Past	{ *might have* (it had been possible for me)³	{ *might have*(it would have been possible for me)

Will = "to be willing," "to like." ⁴

Present	If he { *will* (is willing)	I { *will* (shall be willing)
Past	If he { *would* were to be willing / should be willing	I { *would* (should be willing) ⁴
Compl. Past	{ *would have* (had been willing)	{ *would have* (should have been willing) ⁴

¹ "I *may* come" may mean, either (1) "I am allowed to come," or (2) "It is possible that I may come."

² It is English to say "I am *likely*, I am *sure*, to come." It is a pity it is not English to say "I am *possible to come*." If it were, we might write "If I were *possible*, *should be possible, had been possible*, to come," just as we do with "*may* (to be allowed)."

As it is, a slight change has to be made, and we have to say, not "I am possible to come," but "it is possible for me to come." Hence

³ Forms marked ³ are rarely or never used.

it appears that "may" in the sense of "to be possible" is used only in the Consequent.

⁴ Note that "he would" very often, in the Consequent, corresponds to "I should," and cannot be replaced by "willing," *e.g.*, "If I should see him, he *would* know me." Here "would" is put, out of politeness, for "should," and represents the Conditional (Consequent) Mood. (See Appendix I., Par. 237). But "*I would*" is never (except in Scotland and Canada) used for "*I should*." Consequently in the Scheme above, "he" is placed in the Antecedent, and "I" in the Consequent, to mark the difference of use.

Exercise XXVIII.

171 Replace the italicized Auxiliary Verbs by their equivalents in a non-auxiliary form; and, where they cannot be replaced, state the Mood represented by them:—

1. "If I *might* choose," said the camel to Jupiter, "I *would* have the neck of the swan, and the legs of the horse; then *I should* be the king of the beasts." "You *could* not *have made* a greater mistake," replied Jupiter; "if you had your way you *would be* nothing but a giraffe." 2. "If you *would* but *throw* me into the water," said the gudgeon to the fisherman; "I *should* soon grow fatter and bigger, and then, whenever you wanted me, I *would come* and be caught." "If I *could* feel sure of that," replied the fisherman, "perhaps I *might* let you go; but, as I am not at all sure, I must pop you into my basket." 3. "I *could have* won the race, if I had wished;" said the hare in a rage to the successful tortoise; "but I *would* rather lose the prize, than trudge for a dozen hours together, as you do, over a dozen yards." 4. The ass in the lion's skin *might have* kept the beasts in awe for ever, if he *could have* kept quiet. 5. "If I *could* sell my milk at a good price, I *might* buy a hen; the hen's eggs *would* give me money enough to buy a new gown; then I *should* be the best dressed girl at the fair, and I *would*[1] walk like a fine lady, tossing my head—like this."

172 CAUTION. *Might.*—"I might have" is often used for "I should have had power to," where "power" means "lawful power." It differs very little, in such cases, from

[1] See Par. 173.

"I could have," except that in "could" there is no notion of "lawful" power.

(1) "If he had wished he *might* have helped me."
(2) "If he had not been too scrupulous, he *could* soon have made his fortune."

But the two words are often confused Very often also it is doubtful whether "might" and "could" are not Indicatively, rather than Subjunctively, used. "He *might* have helped me" sometimes (see Par. 175) means "He *had* (Indic.) the power to have helped me (but did not use it)." Since, according to the proverb, "no one knows what he can do till he tries," *power* may always be regarded (1) as *existing* though unused, *i.e. Indicatively;* or (2) as a *possibility*, subject to the fulfilment of *condition*, i.e. *Subjunctively*. Hence, in Latin, the Indicative "potui" is often used in Conditional language.

173 *Will, would.*—Note that—just as "I *may* come" means "I *shall possibly* come,"—in the same way "I *will*, or *would* come" often means "I *shall willingly*, or, *should willingly*, come." In other words, "will" is used for the Future of itself, *i.e.* "I shall will," just as "may" is for "I shall may."

Hence "would" is not quite the same in—

(1) "John *said* he (John) *would* be punctual."
(2) "John *thought* he (John) would take a walk."

In (1) the meaning is little more than "John said he *was going* to be punctual; but in (2) "will" is for "shall will" or "shall like," and "would" is, therefore, for "should will" or "should like," so that the sentence means "John thought he *should like* to take a walk.' This explains the use of "would" for "might" after Verbs of praying (Par. 166). "We begged that he *would* come" is put for "we begged that he *might will*, i.e. *might be pleased* to come."

Indicative Use of Auxiliary Verbs.

The Verbs "can," "may," "shall," "will," together with their Past Tenses "could," "might," "should," "would," being sometimes Indicatively and sometimes Subjunctively used, require much care. Here are examples of the Indicative use of these verbs:—

174 *Can, could*, "to be able."

"He did help me, but he *could* not (*was not able* to) help me much."

175 *May, might* (i), "to be allowed;" "to have power."

(1) "I *may* (*i.e. am allowed* to) play now, because I have finished my work."
(2) "When I was a boy I *might* (*i.e. was allowed* to) always play after I had worked three hours."
(3) "My father says that I *may* (*i.e. am allowed* to) go out."
(4) "My father said that I *might* (*i.e. was allowed* to) go out."
(5) "You *might* (*i.e. had the power* to) have helped me, but you would not."

176 *May, might* (ii), "to be possible."

(1) "He says that he *may* possibly come, but he does not feel certain;" *i.e.* "his coming is possible."
(2) "He said that he *might* come, but that he did not feel certain;" *i.e.* "his coming was possible."

177 *Shall, should* (i), "to be obliged; to be bound."

(1) "You *should* (*i.e. were*, and *are*, *bound* to) control your temper."
(2) "You *should* not (*i.e. were bound* not to) have been so hasty."

178 *Shall, should* (ii), "to be going."

(1) "John says that he *shall*[1] (*is going* to) help me."
(2) "John said that he *should* (*was going* to) help me."

---

[1] There is no rudeness in "shall" here, because John is here avowing his own fixed intention. *You* do not use "shall" about John John uses it about himself.

179 *Will, would,* " to be willing; to wish; to like."

    (1) "He *would* not (*i.e. willed* not, or, *refused* to) help me, although he *could* (*i.e. was able* to) easily have done it."

    (2) "Although he was warned of the danger, yet the foolish boy *would* (*i.e. willed, was determined* to) run upon the thin ice."

    (3) "After breakfast the old man *would* (*i.e. liked* to) generally take a walk."

180 *Caution.*—Notice that Indicative Tenses of "may," "can," "shall," "will," when depending on a Principal Verb in the Present, are Present; but when depending on a Past, are Past :—

    (1) "I say that I *may, can, shall, will,* help you."
    (2) "I said that I *might, could, should, would,* help you."

181 **Rule.**—*The Auxiliary Verbs "can," "could," "may," "might," &c. (when not following "if" or any other Conjunction expressing Condition) are used Indicatively, provided they can be altered into the Indicatives of other Verbs.*

182   **How to Parse the Subjunctive.**

1. Where the Mood expresses *Purpose,* parse the Verb as " Subjunctive of Purpose."

2. Where the Mood expresses *Condition,* but in the Indicative form, *e.g.* "If he *comes, came, had come,*" you may parse the Verb as " Conditional

(Indicative form);" otherwise as simply "Conditional."

3. State whether the Conditional Verb is in the Antecedent or Consequent.

It is good practice to replace Auxiliary Verbs by their equivalents, either in the Indicative or the Subjunctive, as the case may be.

183   EXERCISE XXIX. (SPECIMEN).

State the Moods of italicized Verbs in the following Exercise :—

Hundreds of years ago, in the centre of the city of Rome there suddenly appeared one morning a deep chasm or pit. No one knew what *could have caused* it, and no one could fill it up. If earth or stone *could have filled* it up, it *would* not *have remained* open long ; but, although heaps upon heaps of stone and rubbish were cast down, the pit still remained unfilled. The people now began to fear that the gods of Rome *might intend* to punish the city, and they thought the pit *might be* a sign of their anger. So they went to the priests to ask them what they *ought* to do. The high priest replied that the gods had sent the pit in anger at the citizens ; "Even though you *went on* casting in earth for centuries," said he, "the pit *would* never *be closed :* it will always remain open, until the most precious thing in Rome *is cast* into it." On learning this, the citizens cast in their gold and the women their bracelets and ear-rings, in the hope that thus they *might satisfy* the gods and close the pit. But all was in vain, and it seemed as if nothing *would be* of use. At last a young soldier named Marcus Curtius, clothed in full armour and mounted on his horse, cried aloud that if a brave man *had cast* himself into the pit, it *would have been closed* long ago. Saying this he set spurs to his horse and leaped into the pit; which at once closed, and never opened afterwards.

184 *Could have caused.* "Was able to have caused." Indicative.[1]
Could have filled. "Had been able to fill." Indicative form of the Conditional : Antecedent.
Would have remained. Conditional : Consequent.
Might intend. "It was possible that they intended (put for 'they were possible to intend ')." Indicative.[1]
Might be. "It was possible to be (put for 'was possible to be ')." Indicative.[1]
Ought. "Were bound." Indicative.[1]
Went on. "Should go on." Indicative form of the Conditional : Antecedent.
Would be closed. Conditional : Consequent.
Is cast. "Shall be cast." Indicative form of the Subjunctive.
Might satisfy. "It was possible that they were going to satisfy (put for ' they were possible to satisfy ')." Indicative.[1]
Would be. Conditional : Antecedent. Full sentence is, " as (it would seem) if nothing were going to be of use."
Had cast. Indicative form of the Conditional : Antecedent.
Would have been closed. Conditional : Consequent.

Exercise XXX.

State the Moods of the following italicized Verbs :—

185 "If we *had* but a king," said some noisy frogs in a pond, "we *should* be peaceful and orderly ; as it is, every one

---

[1] Note that the Indicative is used not only in questions, but also after Verbs of fearing, hoping, &c., in many places where it cannot be said to express a *fact*, *e.g.* (1) "I hope he *has* come," (2) " I fear he *has* not come," (3) "I will ask who *has* come, or, if any one *has* come."
In Latin, the Subjunc. would be used in (2) and (3), the Infin. in (1).

may do as he pleases, and say what he likes, and there is as much uproar in our pond as[1] if we *were* a set of noisy ducks, instead of being quiet respectable frogs. A king *would*[2] soon set us to rights. O! that Jupiter[3] *would* give us a king." So they held an assembly and offered up a prayer to Jupiter that he *would*[4] give them a king. Scarcely were the words of their prayer out of their mouths, when down came a big black monster from the sky, splashing the water up like a fountain. Away swam the frogs in a fright. "Jupiter *should* not have sent us such a terrible monster," cried they; "why *could* he not send us a decent quiet king, who *might*[5] keep us in order without frightening us out of our wits? As for this tyrant, if he *terrifies*[6] us thus at his first coming, what will he do when he *is*[7(a)] used to oppressing us?"

186 But the big black monster took no notice of their terror. There he lay silent and sullen, and *would* not so much as move a limb. Astonished at his silence, the frogs, after their first fright, began to wish that their new king *would*[4] say or do something, so that at least they *might be relieved* from their suspense. So they took out of prison a frog that had committed murder, and promised him free pardon if he *would* swim within three frog's leaps of the king. Shivering with terror the poor frog swam towards the king, scarcely daring to hope that he *might*[7(b)] escape, and expecting every moment that

---

[1] *i.e.* "as (there would be) if we were."

[2] Here, as very often, the Antecedent is left out, but can be supplied, "if he were here."

[3] "O! that Jupiter *would*" is a short way of saying "(we pray, desire) that Jupiter *would*." This is a more earnest and less hopeful way of expressing oneself than "we pray that Jupiter *will*, or *may*." If fully expressed, the sentence would perhaps be "if it were possible that one's prayer could be granted, we *would* pray that Jupiter *would* give us a king." This is "would" of *purpose;* Par. 167.

[4] (1) After "prayer" *would* expresses *purpose;* (2) after "wish" it may be changed into "was going to," and treated as Indicative.

[5] "Who *might* keep us in order" is put for "*that he* might" and denotes *purpose.*

[6] "If" here is the same as "since." Hence 'terrifies" is Indicative.

[7] (a) See Par. 80; (b) "might," see Par. 180.

the huge monster *would* dart upon him with open jaws, and swallow him up. Closer and closer he swam ; still the king floated silent, motionless. Taking courage from this, the frog thought he *would*¹ awake his majesty by croaking. He croaked, but the king made no reply. He swam closer, and still closer, and at last, his suspicions being aroused, he extended one of his legs, and stroked the monster's face with it. It was as he had suspected. The king was no king, nothing but a big black log.

187 Immediately the whole tribe of frogs, who had been watching from a distance, lifted up their voices and began to abuse Jupiter : "If he *had wished* to insult us," cried they, "he *could* not have treated us more contemptuously. We *should* not have minded a strong and somewhat fierce king, even if he *had swallowed* up a few of us now and then. Anything *would* be better than this do-nothing, this King Log. Why *may* not we have a king as the birds and the beasts have? Jupiter *should* not have treated us thus ; he *might*² at least have sent us no king instead of thus insulting us. We will pray to him no more until he *sends* ³⁽ᵃ⁾ us a real king." So the frogs shut up all their temples; and for a whole day *would* say no more prayers to Jupiter. But at the end of the day there suddenly hopped down into the pond a monstrous stork to be their king. He began by gobbling up a dozen of the noisiest frogs, and ordered that no frog *should* ³⁽ᵇ⁾ croak in any part of the pond while he was asleep. This pleased the rest, who said, "Now we shall have order : it is worth while having a strong king that we *may* have peace and quiet." But, when they came swimming round

---

¹ "He thought he *would*" is put for "he thought he *should will*, i.e. *should like*." See Par. 173.
² This is Indicative, if you take it to mean "he had the power ;" but, if you take it to be "he would have been able (if he had pleased)," is Conditional, Consequent. See Par. 172.
³ (a) See Par. 80 ; (b) "*should* croak," notion of Purpose.

him next morning, to pay their respects, and to ask him to judge their disputes, he *would* not hear them, but ate them up by scores, quiet and noisy alike, choosing the fattest. So now the frogs saw they had made a mistake, and they said, "If we *were* once rid of King Stork we *would* not find fault with King Log, and indeed we *could* be content to have no king at all."

188 The Indefinite Subjunctive.

Sometimes "should" is used where a Condition is *implied* rather than expressed:—

   (1) "It would be unjust that I *should* suffer for other people's misconduct."

This is really equivalent to—

   (2) "It would be unjust *if* I *should* suffer," &c.

But it is more difficult to explain why we say—

   (3) "It *is* a shame that I *should* be thus insulted," *i.e.* "am thus insulted."

   (4) "I am sorry that my son *should* thus misconduct himself," *i.e.* "thus misconducts himself."

   (5) "To think that he *should have* so far disgraced himself!" *i.e.* "has so far disgraced himself."

In the last three examples *facts* are spoken of: why then is the Subjunctive used?

The answer is, that we desire here to speak of the facts, not as definite facts, but as *possibilities*. In the same indefinite way we sometimes use the Infinitive, as being an Indefinite Mood:—

   (6) "It is a shame *for*[1] me *to be* thus *insulted*."

[1] "For to . . . be insulted" is really here the Old Infinitive with "for to" instead of "to." See Par. 402.

Consequently, this use of "should" may be called the *Indefinite Subjunctive*.

189

Tenses of the Subjunctive.

It is usual to speak of the *Present* and *Past* Tenses of a Subjunctive : but, in reality, "if *he comes*" refers to *future* time, and so does "if he *came* or *should come.*"

It may perhaps be said that, in "if he come(s), I will see him ;" the Condition, though having to do with the Future, is regarded as *Present* to the speakers. Nevertheless, the fact that the Elizabethan writers often used to say "if he shall come," indicates that this form is more like a Future than anything else.

The form "if he *should* come" seems to be a combination of Future and Past—the Future being represented by the *shall*, and the Past by the Inflection *-d*—as though with the intention of making a Condition that should apply to no time in particular, but to all time.

The same intention seems obvious in "if he *were to* come," where the Past time is included in "were," and the Future in "to," which looks "*to*-ward" the future.

The False Subjunctive.

190

"If" is sometimes used not in its ordinary Conditional sense, nor, on the other hand, exactly like "since," but rather in the sense of "assuming as a fact." In such cases it is followed by a true Indicative (not an Indicative form of the Conditional), and the Indicative (Present or Past) is also used in the Consequent :—

(1) "*If* he *says* that, he *is* more ignorant than I supposed."

(2) "*If* he *said* that, he *was* more ignorant than I had supposed."

This must not be confounded with the true Subjunctive.

Pope seems to use the Present and the Future indifferently after "while" in—

"While *lasts* the mountain or while Thames *shall flow.*"

CHAPTER VII.

IRREGULARITIES.

191 REGULARITY means that which is *like a ruled line*, for "regular" means "ruled." Irregularity, therefore, means that which is *not like a ruled line*. Language is said to be regular when it follows *straight fixed rules*.[1]

Irregularity of Idioms.

192 For example, it is *regular* to say, "I have a score of sheep." Here "score" is a Noun, and therefore is regularly followed by "of." On the other hand, it is *irregular* to say, "I have a dozen marbles," leaving out "of."

Now bear in mind—

Whenever language is irregular, there is some cause for the irregularity.

---

[1] For a Summary of the Rules of Syntax, see "RULES AND DEFINITIONS," p. xxviii.

Language does not bend away from its straight fixed rules for nothing; there is some *cause* that makes it bend.

193 In the last example there are perhaps two causes: (1) when we say, "I have a dozen," we *confuse* this with "I have twelve," that is to say, we confuse the use of a Noun with the use of an Adjective. So we treat "dozen," partly as though it were an Adjective, leaving out the "of" after it, and partly as though it were a Noun, keeping the "a" before it.

We do the same thing in "I have a hundred sheep;" we ought to say, by rule, "I have a hundred (*Noun*) of sheep," or, "I have hundred (*Adjective*) sheep;" but we keep the "a," as though "hundred" were a Noun, and yet leave out "of" as though "hundred" were an Adjective. Thus we *mix or confuse two constructions*. (2) Another reason why the "of" is omitted after "dozen" and "hundred" is probably *the desire to be brief*.

194 Here then there are two causes, and they are very common causes, of irregularity: (1) **Confusion of two constructions, (2) the desire to be brief.** (3) **The desire to avoid harshness of sound or of construction,** and (in Poetry more especially) the desire to give special emphasis to certain words, are also causes of irregularity.

195   Irregularity of Words.

The "confusion of two constructions," or rather the "reduplication of constructions," affects the formation of *words*, as well as of *idioms*. It is very common for an Inflection to become obsolete and forgotten, and then to receive a second Inflection as an appendage, the two being blended or "confused" together.

196   For example (1) the old Genitive in '*s*, which is now retained only in our " Possessive Inflection," had once a wider use, so that it represented our " at" or "by," and was used for an Adverbial termination.   Hence were formed :

   (1) "One-*s*" or "once ;" "unaware-*s* ;" "door-*s* ;" "day-s ;" *i.e.* "by day."

In time, the Adverbial use of the Inflection becoming obsolete, a Preposition was inserted, but the old useless Inflection was retained :

   (2) "At once ;" "at unawares" (Spenser); "in doors ;" "now-a-days." [1]

197   In the same way (1) " near " was recognised as a Comparative form, from " neah" nigh : (2) "songster" was recognised as a Feminine, with the old Feminine termination -*ster*.   But, as the sense of

---

[1] Occasionally there is found " by littles and little-."

the Inflection in each word became lost, new Inflections were added :

(1) "Near-*er* ;"   (2) "Song-str*ess*."

In this way may be explained the use of "yours" in "a friend of *yours*." (*See* Par. 434). The use of "yours"[1] for "your," is in part explained by "confusion," and in part by Law III.

Law III, the "Desire to avoid harshness," accounts for the irregular retention of the following old forms for emphasis :—

(1) "I want a book, give me *one* (emphatic form of *a, an, ane*)."
(2) "Give me a book, for I have *no(ne)*."
(3) "Keep my book, and I will keep *your(s)*,[1] till you have done with *mi(ne)*."

198   How to Explain Irregularities.

Just as the attraction of the earth makes a bullet deviate from the straight line in which it is discharged, so some attracting cause makes language deviate from the straight path, *i.e.* from *regularity*, into a path that is not straight, *i.e.* into *irregularity*.

---

[1] "Yours was early used in the Northern Dialects

This may be illustrated by a diagram :—

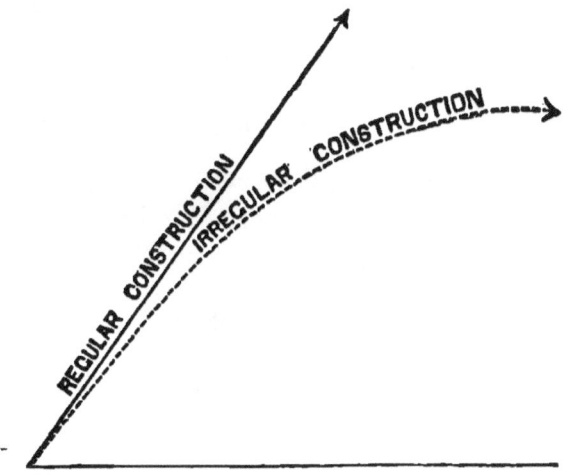

Attracting force :—
    I. Desire of Brevity.
    II. Influence of some other construction.
    III. Desire to avoid harshness of sound or of construction, &c. &c.

First, therefore, ascertain the *regularity* from which the *irregularity* in question has deviated.

Secondly, ascertain the *cause of deviation*, whether it be (i) desire of brevity ; (ii) confusion of two constructions ; (iii) desire to avoid harshness of sound or of construction.

    (1) "He loved her *as* his own daughter," *i.e.*, "as (he would have loved her, if she had been) his own daughter." (Brevity).
    (2) "*All of* us remonstrated," *i.e.*, confusion of the two constructions : "All[1] we remonstrated," and "*some, many, ten*, &c. *of* us remonstrated."
    (3) "It is you that say so."

[1] Compare "*All we*, like sheep, have gone astray

In this last example two principles are at work. The regular construction would have been—

(1) "It that says so is you."

Here steps in (III) the desire to avoid the harshness of "it," used so emphatically; hence "it" is deprived of its emphasis by being separated from its Relative "that."

(2) "It is you that says so."

Here steps in (II) "confusion" between this construction and the straightforward construction "You say so"—resulting in the idiom logically incorrect, but by process of custom stamped as perfectly good English :—

(3) "It is you that *say* so."[1]

200 Irregularities are very common (i) with the Relative Pronouns and Relative Adverbs, (ii) with Adjectives and Adverbs of Number and Amount. A few of these irregularities are given below, in order to prepare the reader for dealing systematically with all irregularities in the English language.

In every case the same method will be adopted, viz. to ask—

I. *What would be the regular construction?*

II. *What is the cause of irregularity?*

[1] See also Par. 160.

Relative Pronouns and Adverbs.

201 1. "*That*" is often omitted as the Object, and sometimes (rarely except in Poetry) as the Subject:—

(1) "'Twas you (*that*) I saw."
(2) "'Twas you (*that*) said so, not I."

The regular construction inserts "that."

The cause of irregularity is (I)[1] "the desire of brevity," and (II)[1] "confusion" with the straightforward construction "You said so."

202 2. "*But* "seems put for "that...not" or "who ...not," *e.g.* in—

(1) "There is no one here *but* hates you," *i.e.* "that does not hate you."

The radical meaning of "but" is "be-out" or "with-out;" hence "except." And therefore the regular construction is—

(2) "There is no man here *but* or *except* (he) hate you."

Compare *Julius Cæsar*, v. 5, 35 :—

(3) "I found no man *but he* was true to me."

Brevity steps in and omits "he." Also "but" is *confused* with a Relative Pronoun, just as "as" is. (See next Paragraph).

For other uses of "but," see Index.

[1] These Numbers refer to the Laws of Irregularity mentioned in Paragraph 198.

203 3. "So." The radical meaning of "so" (Early English "swa") is "in that way;" and the radical meaning of "as" (which is a contraction of an emphatic form of "so," Early English "all-swa," "alse," "als," "as") is "in which way," or "in that way." Consequently, "as" has the Demonstrative meaning of "so," besides having its own Relative meaning.

(1) "If you are busy, say *so*."

(2) "I thought he was a rascal, and he is *so*."

The Regular Construction would be—

(3) "He is *it*."

But (Law III)[1] the *harshness* of "it" in so emphatic a position has tended to irregularity; and (Law II) this construction has been *confused* with—

(4) "I thought he was a rascal and he turned out *so*, proved *so*," &c.

In (4), "so" is used in its proper sense, viz. "in that way," and it has been confused with and substituted for "it" in Example (2), in which "so" must be parsed as "used for *it*."

204 4. "So as-to."

(1) "The sailors furled the sails *so as* to be prepared for the storm."

[1] These Numbers refer to the Laws of Irregularity mentioned in Paragraph 198.

The Regular Construction would be—

(2) "The sailors furled the sails *so* (in the way) *as* (in which way) [they would furl the sails] to be prepared for the storm."

Brevity (Law I), disliking the repetition, omits the bracketed sentence. In the same way we say—

(3) "I am not *so* credulous *as* (I should have to be) to believe this."

The words "so as" add indefiniteness, by suggesting *condition*. If they had been omitted :

(4) "The sailors furled the sails *to be* prepared for the storm."

—the *purpose* of the sailors would have been definitely expressed. But the insertion of "so as" implies rather that the work was of a nature tending towards a certain result, without distinctly stating the *purpose*.

205

5. **"As."** "In that way," "in which way."

(1) "I have not such kind treatment *as* I used to have."
(2) "Bring such books *as* you have."
(3) "Parse such a sentence *as* this (is)."
(4) "Such *as* it is, I give it you."

The Regular Construction would be (since "such" means "so-like," and is the Demonstrative corresponding to the Relative "which," *i.e.* what-like) :—

(5) "I have not such kind treatment *which* I used to have."

206 Hence, in Shakespeare, we often find "such" followed by "which" and "that" (Relative Pronouns):—

> (6) "Such an affection *which* cannot choose but branch."
>
> (7) "You speak to Casca, and to *such* a man
> *That* is no fleering tell-tale."

But (Law II)[1] the Regular Construction in (5) is *confused* with—

> (8) "I have not kind treatment *as* (*i.e.*, in the way in which) I used to have."

207 The result is the irregularity in (1), which is now recognized as good English. But while this process of "confusion of constructions" was going on, many idioms were formed that have been discarded, and are not recognized as good English. We all know that it is vulgar to say—

> (9) "This is *the* boy *as* I saw yesterday."

Yet Shakespeare, using "as" for "that," precisely in this way, writes—

> (10) "I have not from your eyes *that* gentleness
> And show of love *as* I was used to have."

208 Hence we can explain the use of "as" in parentheses, as follows:—

> (11) "So you are late again, *as* (is) usual."
>
> (12) "*As* I told you before, you must work before you play."

---

[1] These Numbers refer to the Laws of Irregularity mentioned in Paragraph 198.

In both (11) and (12) "as" is used for the Relative Pronoun "which," while the Antecedent (see Par. 25) must be supplied from the context, thus :—

> (11) in full, "So you are late again, *which* (lateness) is usual with you."
>
> (12) in full, "You must work before you play, *which* (saying) I told you before."

209 6. "As" redundant.
> (1) "He was appointed *as* general."
> (2) "We will have him *as* our leader."
> (3) "I esteem him *as* a rascal."
> (4) "This shall serve us *as* ink."

In (3) and (4) the Regular Construction would be—

> (3) in full, "I esteem him *as* (I should esteem) a rascal."
>
> (4) in full, "This shall serve us *as* ink (would serve us)."

It is more difficult to give the Regular Construction for (1) and (2), and probably the irregularities of (1) and (2) are caused not only by (I) *desire of brevity*, but also by (II) *confusion of construction*. For example, it is an easy transition to "We will *have* him *as*" from :—

> (5) "We will obey him, serve him, honour him, treat him, hold him, *as* (we would obey, serve, honour, treat, hold) our leader."

210 "As," in many similar sentences, is used to give the impression that the writer is not stating a *fact*, but *somebody else's opinion* :—

    (1) "He considered pleasure *as* (it would be considered if it were) the object of life."

    (2) "He represented the results of the expedition *as* (they would be represented, if they were) most disastrous."

In all these cases "as" may be parsed as "redundant." The full construction should be given, or the construction that has caused the irregularity by "confusion."

For "as yet" and other uses of "as," see Index.

211 7. "**As if**," "**as though**," are often used where (I) the Consequent is omitted :—

    (1) "He loved her *as* (he would have loved her) *if* she had been his own daughter."

    (2) "He loved her *as* (much as he could have loved her, for he could not have loved her more) *though* she had been his own daughter."

In both examples, Brevity is the Cause of Irregularity.

212   Words of Number.[1]

Some much-used Adjectives and Adverbs of

---

[1] (I), (II.), (III), refer to the "Laws of Irregularity," mentioned in Par. 198.

Number and Amount present many irregularities. The same word is used sometimes—

1. As a *Numeral Adjective*, answering the question " How many ? "

2. As an *Adverb*, answering the question " How much ? " " In how great a degree ? " &c.

3. As a *Noun*, being the name of a collection, *e.g.* " score."

213 Hence the principal " Cause of Irregularity " here will be the " Confusion of Constructions," viz. the Constructions of an Adjective, Adverb, and Noun.

(1) " A dozen (of) pens, a hundred (of) men, half (of) the country,[1] all (of) the men, more (of) pudding a little (of) pudding." [2]

Here the Regular Construction would have been—

(2) " Hundred men, twenty men," &c.

But a feeling that each number represented a single " collection " led to the insertion of " a " without the grammatically consistent and necessary insertion of " of," so that the Noun Construction

---

[1] Note that you cannot say "quarter the country." Why ? Because "half" is *more commonly* used than "quarter" (insomuch that "half" is sometimes used for " part," *e.g.* " the larger half "); and remember *irregularities feed upon custom.* It is where men have to say the same things *often and quickly,* that men are most apt to cut and clip and modify their language to suit their convenience. Hence, in Latin, " venio Romam," but " venio *ad* Italiam."

[2] See Par. 217.

was confused with the Adjective. In the same way, in earlier English, we find—

(3) "A *score* sheep," "a ten furlongs."

And even in our Authorized Version of the Bible we have—

(4) "About *an* eight *days* after these sayings."

214 In some of these cases probably the Adjective and Noun are regarded as *one* Compound Noun. Compare "*a* fortnight," *i.e.* "*a* fourteen-night," "*a* twelve-month."

But in modern English the irregularity is only licensed with a few much-used Adjectives—"dozen," "hundred," "thousand" (perhaps "million").

215 1. "All."

(1) "All *of* us rejoiced."

Regular Construction "All we." Cause of Irregularity, partly (III) the *harshness* of "all we," partly (II) Confusion of (1) with "ten, twenty, many, &c., *of* us." Note the following various uses:—

(2) "He rushed up *all* out of breath," "*all* the better," Adverb.
(3) "*All* is in vain: he will not help us at *all*," Noun.
(4) In "The men *all* perished"

—"all" may be parsed as an Adjective, just as we can say "The men—twenty in number—perished."

But undoubtedly "all" owes its position in (4) to a *confusion* of its Adjectival use with its Adverbial use, viz. "altogether."

216 2. "Enough:"—
  (1) "He has been punished *enough*," Adverb.
  (2) "We have had *enough* of wandering," Noun.
  (3) "We have not *enough* men," Adjective, though really a Noun with "of" omitted ; (II.)
  (4) "I have not men *enough*," Adverb in position, Adjective in use ; (II.)

217 "Few," "little:"—
  (1) "A *few* (of) men," "a *little* (of) pudding."

Adjectives, with (II.) Confusion of Noun Construction. Distinguish "a *little* (of) pudding" from "a little," *i.e.* "a *small* pudding." See Pars. 213—14.

218 3. "Many:"—
  (1) "*Many* a man has tried, but few have succeeded."

The Regular Construction would be "Many men;" but this appears to have been confused with—
  (2) "*Many times* a man has tried."

The *-y* termination of "many" has doubtless favoured this Adverbial use.

There is abundant proof that in Early English "many" was used either as an Adverb, or as part of a Compound Adjective "many-one," *i.e.* in Modern English "many-a." (See *Shakespearian Grammar*, Par. 85.) This began in the thirteenth century.

In the same way the Germans say "mancher (Adj.) mann," but "manch (Adv.) *ein* mann."

The insertion of "a" is common after Adjectives that are Semi-Adverbial. Compare—

(3) "*What a* man he is!"
(4) "*Such a* man as he is ought to know better."

And, in Early English :—

(5) "*Each a* man," "*which a* wife," *i.e.* "*what a* wife."

Shakespeare also has—

(6) "*Poor* (*i.e.* barely) *a* thousand pounds."

It is rare to find "many" (like "few") now treated as a Noun (Shakespeare has "a *many* of our bodies") :—

(6) "A *many* (of) men."

219   4. "More:"—

(1) "Give me some, no, much, &c. *more* pudding."
(2) "Give me three *more* books, one *more* book."

Here "more" is an Adverb, and means "besides." But it owes its position to a confusion of the Adverbial with the Adjectival use of "more." Hence, instead of saying "Some pudding *more*, *i.e.* in addition," we say "some *more* pudding."

220 "No," "any," "some," are used as Adverbs answering to the question "How much more?" in—

> (3) "He slept *no more*," *i.e.* "*no* longer;" "did not sleep *any more, much more*," i.e. "*any, much,* longer."

221 "More" is used as a Noun in—

> (4) "He is always asking for *more*."
> (5) "I want, (or) I said, no *more*."

Here "no" may be regarded either as an Adjective making up part of a Compound Noun, "no-more," or perhaps, more correctly, as an Adverb modifying the anomalous Adverbial Noun "more."[1]

222 "Some:"—

> (1) "I had *some* difficulty," Adjective of Amount.
> (2) "I saw *some* children," Adjective of Number.
> (3) "He will come *some* time or other," Adjective of Indefiniteness.
> (4) "*Some* one or other said so," Adjective of Indefiniteness.
> (5) "*Some* twenty men arrived," *i.e.* "about," Adverb.

Compare, for the Adverbial use of "some," Shakespeare's use of the word :—

> (6) "I would detain you here *some* month or two."
> (7) "*Some* hour (*i.e.* about an hour) before you took me."

[1] For the Adverbial use of "no," see Index.

And Early English (modern Scotch) use :—

(8) "It is-*some* late." "Five mile or *some* (*i.e.* thereabouts)."

"Each," "every," "one," "none," "other."

223   1. "Each," "other :"—

(1) "They hated *each other* (or) *one another*."

This is (I) a contraction for—

(2) "They hated, each (hated) other," or, "They hated, one (hated) an other."

In the same way we must explain (I) by the *Desire of Brevity:*—

(3) "They inquired after — each (inquired after) other's health."

Here, in modern English,[1] we are inclined to treat "each other" as a Compound Noun; but it is not so. "Each" is in Apposition to "they," or Subject to "inquired" understood.

224   *Caution.* It is a common fault to use "each" with a Plural Verb. Where "each" appears to be the Subject of a Plural Verb, it is really not so, but only in apposition to the true Subject, *e.g.* :—

(4) "They are *each* going to their several homes."

[1] See Par. 530.

Here also "their homes" for "his home" is hardly logically correct.[1]

The following line of Pope is an example shewing that, though "all" takes a Plural, "each" does not:—

(5) "*All join* to guard what *each desires* to gain."

225 2. "Every" (once "ever-each,") is used like "a" before a Numeral Adjective and Noun:—

(1) "There is a lamp-post *every* hundred yards."
(2) "He wakes up *every* ten minutes."

In such cases probably "ten-minutes," "hundred-yards," are Compound Nouns like "fo(u)rt(een)-night," "twelve-month." See Par. 214.

226 3. "One" (which is the same word, by derivation, as "ane," "an," "a") may mean (*a*) a particular "one;" (*b*) any "one" you like; (*c*) a single "one;" (*d*) being used for "one person" or "one thing," it has come to mean a "person," "animal," (*e.g.* "young *ones*,") or "thing":—

(*b*) "*One* knows very well that perseverance *is* necessary for success," Pronoun: "any one."
(*d*) "All creatures love their young *ones*," Noun.
(1) "I do not like this book; give me that *one*."
(2) "I have no book; give me *one*."

In (1) "one" is a Pronoun put for "book;" in (2) an Adjective (with the Noun to be supplied) put for "*one* (book)" or "*a* (book)." Sometimes the meaning of "one" depends on its emphasis.

[1] The Latins would have used the Singular, "domum."

For example, in (2) "one" is unemphatic, and means "a"; but where it is emphatic, it may mean "a single one," *e.g.* in—

(3) "Lend me a book; I have not *one* left."

227 4. "**None**," when used as a Subject, ought to be followed by a Singular Verb, as in Dryden:—

(1) "None but the brave *deserves* the fair."

But when you are denying something about a number of persons, the Verb falls naturally into the Plural:—

(2) "*None* of my friends *were* at home."

This arises from a confusion (II) between "*none was* at home" and "*all were* not-at-home."

228 It is a common fault (not quite sanctioned by custom), to say:—

(3) "Neither you nor he *were* to blame," for "*was* to blame."[1]

This arises from a confusion (II) with—

(4) "You and he *were* both not to blame."

229 "None" was once used as an Adjective; and this usage is still retained in—

(5) "Where is your book? I have *none*."
(6) "Hope have I *none*."

---

[1] The Rule is that when two Subjects are separated by "nor," or "or," the Verb agrees with the latter.
There is a little harshness in the correct "was." The harshness may be *evaded* by writing, "Neither he nor you were to blame." Here "were" *must* be right, whether the Subject be regarded (incorrectly) as Plural "he nor you," or (correctly) as "you."

Here "none" is used *for the sake of emphasis*. "I have *no* book" would not lay emphasis enough on "no." "Book have I *no*" would be intolerably harsh. And therefore we use the old emphatic form "none;" just as we cannot say "this book is *my*," but have to say "this book is *mine*."

"None" is Adverbial in—

(7) "He is *none* the happier for all his wealth," *i.e.* "no one whit," or "naught," Adverb.

230 5. "**No.**" If in the last example "the" were omitted, we should use, instead of "none," the less emphatic form "no" :[1]—

(1) "He is *no* happier for all his wealth," Adverb.

"No" does not seem to be a Numeral Adjective in—

(2) "You are *no* soldier."

It is rather Adverbial : "You are *in no way, in no respect*, a soldier."

---

[1] Compare "*none* the less" with the less emphatic form of "none" in "*nathless*."

APPENDIX I.

THE SUBJUNCTIVE MOOD.

It is interesting to trace the processes that have shaped our modern anomalous Conditional Mood. For this purpose we will compare the Mood "as it is," with the Mood "as it might have been."

Conditional Mood, as it is.

231

Antecedent.	Consequent.
If he { *sees* / were to see / should see / *saw* / *had seen* } me,	he { *will know* / would know / would have known } me.

As it might have been.

232 Out of the five forms of the Conditional Antecedent, three (those italicized above) are identical with the Indicative; and out of three in the Consequent, one is Indicative. Once there were many more separate Conditional forms; but they have now fallen into disuse, and the Conditional Mood is assimilated to the Indicative.

233 The reasons for this are (1) the general tendency in every language to drop distinctions wherever they can be dropped; (2) the " if," expressing the Condition by itself, has enabled us to dispense, *in the Antecedent*, with the Verbal forms; but, *in the Consequent*, there being no " if," the Verbal forms have been retained.[1] There is no ambiguity in " if he had seen me" used in the Antecedent; but, were that form used in the Consequent, *e.g.* " he had known me," there would be danger of ambiguity.

It is neither possible nor desirable to revive the old forms, but it is of use to perceive their regularity. There are two ways of expressing the Conditional: (1) by Inflections, (2) by the use of Auxiliary Verbs. Supposing the Conditional Mood were regularly formed by Inflections, it would be—

234 ## I. A. Regular Conditional Mood with Inflections.

Antecedent.	Consequent.
(If it) { be / were[2] / had been } (true),	(he) { [be] / were[3] / had been[3] } (guilty.)

[1] Similarly, in the Antecedent when the "if" is omitted, the distinctive form of the Conditional must be used. "Should I, *or*, were I to, see him"—not "saw I him."
[2] Generally used of an unfulfilled condition.
[3] Still used in Poetry.

Or, taking another Verb, *e.g.* " come " :—

Antecedent.	Consequent.
(If he) { come [1] / came / had come }	(he) { [see [2]] / [saw [3]] / had seen [4] } (me.)

235 I. B. Modern Conditional Mood with Inflections.

With the general decay of Inflections, the Conditional " if he *come* " has fallen into such disuse that it may now be called extinct. Hence the new scheme *with Inflections* is—

Antecedent.	Consequent.
(If he) { comes / came / had come }	(he) { (no form) / (no form) / had seen [4] } (me).

[1] Rarely used, except by pedants. But "be" is still allowable as an exception: "if it *be* true."
[2] Not used.
[3] This ambiguous form of the Subjunctive is used two or three times by Shakespeare. See *Shakespearian Grammar*, Par. 361, "If I rebuked you, then I *check'd* (i e. *should check*) my friends."
[4] Used only in poetry, and archaic or elevated prose.

236 II. A. Regular Conditional Mood with "shall."

Bearing in mind that "shall" and "should" are nearly equivalent to "am to" and "were to," the reader will perceive the regularity of the following:—

Antecedent.		Consequent.	
If he	$\begin{cases} shall,^2 \ [be^1 \ to] \\ should, \ were \ to \\ should^2 \quad have, \\ or \ [had \ been^1 \ to] \end{cases}$ come,	he $\begin{cases} shall \ \text{see} \\ should \ \text{see} \\ should \ have \ \text{seen} \end{cases}$ me.	

237 II. B. Modern Conditional Mood with "shall."

In course of time people came to think "shall" and "should" harsh words to use to any one *to whom* (Second Person), or *about whom* (Third Person), they were speaking. But when "shall" and "should" were preceded by "if," the "if" removed the notion of compulsion. Consequently "shall" and "should" were replaced by "will" and

[1] Rarely, or never used.
[2] Used by Shakespeare. Compare "If you *should have* taken vengeance on my faults, I never had (*i.e.* should have) lived."—*Cymbeline*, v. i. 8. "If he shall come" is common in Shakespeare.

"would" *in the Consequent, (with the Second and Third Persons), but not in the Antecedent.* Hence arose the following scheme:—

Antecedent.	Consequent.
If he shall, should, or were to come, should have	he will see, would see, would have seen me.

238   III. Modern Mixed Conditional Mood.

This is formed by blending the New Inflectional Mood with the New Auxiliary Mood, as follows:—

Antecedent.	Consequent.
If he comes, came, or { should come / were to come }, had come	he { will see / would see / would have seen } me.

Hence we see that the Inflectional Mood, having been assimilated to the Indicative, and being superior in brevity to the Auxiliary form, has gained the victory, as it were, in the Antecedent, where the resemblance to the Indicative does not cause much danger of ambiguity; but the Auxiliary form has gained the victory in the Consequent.

APPENDIX II.

ON THE ANALYSIS OF SENTENCES.

239   Hitherto we have treated a sentence as composed of *words*: now we shall treat it as composed of *groups* of words.

Sentences, Phrases; Clauses.

Def. *A group of words expressing a statement, command, or question, is called a "Sentence."*

Def. *A group of words expressing a meaning, but not a statement, &c., is called a "Phrase."*

Def. *A "Phrase" that includes a "Sentence" may be called a "Clause."*

(1) "He came." *Sentence.*
(2) "To come;" "Upon his coming;" "In a short time." *Phrases.*
(3) "That he came;" "When he came;" "Because he came;" "If he had come." *Clauses.*

Note that some Phrases, *e.g.* those in (3), *include* Sentences. But they *are not* Sentences; for they are neither *statements*, nor *commands*, nor *questions*.

Such Phrases as those in (3), are sometimes, however, called, for shortness, *Noun-Sentences*, because they *include* Sentences. But it must be always borne in mind that they are not really sentences, though they become Sentences if the Conjunction is removed.

240   Phrases and Clauses.

A Phrase or Clause may express :

    1. *A Noun.*
    2. *An Adjective.*
    3. *An Adverb.*

1. Noun Phrases[1] are exemplified by the italicized words in the following sentences :—

1. *To be anxious* is useless. 2. *That he is in error* is certain. 3. *Why you act thus* I cannot understand. 4. I like *a rascal to be punished*. 5. *What is done* cannot be undone. 6. *Whether he meant what he said*, it is hard to determine. 7. *Walking to school* is being injuriously superseded by trains and omnibuses.

Exercise.

The pupil should construct other sentences on the model of each sentence above, having Noun-Phrases[1] for Subjects and for Objects. For example, beginning with (1), the pupil should make Noun

[1] For brevity, the word "Phrase" is used to include "Clause."

Phrases out of Infinitives; then passing to (2), let him use the Conjunction "that," and so on.

241   2. Adjective Phrases or Clauses :—

> 1. The monkey *with the long tail.* 2. The monkey *that has the long tail.* 3. A man *without principle.* 4. A man *of honour.* 5. Sing for the oak-tree, *the monarch of the wood.* 6. The light *of the sun.* 7. *The moon's* orbit. 8. The book *belonging to my uncle.* 9. The cow *in the paddock.* 10. The business *in which I am engaged.* 11. The painter *of that celebrated picture.* 12. This is an action *to be deplored.* 13. I have water *to wash* (*i.e.* washing water), but none *to drink* (*i.e.* drinking water). 14. The boy *at the top.*

Exercise.

As with the Noun Phrases, so with the Adjective Phrases, the pupil should construct other phrases according to the several models above.

242   3. Adverbial Phrases or Clauses :—[1]

> 1. *Knowing*[2] *this* (*i.e.* since I knew this) I was not surprised. 2. *Surprised at his answer,* I knew not what to reply. 3. *When, while, after, before, as, since, I perceived my mistake,* I

---

[1] Note that an Adverbial *Clause, e.g.* "when I came," becomes, if the Conjunction is removed, a *Sentence.*

[2] One of the first things to be done in the Analysis of Sentences is to understand the difference between (1) a Participle implying a Conjunction, and (as here) representing an *Adverbial Clause,* and (2) a Participle implying the Relative Pronoun "that," and representing an *Adjectival Clause.*

243 apologized. 4. I am living *in, near, not far from, &c. St. John's Wood.* 5. I go daily *to, from, past, across, &c. the city.* 6. *This done,* they departed. 7. This house was built, (Cause) *owing to the increase of the owner's family;* (Purpose) *to command a view of the river;* (Agency) *by a wealthy man:* (Instrumentality) *by foreign workmen:* (Means) *with timber off his own estate;* (Source) *out of his capital;* (Place) *near London;* (Time) *ten years ago;* (Manner) *with great haste;* (Circumstance) *amid the derision of the neighbours, in spite of the opposition of his friends, though he was in debt at the time;* (Result) *to the great detriment of his fortune, so expensively that he ruined himself by it.* 8. I am moving (Purpose) *in order to be nearer to my friends,* or (Cause) *because I am too far from my friends.* 9. He is unwise *to say this,* i.e. "for saying this." 10. *Wherever he goes* he prospers. 11. He is too foolish *to succeed,* i.e. "for the purpose of success."

244 Note especially the following :—

12. The soldiers disliked their general, *who seemed to take a pleasure in exposing them to hardships,* i.e. "*because* he seemed—." 13. (Circumstance)[1] *Admitting that your facts are correct,* I still deny your inferences. 14. (Circumstance)[1] *If he comes,* I will come.

EXERCISE.

Make Adverbial Phrases and Clauses on the model of the above.

---

[1] The *condition* subject to which anything happens, may conveniently be called a "circumstance."

Sentences.

245   1. **A Simple Sentence.**—*A Sentence that has only one Subject and only one Stating, Questioning, or Commanding Verb is a Simple Sentence :*—

"John struck Thomas."

Note that "John came, but soon departed," is not "simple," because (though it has only one Subject) it has *two stating Verbs*; again, "John came that Robert might take a holiday," is not "simple" because, though there is only one stating Verb,[1] yet there are *two Subjects*.

246   2. **A Co-ordinate Sentence.**—*When several Simple Sentences are connected by "and," "but," "so," "then," &c.,*[2] *so that each Sentence is, as it were, independent, and of the same rank as the rest, each is called a Co-ordinate Sentence :*—

"John struck Thomas, *so, and, but,* &c. Thomas struck John again."

The mark of a Co-ordinate sentence is that *it can generally stand as a sentence by itself*, preceded by its Conjunction, *e.g.* :—

"He made all possible haste. *For he was afraid of being late.*"

---

[1] In "Robert *might* take," "might take" may be (Par. 174) a stating Verb: but, when preceded by "that," the Verb ceases to *state*.
[2] The Co-ordinate Conjunctions are *and, also, besides, moreover, too, for, accordingly, consequently, hence, so, then, now, therefore, but, however, nevertheless, notwithstanding, or*.

247 3. A Compound Sentence.—*A Sentence made up of Co-ordinate Sentences is called a Compound Sentence :—*

"John struck Thomas, and Thomas struck John again."

248 4. The Principal Sentence.—*When a number of Sentences are connected by Conjunctions that are not Co-ordinate, the Sentence that is not introduced by a Conjunction is called the Principal Sentence.*

249 5. Subordinate Sentences.—*Sentences connected with a Principal Sentence by Conjunctions that are not Co-ordinate are called Sub-ordinate.*[1]

The *Sub-ordinate* Conjunctions are "that" (introducing (1) Subject or Object, (2) Purpose, (3) Result) ; " because," " when," " how," " since," " as " in the sense of " since," " after," " before," " while," &c. ; and they are so called because " purpose," " time," " circumstance," &c., are regarded as being *Sub-ordinate* to the statement, question, or command expressed in the Principal Sentence.

"Before (Subord.) he had heard the evidence (Princip.) he asserted that (Subord.) the prisoner was guilty."

The mark of a Sub-ordinate Sentence is this, that,

---

[1] *Implied* Sub-ordinate Sentences are sometimes introduced without Conjunctions, by means of Interrogative and Relative Pronouns and Adverbs, *e.g.* "He asked *what John said,*" where the italicized words *imply* the Sentence "What did John say?" See Par. 28.

when preceded by its conjunction, *it cannot generally stand as a Sentence by itself.* You cannot write:

"He made all possible haste. *Because he was* afraid *of being late.*"

N.B. All Sub-ordinate Sentences, when preceded by their Conjunctions, or introduced by their Relative Pronouns, become either :—

(1) *Noun-Clauses:*
"*That he was guilty* is certain."

(2) Or, *Adjective Clauses or Sentences:*[1]
"The boy *that cleans the boots.*"[1]

(3) Or, *Adverb Clauses:*
"I will come *when I can.*"

250 6. **The Complex Sentence.**—*The whole sentence formed by the combination of the Principal and Sub-ordinate Sentences is called a Complex Sentence.*

Now construct "Complex Sentences" using:

1. **Noun Phrases** or **Clauses** for Subjects, &c.
2. **Adjective Phrases** or **Clauses** to qualify the Noun Phrases.

---

[1] It may be said that the italicized words are a *Sentence* not a *Clause.* Taken by themselves, if "that" be regarded as Demonstrative, they undoubtedly constitute a Sentence : but, when attached to a Principal Sentence, they cease to make a statement, and therefore cease, strictly speaking, to be a Sentence. See Par. 239.

3. **Adverbial Phrases or Clauses,** the Clauses being Sub-ordinate Sentences preceded by Conjunctions, thus :—

"After the capture of this important city (*Adverb*[1] *of Cause or Time*), this great general (*Subject*)—the Hannibal of his day (*Adjective qualifying Subject*)—unsurpassed for military intuition and promptness of action (*Adjective qualifying Subject*), incurring the suspicion of having betrayed the town (*i.e.* "since he incurred," therefore *Adverb of Cause*) was (*part of Principal Verb*) so completely (*Adverb*) distrusted (*rest of Principal Verb*) even by his own soldiers (*Adverb of Agency*) who had won so many battles under him (*i.e.* "though they had won," therefore *Adverb*[2]) that he was deprived of his command, and would have been executed, but for the influence of his wife (*Adverb of Result*)."

251

EXERCISE.

Expand the following Simple Sentences into Complex Sentences by introducing Adverbial Phrases to describe *cause, purpose, material, agency, instruments, manner, place, time, circumstances, i.e., condition, obstacle, &c.* :—

1. The house was built.   2. Napoleon died at St. Helena.
3. Charles I. was executed.   4. James II. was deposed.

---

[1] For brevity, the terms *Adverb, Adjective,* &c., are used for *Adverbial Phrase, Adjectival Phrase,* &c.
[2] If it had been "The soldiers *that* had won", the Relative Clause "that had won," &c. would have *described* the soldiers ; therefore it would have been an *Adjective Clause*. But "who" also sometimes introduces an *Adjective Clause*.

5. Elizabeth was respected.   6. David killed Goliath.
7. Alfred defeated Guthrum.   8. Columbus discovered America.   9. The Spanish Armada was defeated

252 **Contracted Sentences.** When two Sentences are connected by (1) the Co-ordinate Conjunctions "and" and "but;" (2) by Comparative Conjunctions, *e.g.* "as," "than;" the Verb in the second Sentence is often omitted and sometimes the omission extends to other words :—

(1) "I saw John yesterday *and* (I saw) Thomas the day before."
(2) "He is taller *than* I (am tall)." See "than," Index.
(3) "I have as many apples *as* you (have apples)."

In all such cases the full Sentences should be expressed if the whole Sentence is to be analysed. See Par. 209.

The Sentences introduced by "than" and "as" (in this sense) are Subordinate; for "than" and "as" (in this sense) cannot stand at the head of a Sentence placed by itself.

253 Degrees of Subordination (Synthesis).

Note that a Complex Sentence may contain (1) a Principal Sentence; (2) a Sub-ordinate Sentence depending on the Verb[1] in the Principal Sentence; (3) a second Sub-ordinate Sentence depending on the Verb in the first Sub-ordinate; (4) a third Sub-ordinate depending on the Verb in the second Sub-ordinate; and so on

[1] Not always on the *Verb* The implied Sentence in a Relative Phrase may qualify a *Noun*

The degrees of sub-ordination may be indicated by lines in the following way :—

1st Degree of Subordination			"Socrates knew that he knew nothing."
2nd	,,	,,	,,	"Socrates was declared by the oracle to be the wisest of men, because he knew that he knew nothing."
3rd	,,	,,	,,	"Socrates said that he was declared by the oracle to be the wisest of men, merely because he knew that he knew nothing."
4th	,,	,,	,,	"We are told that Socrates said that he was declared by the oracle to be the wisest of men, merely because he knew that he knew nothing."

The process of putting a Sentence together as above is called *Synthesis* (*syn*, together; *thesis*, putting).

The reverse process of taking a Sentence to pieces again, *loosening* its structure as it were, and exhibiting the different parts and joints of the Sentence, is called *Analysis* (*ana*, "back again;" *lysis*, "loosening)."

254 Degrees of Sub-ordination (Analysis).

Reversing the process in the last paragraph, we can take a Complex Sentence to pieces, beginning first with the Principal Sentence, then taking the first degree of Sub-ordination, then the second, and so on. Take, for example—

> "He said that I did not come last Tuesday though I had promised that I would come to see him before he left town."

1. The Principal Verb is "said." Read on from "said" to the first Sub-ordinate Conjunction "that." "That" introduces the *Object* of "said," viz., the following Sub-ordinate Sentence: "I did not come last Tuesday, though I had promised...town." This is a Sub-ordinate Sentence of the *first Degree*, which is therefore underlined *once*.

2. The Principal Verb in the first Sub-ordinate Sentence is "did (not) come." Read on from this to the next Sub-ordinate Conjunction "though." The following words, "I had promised...town," make up a Sub-ordinate Sentence of the *second Degree*, and must be underlined a *second* time.

3. The Principal Verb in the second Sub-ordinate Sentence is "had promised." Read on to the next Sub-ordinate Conjunction "that." The words "I would come...town" make up a Sub-ordinate Sen-

tence of the *third Degree*, and must therefore be underlined a *third* time.

4. The Principal Verb in the third Sub-ordinate Sentence is "would come." Read on to the next Sub-ordinate Conjunction "before." The following words, "he left town," make up a Sub-ordinate Sentence of the *fourth Degree*, and must therefore be underlined a *fourth* time.[1]

255 Relative Clauses.

A Relative Clause sometimes introduces (1) an *implied Co-ordinate*, sometimes (2) an *implied Sub-ordinate* Sentence. The Sub-ordinate Sentence may form part, sometimes of (2) an Adverbial, sometimes (3) of an Adjectival Clause.

(1) "I heard it from the landlord, *who* heard it from the policeman," *i.e.* "(*and*) he," &c. ; a *Co-ordinate Sentence*, "who" being put for "and he."

(2) "I ought not to have been beaten by John, *who* has never beaten me before," *i.e.* "(*since*) he has, &c. ;" *Subordinate Sentence*. (Adverb.)

(3) "I heard it from the boy *that* cleans the boots," *Sub-ordinate Sentence*. (Adjective.)[2]

---

[1] Note that, if the meaning had been "Though I had promised...town, yet he complained," then the words "though...town" would have made up an Adverb of Circumstance, modifying "complained." In that case, "(though) I had promised" would have been in the *first* Degree (not the *second*) of Subordination.

[2] "That (boy) cleans the boots" may perhaps be called a Subordinate Sentence introduced by the Conjunctive force of the Relative "that." See Par 249. Note.

In Sentences (2), (3), (4), and (5) of the next Exercise the Relative introduces an Adjective Clause ; in Sentence (6) "which" is the same as "and these," and therefore the words "might be sold" make up an *implied* Sentence *Co-ordinate* with "she could get."

256 The different degrees of Subordination may be indicated in the implied Sentences of Relative Phrases by underlining, as above. For example :

(1) "The man that will not accept what is offered to him by opportunity, often lives to seek opportunity in vain."

Here the two Sentences are (1) "That (man) will not accept what is offered to him by opportunity ;" (2) "What is offered to him by opportunity ?" [1]

(2) "The man that ought to have met me at the station where I got out was not to be found."

Here the two Sentences are, (1) "That (man) ought to have met me at the station where I got out;" (2) "I got out."

EXERCISE.

257 Express, by underlining, the Degrees of Subordination in the following Sentences : —

1. He asked me whether I had said that I should not come. 2. You would have acted wrongly if you had

[1] For the originally interrogative use of "who," "what," "which," see Par. 27.

refused help to the friend from whom you obtained help when you needed it. 3. When I heard that the train had started before I had arrived at the station where we had agreed to meet, I at once telegraphed. 4. Though you asked me when I would come and pay you the visit that I had promised, you did not mention a definite day. 5. I confess that I was irritated when I heard that my cousin, after he had accepted my invitation, wrote to decline it, because he had been subsequently invited by some one whose society he preferred to mine. 6. The market-girl reckoned that, if her milk sold well, she could get at least six dozen eggs, which, when they were hatched and grown to be chickens, might be sold, before May came round, for as much money as would buy her the best dress that could be found in the village.

258 Analysis of Sentences.

Reversing the process in Paragraph 250, we can *analyse* a Sentence into—

I. Principal Verb.

The term Principal Verb includes the "Subjective or Objective **Supplement**," *e.g.* in "He *was appointed general*," " was appointed general " will be called the " Verb ; " and so, in " They *appointed* him *general*," " appointed general " will be called the " Verb." See the Scheme on page 168.

II. Subject.

The terms Subject and Object here include their "Complements"; *e.g.* " a rascal to be punished " is the Subject in " *A rascal* is expected *to be punished*," and the Object in " I like *a rascal to be punished.*"

III. Object.

The Indirect Object may either be treated separately, or be treated as an Adverb. If we can say, in " The house was built *by Thomas* " that " by Thomas " is an " Adverb-Phrase of Agency," there seems no reason why we should not say " for Thomas " and " to Thomas " are "Adverb-Phrases of Reception." Hence in " Give *me* the book," we may call " me " either Indirect Object, or an abridged " Adverb-Phrase of Reception." The latter would probably be found, in the end, the simpler course.

IV. **Adjectives**, or Adjective Phrases.
V. **Adverbs**, or Adverb Phrases.

259   SPECIMEN EXERCISES.

1. "Not knowing the value of his prize, the cock gave away the diamond that he had found for a single grain of barley, when he saw that the jewel did nothing but shine, and was not good to eat."

I.	Verb	"Gave away."
II.	Subject	"The cock."
III.	Object	"The diamond."
IV.	Adjectives	"That he had found" qualifies Object.
V.	Adverbs: (a) of Cause	"Not knowing—prize," *i.e.* "since he did not know."
,,	,, : (b) of Circumstance	"For a single grain of barley."
,,	,, : (c) of Time or Cause	"When he saw—to eat."

If further Analysis is required, the Adverbial Clauses may in turn be analysed, as in the following Example:—

260 2. "A reader acquainted with the treasures of English literature will not unnaturally feel surprised, when he sees that so large a portion of time is devoted to the inadequate study of a few ancient authors, whose works have no direct bearing on the studies and duties of our own generation, while our English classics are comparatively neglected."

First Analysis.

I.	Verb	"Will feel surprised."[1]
II.	Subject	"A reader."
III.	Adjective	"Acquainted with—literature," qualifies the Subject.
IV.	Adverb (a) of Cause	"When he sees—neglected."
,,	,, (b) of Manner	"Not unnaturally."

Second Analysis.

"He sees that so large—neglected."

I.	Verb	"Sees."
II.	Subject	"He."
III.	Object	"That so large—neglected."

Third Analysis.

"So large a portion—neglected."

I.	Verb	"Is devoted."
II.	Subject	"So large a portion of time."
III.	Adverbs (a) Manner or Purpose	"To the study—generation."
,,	,, (b) Circumstance	"While[2] our English — neglected."

No further *Sentence* remains for analysis; but it may be well to mention that, in Clause (a) the Relative Clause "whose works—generation," is an Adjective Clause qualifying "authors"; and that the Phrase "of a few ancient authors" is an Adjective Phrase, qualifying "study."

---

[1] "Feel surprised" is a Compound Verb, like "He *fell lame*," "He *grew tall*."

[2] "While" may either mean "at the very time when " (as perhaps here,) or "although," or simply "but on the other hand." In the last case "while" approaches a Co-ordinate Conjunction in meaning, for is nearly the same as "but, on the other hand."

Caution.

261 The principal difficulty in the Analysis of Sentences consists in distinguishing between Participles implying an Adverbial Phrase and Participles implying an Adjectival Phrase. The same difficulty exists in distinguishing between Relative Phrases. As "who" (or "which") and "that" are loosely used by many writers, the pupil must not depend on these words for help, but upon the *sense* of each passage :—

(1) "I saw a ship *sailing into harbour*," *i.e.* "*that was sailing*," Adjective Phrase.
(2) "*Sailing too near the rocks* the ship went down," *i.e.* "*because she sailed*," Adverbial Phrase.
(3) "Yesterday I saw a schooner here, *which has now sailed away*," *i.e.* "*and*, or but, it has sailed," Co-ordinate Sentence.
(4) "The schooner *that* was here yesterday," Adjective Clause.

262 (5) "The potent rod
Of Amram's son in Egypt's evil day,
Waved round the coast, up-called a pitchy cloud
Of locusts, warping in the eastern wind."

In the last example, "waved round the coast" seems to mean "*when* or *after* it was waved," and not "the rod *that was waved.*" Consequently it seems far better to treat the italicized words as an *Adverbial* and not as an *Adjectival* Phrase. But "warping" may fairly be replaced by "that came warping," and may therefore be treated as an Adjectival Phrase qualifying " locusts."

> (6) "But me, scarce hoping to attain thàt rest,
> Always from port withheld, always distressed—
> Me howling winds drive *devious*—tempest-tossed,
> Sails rent, seams opening wide, and compass lost."

Here the second line is clearly Adjectival to "me;" but "devious" is not Adjectival, it is the Supplement of the Verb "drive;" to "drive devious" is to "drive out of the way," and is as much a Compound Verb as to "drive mad." On the other hand the abrupt pause between "devious" and "tempest-tossed" allows us to treat "tempest-tossed" as co-ordinate with "withheld" and "distressed," and therefore as Adjectival to "me."

"Sails rent" is of course an Adverbial Phrase, and "sails" is an "Adverbial Subject." See Par. 135.

Phraseology of Analysis.

263 The Principal Verb of a Sentence is sometimes called the Grammatical Predicate, or, simply, *Predicate*.

Adjectives and Adjective Phrases are called, as the case may be, Attributive Adjuncts to the Subject or Object; and, when attached to the Predicate, Adverbs are called **Adverbial Adjuncts** to the Predicate.

Again, Adjectives and Adjective Phrases are sometimes called "**Enlargements of the Subject or Object;**" and, when attached to the Predicate, Adverbs are called "**Extensions of the Predicate.**"

This phraseology does not appear to be necessary; but, if thought desirable, it can easily be substituted for the terms "Adjective," "Adverb," &c. used in the Scheme appended below.

264. Summary of the parts of a Sentence.

The following Summary will be a useful preparation for the "Scheme of Analysis" on Page 172, and will also illustrate the comparison of the different technical terms of Analysis.

In all Sentences:
- SUBJECT . . . **Noun;** or Pronoun; or Adj. put for Noun; or Noun Phrase.[1]
- PREDICATE . **Verb.**

COMPLETION OF PREDICATE
- **Object, Direct**[1] (If the Verb is Trans.)
- **Object, Indirect** (With some Verbs.)
- **Supplement** (If the Verb is Intrans. or Pass.)

Not in all Sentences:
- EXTENSION OF PREDICATE. — **Adverb;** or Adverbial Phrase.
- ATTRIBUTIVE ADJUNCT, or ENLARGEMENT OF NOUN — **Adjective;** or Adjective Phrase.

[1] Note that the Subject or Object may sometimes consist of a Noun or Pronoun with a Complementary Infinitive, *e.g.* "I know *him to be in* error." "*He* was believed *to be dishonest*." See Par. 97.

265 SCHEME OF

For convenience, in order to preserve the order of the sentence as
In order to distinguish the *Adjective* or *Complement* from the rest
Object from the Adverb, underline Adjective, Complement, Supplement,

Analyse the following passage:—
"In one of the large rich cities of China there once lived a tailor named Mustapha.
wife and one son. This son, who was a very idle fellow, was called Aladdin.
his shop, to learn the use of the needle; but all his father's endeavours to keep
was gone. Soon after Aladdin was thirteen years old, poor Mustapha—who was

Adverb.	Subject (including Adjective, or Complement.)	Verb with Supplement.
(1) In one of the large rich cities of China (2) there (3) once	a tailor *named Mustapha*	lived
Being, *i.e.* (since he was) very poor	he	could maintain [1]
	This son *who was a very idle fellow*	was called *Aladdin*
When he was old enough to learn a trade	*his* father	wished
	(1) *all his* (2) *father's* endeavours *to keep him to his work* [2]	were *vain*
	his back	was turned
Soon after Aladdin was thirteen years old.	*poor* Mustapha	fell *sick*
	(Mustapha)	died
	(he) . . . (Compl.)[3] *to predict that his son would come to no good*	was heard

[1] The Auxiliaries *could, would, can, will, may, might,* &c. may be treated as
[2] This Infinitive describing the nature of the "endeavours" may be regarded
[3] These words might be analysed still further if desired. Any subordinate
be analysed as a separate sentence.
[4] It will generally be advisable to analyse a Parenthesis *after* the rest of the

SIMPLE ANALYSIS.

far as possible two columns are made for the Adverb.
of the Subj. or Obj., the *Supplement* from the Verb, and the Indirect
and Indirect Object. Write (*Compl.*) before the *Complement.*

Being very poor he could hardly maintain his family, which consisted only of his
When he was old enough to learn a trade, Mustapha wished the boy to enter
him to his work were vain; for no sooner was his back turned than Aladdin
often heard to predict that his son would come to no good—fell sick and died."

Object (including **Adjective,** or **Complement.**)	1. **Adverb,** or 2. **Indirect Object.**	**Conjunction,** (introducing next Sentence.)
. .		
his family, *which consisted only of his wife and one son*	(1) hardly	
the boy (*Compl.*) *to enter his shop*	to learn the use of the needle	but
		for
	no sooner than (3) Aladdin was gone	
		and
		["who" = "and, or now, he " 4
	often.]	

parts of Compound Verbs.
as an Adjective, see Par. 100.
sentence may be taken out of the Adjective, Adverb, or other column and may

sentence.

APPENDIX III.

HINTS ON SPELLING.

266 English Spelling is so irregular that no systematic rules can be laid down for it. The knowledge of the derivation of a word is often a help towards the spelling of it; but this is not always the case. The best way to spell well is to read often, and so to become familiar with words. Thus misspelt words will be detected by their *strange look*.

Change of Letters.—The following principle will explain many of the variations in the spelling of words:

Rule.—*A letter is often changed or doubled in passing from one form of a word to another, in order to preserve the original sound.*

267 I.—y. For example, -*y* final preceded by a consonant, as in "happ*y*," is changed into *i* upon the addition of -*er*, -*est*, -*al*, -*ed*, -*ous*, or of any other affix (except -*ing*) beginning with a vowel. Other-

wise the sound of the word might be altered, *e.g.*
"happ-*yer*," "gidd-*yest*." Hence—

> Def*y*, defi-ance ; eas*y*, eas*i*-est ; remed*y*, remed*i*-al remed*i*-ed ; merr*y*, merr*i*-er; countr*y*, countr*i*-es.

In many of these words the original termination was -*ie*, which indeed was the regular English equivalent of the French -*é* :

> Citie ; nobilitie ; felicitie ; clergie.

From a very early period *y* and *i* were interchanged (for example in the Present Participle which ended in *–inde* or *-ynde*) so that in the *Utopia* (1516 A.D.) we have "writynge," "myghte," "thynge," "fyne." Hence *y* began to supersede *i* in these terminations, so that in the *Utopia*, we find on the same page, "felicitye" and "felicitie." By degrees, the *e* after *y*, being found unnecessary, was dropped. It might have been expected that the same curtailment would have been attempted in the Plural : and accordingly in the *Utopia* we find "qualityes." But, owing perhaps to the danger of mispronunciation, "qualit-yes"—the innovation—did not succeed in supplanting the old Plural "qualit-ies."

This rule is also extended to -*y* before other affixes, viz. -*ment*, -*ly* -*ful* :—

> Necessar*i*-ly ; greed*i*-ness ; beaut*i*-ful.

II.—y. When (1) the affix is -*ing*, or (2) -*y* is already preceded by a vowel, or (3) -*y* terminates a monosyllable—in all these cases -*y* remains generally unchanged :—

> (1) Pity-*i*ng (not "pit*ii*ng") ; (2) enjo*y*-ment, val-le*y*s ; (3) dr*y*-ness.

The reasons are in (1) the desire to avoid *ii* ; in

(2) and (3) *because the sound is not altered by the retention of -y.*

Exceptions.—Nevertheless, out of conformity to other words—

"Dry" makes "dri-er," "dri-est;" "try," "tri-al;" "tri-er;" "day," "dai-ly;" "pay," "pai-d;" "fly," "fli-es;" "lay," "laid;" "lay" (Past Tense of "lie") "lai-n;" "say," "sai-d;" "gay," "gai-ly," "gai-ety."

N.B. Pite-ous, plente-ous, from "pity," "plenty."

269 III. When a word ends in -*ie*, the juxtaposition of *iei* in the Active Participle is avoided by changing -*ie* into -*y:*—

Die, dy-ing; lie, ly-ing, *but* li-ar.

270 Omission of Letters.—Rule. -e *final is* (IV.) *dropped before an affix beginning with a vowel; but* (V.) *retained before an affix beginning with a consonant.*

IV. Instances of Rule IV. are—

Griev*e*, griev-*ance;* fam*e*, fam-*ous;* sens*e*, sens-*ible;* judg*e*, judg-*ing;* pleas*e*, pleas-*ure;* remov*e*, remov-*able;* blam*e*, blam-*ing;* spher*e*, spher-*ical.*

271 *Exceptions to IV.*—(*a*) *C* and *g*, though soft (*e.g.* in "service," "outrage") must necessarily become hard if followed by an affix beginning with *a, o,* or *u.* To prevent (1) this and (2) other changes of sound, final -*e* is sometimes retained :—

(1) Service, service-*able;* outrage, outrage-*ous.*
(2) Unsale-able.

272 *Exceptions to IV.*—(b) When *-e* is preceded by *-i, -o, -e, -y,* it is often retained before *-ing, -able.* This is in order to preserve the sound :—

Shoe-*ing* (not "sho*ing*"); agree-*able* (not "agrea-ble").

273 The *-e* is also retained in "dye-*ing*," "singe-*ing*," "swinge-*ing*," in order to distinguish them from "dy-ing," "sing-ing," and "swing-ing."

274 *Exceptions to V. :—*

Abridg-ment, acknowledg-ment, argu-ment, aw-ful, du-ly, judg-ment, tru-ly, whol-ly.

275 Rule VI.—*Monosyllables ending in* -ll (1) *when followed by an affix beginning with a consonant, or* (2) *when used as affixes, generally drop one* -l :—[1]

Al-most, *al*-though, *al*-ready, *al*-beit, *al*-mighty, *al*-so, *al*-together, *al*-ways, *bel*-fry, *ful*-fil, *wel*-fare, *el*-bow, *ful*-ly, *drol*-ly, *ful*-ness, re-*cal*.

276 The old affixes and prefixes with single *-l* appear to have been so common that they assimilated to themselves other words (*e.g.* re-*cal*) in which an *l* was really dropped. But in some words the syllable in *-ll* has not coalesced so completely with the other syllable as to be regarded as a prefix or affix. Consequently the syllable in *-ll* is treated as a separate word and retains *-ll.* Hence—

Under-*sell* (and several words ending in *-ness*), *tall*-ness, *small*-ness, *ill*-ness, *shrill*-ness, *droll*-ness, fare-*well*, un-*well*, be-*fell*, down-*fall*, cat-*call*.

[1] This is the shape in which the rule would suggest itself to modern Englishmen. But, in reality, the old spelling was *al, wel, el,* and this is *retained* in "*al*-though," "*wel*-fare," "*el*-bow." "*Bel*-fry" was not in reality derived from "bell" (See *Etym. Dict.*)

277 Doubling Letters.—Rule VII.

If the termination of a word is a consonant preceded by a vowel (e.g. " -it "), then, on receiving an affix beginning with a vowel (e.g. " -ing "), the final consonant in the word is doubled (e.g. " -itting "), provided that the word is a monosyllable (e.g. " sit "), or a polysyllable accented on the last syllable (e.g. " remit ").

This is *in order to preserve the sound.* If the consonant were not doubled, " hop-ping " would be confused with " hop-ing " :—

(1) Hop, ho*p-p*ing ; thin, thi*nn*er ; fat, fa*tt*est.

Accent on the last.	Accent not on the last.
forge*tt*ing, remi*tt*ing	brack*et*-ing, debi*t*-ing
infer-*r*ing, refer-*r*ing	cover-ing, offer-ing
occur-*r*ing, acqui*tt*ing	sever-ing, credi*t*-ing

278 *Exceptions to VII.*—Words ending in *-l*, although not accented on the last syllable, nevertheless double *-l* :—

Trave*l-l*ing, -*l*er ; counse*l-l*ing, -*l*or ; reve*l-l*ing, -*l*er ; marve*l-l*ing, -*l*ous ; riva*l-l*ing ; leve*l-l*ed ; unramme*l-l*ed. Also, wershi*p-p*ing.

Unparallel-ed is an exception.[1]

Exercises.

279 I. and II. Add as many as possible of the affixes

---

[1] Possibly, owing to the fact that "unparalleled" is of Greek derivation, containing the Greek long *e*, it may have been once pronounced "unparall*ee*led," and spelt accordingly.

-al, -ed, -er, -s, -ly, -ness, -ous, -s, to the following words :—

Lonely, employ, gaudy, daisy, decay, steady, accompany, enjoy, effigy, silly, occupy, busy, giddy, jelly, colloquy, chimney, ready, journey, shabby, annoy, prophesy, felony, try, lovely, efficacy, convey, lofty, supply, dismay, defy, gay, vary, penury, stately, day, accompany, pity, marry, plenty, continue.

280   IV. and V. Add as many as possible of the affixes -able, -ing, -ly, -ment, -ous, -er, -y, to the following words :—

Love, peace, move, blame, marriage, whole, sole, decree, ease, feeble, advantage, true, spice, village, due, charge, trouble, trace, pledge, judge, guarantee, manage, abridge, disagree, excuse.

281   VII. Add -ing, -ence, -er, -ous (where possible), to—

Control, bargain, ~~~~, peril, benefit, admit, ballot, danger, infer, pencil, debit, acquit, abhor, glutton, begin, poison, suffer, traitor, gambol, extol, rebel, travel, compel, level, worship, cancel, model, sever, equip, allot, riot, murder, befit, ruin, sin.

Reasons for apparent Irregularities.

282   I. -eive, -ieve.—It is sometimes difficult to decide, in such words as "receive," "believe," &c., whether the *e* or *i* should come first; but the difficulty will vanish if it is borne in mind that (except after *c*) *i* comes first :—

(1) Believe, reprieve, retrieve, grieve, mischief, mischievous.

(2) Deceive, deceit, conceive, conceit, receive, receipt.

The reason for the exceptional spelling of *-ceive* is that this termination represents the Latin *cap-*, French *cev-*; whereas *-ie* is the non-Latin termination.

283   II. -eed, -ede.—A few compounds from the Latin ced- were introduced early and received the English spelling :—

Succeed, proceed, exceed.

These words are very common in Shakespeare's plays. Other compounds were not introduced till afterwards, when it was no longer the custom to Anglicize the spelling of foreign words. Hence the Latin or French spelling is retained in—

Accede, concede, precede, recede.

These four are not found in Shakespeare's plays.[1] The English spelling also accounts for the double *e* in "agreeable" (Fr. *agréable*), "degree" (Fr. *degré*).

---

[1] "Preceding" is used once as an Adjective, and once as a Participle; in the latter case it is spelt "preceading."

284 III. -or, -our, -er.—These terminations are from different sources: *-or* is Latin; *-our* is Latin through French; *-er* is English. Hence—

Latin : (1) Actor, collector, demonstrator.
French : (2) Colour, honour, odour.
English : (3) Painter, player.

Note that, wherever a Noun is formed according to English and not according to Latin rules, then, though the Verb be of Latin or French-Latin origin, the terminat is generally *-er*; *e.g.* "defend-er," "extinguish-er" (the Latin Nouns would be *defens-or, extinct-or*); "vict-or," but "vanquish-er."

There is a tendency, especially in advertisements, to save space by omitting the French *-u*. "Governor" (for "governour") is now recognized as correct, and "honor" is aspiring to correctness.

285 IV. Latin : -(a)ble, -ible.—Strictly speaking, *-ble*, and not *-able*, is the Latin termination, *a* being part of the Root. Thus the Latin word was *penetra-*, and the termination *-ble*. In the same way, in a few cases, but not many, *i* is part of the Root, and *-ble* is the termination :—

(1) Penetra-ble, indisputa-ble, delecta-ble, indispensa-ble, inconsola-ble, indomita-ble, insupera-ble, demonstra-ble.
(2) Audi-ble, ed-ible, incorrupt-ible, indigest-ible, indestruct-ible, reprehens-ible, incomprehens-ible, incompress-ible.

286 V. English : -able.—This termination is used with English Verbs, *e.g.* "lovable," and also with many Latin Verbs (even where the Root does not end in -*a*), *provided that the Verb is so common as to be regarded as English* :—

Latin words with English termination :
Indefinable, inextinguishable, redeemable, perishable, attributable, disposable.

287 VI. **Latin** (1) -(a)nt, (2) -ent, represent the Latin terminations for the Active Present Participles from (1) Verbs whose roots ended with -*a*, (2) other Verbs :—

(1) "Litiga-nt," "disputa-nt," "recalcitra-nt."

(2) "Immine-nt," "reg-ent," "trans-ient."

288 VII. **Latin-French -ant.**—The French have but *one termination, -ant,* to represent *the two Latin terminations.* Hence, sometimes, similar words are spelt differently: where direct from Latin, *-ent;* where through French, *-ant.*

(1) Transcend*ent.*

(2) Defend*ant*, descend*ant.*

Hence the Latin *dependens* has, curiously enough, given rise to two English words, with different terminations: (1) "depend*ent*," Adjective, direct from Latin, and with Latin spelling; (2) "depend*ant*," Noun, through French, and with French spelling. Similarly, "ascendant" (though used by Pope as an Adjective) is now only used as a Noun.

289 VIII. (1) -ise, (2) -ize.—If *-ize* is to be retained, it ought, in strictness, to be retained only as the affix for Greek Roots :—

(1) Equalise, recognise.

(2) Baptize, emphasize.[1]

290 IX. (1) -se, (2) -ce.—Distinguish between (1) the termination of the *Verb* in *-se*, and (2) the termination of the *Noun* in *-ce* :—

(1) Advise, license, practise, devise, prize. (Verbs.)

(2) Advice, licence, practice, device, price. (Nouns.)

Spelling List.

The following words should be noted. They may be combined in sentences for dictation, or may be set by the pupils to one another. They are purposely unarranged :—

291 Niece, awkward, seize, courageous, ceiling, league, colonel, leisure, almond, treasure, intrigue, kernel, clothing, grandeur, ghastly, heifer, punishment, intelligence, villains, gardener, realm, principal, mountainous, principle, friar, poniard, sergeant, abhorrent, pony, necessarily, unparalleled, quarrelling, ecstasy, cavilling, kidnapping, limiting, dignitary, practice (Noun), reprieve, continually, character, potato, pedlar, annually, anomaly, business, mischievous, indictment, onions, cabbages, vengeance, deign (Verb), embarrassment, anonymous, committee, couple,

---

[1] "Analyze" is a mistake. The word is Greek, but contains an justifies no *z*. It should be spelt "analyse."

camphor, giraffe, syrup, guerilla, mosquito, verandah, azure, hammock, phosphorus, apartment, annalist, apparition, license (Verb), recede, decalogue, etymology, apparel, courteous, succeed, furlough, miscellany, scythe, morocco, chocolate, cemetery, proceed, accessory, bouquet, paroquet, exchequer, banquet, masquerade, accede, gelatine, obsequies, gazette, effigies, etiquette, balloon, encyclopædia, leopard, gudgeon, counterfeit, pigeon, menagerie, besiege, bereave, concede, inveigle, obeisance, complaisant, bivouac, neighbour, pleurisy, journeys, quarantine, unique, cylinder, symptom, hydrophobia, rubies, valleys, mimicking, noticeable, milliner, sepulchre, available, sedentary, peremptory, pelisse, analyst.

APPENDIX IV.

HINTS ON PUNCTUATION.

292   Stops, or Marks of the Division of Sentences.

1. Full Stop . . (.)
2. Colon . . . (:)
3. Semi-colon . (;)
4. Comma . . (,)
5. Note of Interrogation . (?)
6. Note of Exclamation . . (!)
7. The "dash" or "break". (—)
8. Marks of Parenthesis . ( )
9. Inverted commas, or, Marks of Quotation (" ")

293   **Use of Stops.**—The meaning of a sentence often depends on the pauses after certain words. These pauses are represented by marks, sometimes called (from their effect) *Stops*, and sometimes (from their appearance) *Points*. The Latin for "point" is *punctum*, and accordingly the arrangement of *points* in a sentence is called **Punctuation** :—

"John," said Thomas, "would come if he could."

Omit the *points* in the foregoing sentence, and it becomes ambiguous.

294   **The Comma.**—The Comma (meaning "that which is cut off") marks the smallest "cutting off," or division of a sentence.

I. **Rule.**—*When a word is separated from its grammatical adjunct by any intervening phrase, the phrase should be preceded and followed by a Comma :—*

Verb
separated
from
Subject.
{ "The *traveller*, after alighting from his horse, *entered* the inn."
"His *conduct*, according to his own account, *is* inexcusable."
"The *king*, wearied by the woman's importunity, *granted* her request." }

Verb
separated
from
Object.
{ "He *endeavoured*, in every possible way, *to undermine his rival.*" }

Verb
separated
from
Conjunction.
{ "*When*, after hearing your explanation, *I promised* to forgive you, *I believed*, in accordance with your assurance, *that* this was your first offence."¹ }

Verb
separated
from
Adverb.
{ "*Now*, thought he, he had succeeded."
"He *frustrated* all the efforts his friends were making for him, *by his silly vanity.*" }

295 II. Hence the Comma is often used before and after an Adverbial Clause, including a Subordinate Sentence, whether the sentence be (1) introduced by a Conjunction, or (2) implied in a Participle :—

(1) "I replied, *as soon as I had recovered my presence of mind*, that I could not consent."
(2) "I replied, *on recovering my presence of mind*, that I could not consent."

¹ The Conjunction "that," not being capable of much stress, nor allowing much pause after it, often dispenses with the comma :—
"Remember *that* in almost all business, it is best to make haste slowly."

296 A Comma will therefore necessarily be inserted *between two Conjunctions* :—

> "It was said *that, when* the Capitol was built, a human head was discovered amid the foundations."
>
> "It cannot be denied *that, if* this statement is true, your brother has acted most culpably."

When a Subordinate Clause or Adverbial Phrase comes at the beginning of the sentence, the Comma is inserted after it, *if the Clause or Phrase precedes the Subject of the Principal Verb* (see Par. 306) :—

> (1) "*When I recovered my presence of mind,* I replied, &c."
> (2) "*On recovering my presence of mind,* I replied, &c."
> (3) "*Having recovered my presence of mind,* I replied, &c."
> (4) "*To be brief,* there are but three courses open to us."
> (5) "*The colonel having fallen,* the major took the command."

297 III. The Comma is often used between co-ordinate sentences connected by Conjunctions :—

> "*He went back to his home, and I went forward on my journey.*"

In accordance with the Rule in Par. 294.—

298 IV. When a number of co-ordinate words have

the same grammatical adjunct, all but the last are followed by a Comma:—

(1) "*John, Thomas,* and *Henry* came."
(2) "I saw *John, Thomas,* and *Henry.*"
(3) "He was *dutiful, kind,* and brave."
(4) "He is acting *wisely, justly,* and mercifully."
(5) "She *loved, honoured,* and obeyed her husband."

299 But, if words are in *pairs*, then *each pair* (even the *last*) is followed by a Comma:—

(6) "*To carp and to criticize, to slander and to rebuke, to warn and to discourage,* are very different actions."[1]

300 But sometimes, where "and" is repeated between a number of Co-ordinate Nouns the writer may regard them (1) as a mere list of names, *all of one kind,* requiring rapid enumeration, and therefore may omit the comma, or (2) as expressing *different* notions and may therefore insert commas. Compare—

(7) "Havoc and spoil and ruin are my gain."—*P. L.* ii. 109.
(8) "Where all is cliff, and copse, and sky."[2]—*Scott.*

No doubt the omission of the comma here, as in Par. 306, is more easy *before the Verb,* when the reader is hurrying on to the Verb, than after the Verb, where pauses are more natural.

301 V. A Noun used Vocatively or Appellatively must necessarily have no grammatical adjuncts,

---

[1] The reason is that in this case "and" is not inserted before the last *pair.* Hence the termination is somewhat abrupt; and, after an enumeration of the *pairs,* the reader requires a pause, as though to insert "these": "—— (these) are very different actions."
[2] Quoted by Mätzner.

and should therefore (unless uttered very passionately; Par. 313) be marked off by Commas :—

"Your conduct, Thomas, surprises me."

302 VI. In all the above Examples the principle is the same, that the Comma denotes *separation from the grammatical adjunct*. But sometimes the Comma denotes the *omission* of the grammatical adjunct :—

"To carp is easy; to criticize, difficult."

303 VII. When a Subject is a lengthy Phrase, it is often separated from the Verb by a Comma, especially when the Subject-Phrase contains some Noun that might at a hasty glance be supposed to be the Subject of the Verb. The object of the Comma is to indicate that *not the word immediately preceding the Verb, but the whole of the preceding phrase is the Subject of the Verb* :—

(1) "*To resent injuries inflicted on the weak and helpless*, is the duty of all."

(2) "*That he made a very great mistake*, is clear."

304 VIII. A Comma is sometimes employed when a statement or speech is introduced as the *Object* of a Verb, to mark a pause before the statement. But this is scarcely necessary or justifiable, *except where the statement is in Apposition to a previous Noun* :—

(1) "Who does not know the well-known proverb, that seeing is believing?"

(2) "Some people seem scarcely aware of this *principle*, that all men are better contented to make progress in small matters than to remain at a stand in great."

Where the Noun in Apposition intervenes between the Verb and its Object, the Comma is justifiable on the principle stated above, Par. 294; where there is no intervening Noun, the Comma is unjustifiable.

305 IX. It has been seen, from Example (5) in Par. 298, that, when the same Object follows several Verbs, the Comma is *not* inserted after the last *Verb;* but, when the same Object follows several Prepositions, the Comma *is* inserted after the last *Preposition :—*

(1) "I am desirous *of*, and earnestly hoping *for*, an amicable settlement."

2) "I am sent by, and acting as the representative *of*, a large number of my fellow-citizens."

The reason is that a Verb, being a more emphatic word than a Preposition, allows a greater stress to be laid upon it, and a longer pause after it. The Preposition, not allowing this, requires the aid of a Comma to denote the necessary pause. The purpose of the pause is to summarise, as it were, what has preceded, and to indicate that the Object is the Object not of the last Preposition alone, but of all the Prepositions.

306 Omission of the Comma.—I. When (1) an Adverb *follows* its Verb, or when (2) a subordinate sentence *follows* its principal Verb, there is not so much need of a pause or division, and consequently the Comma may be dispensed with. Compare—

(1)
- "Very gradually, his health and strength returned."
- "His health and strength returned very gradually."

(2)
- "As soon as he caught sight of me, he ran away."
- "He ran away as soon as he caught sight of me."

307 II. When the Subject-phrase is short, and the omission of the Comma produces no ambiguity, it is omitted :—

(1) " What you say is very sensible."

(2) " To be ignorant is to be weak."

308 III. *Caution.*—The Comma ought not to be inserted (1) before "that" introducing an Object-phrase, nor (2) before "that" introducing a Subject after "Preparatory *it.*" Avoid the following :—

(1) "The ambassador *replied, that* no interference was needed."

(2) "It was the common *belief, that* the house was haunted by the ghost of a murdered woman."

309 **The Colon and Semicolon.**— The *Colon* (meaning "limb" or "member") is used after a "member" of a sentence ; that is, after a portion that has a complete sense by itself. The Colon is therefore used to shew some close relation between two or more sentences by combining them in one. The relation indicated may be *consequence, cause, antithesis, similarity,* &c. :—

> "How the door was opened no one knew : on the evening of the robbery it had been locked as usual."

310   The *Semi-colon* ("half-member") is used between co-ordinate statements where a shorter pause is desired than that marked by the Colon. Generally, where there are *more than two* co-ordinate statements *in a graphic description,* the Semi-colon would be preferred to the colon :—

> "After a terrific struggle, the infantry were forced back into the gates ; the combined fleet and army opened fire upon the city ; and preparations were made for an immediate assault."

311   If the Co-ordinate Conjunction is inserted, the Semi-colon is generally preferred to the Colon :—

> "Trial by jury is popularly attributed to Alfred the Great ; *but* this is only an instance of the common tendency to associate popular institutions with popular names."

The **Full-Stop** requires no comment.

312   The **Note of Interrogation** is used, not only after questions asked for information, but also after "questions of appeal," where no answer is expected :—

"What can be toilsome in these pleasant walks?"
Paradise Lost, x. 179.

"O Grave! where is thy victory?
O Death! where is thy sting?"—*Pope*.

313 The Note of Exclamation is used (1) after Vocatives ; (2) after words or sentences uttered with sudden emotion ; (3) very rarely after semi-interrogatory exclamations :—

(1) "Go, *wondrous creature!* mount where science guides ;
Go, measure earth, weigh air, and state the tides."—*Ib*.

(2) "But *hark!* he strikes the golden lyre ;
And *see!* the tortur'd ghosts respire,
See, *shady forms advance!*"—*Ib*.

(3) "What sounds were heard,
What scenes appear'd,
O'er all the dreary coasts!"—*Ib*.

314 The Dash is used (1) to mark a very abrupt break in the sentence, often introducing some quite unexpected word ; (2) in a long sentence, to mark a return to the thread of the principal sentence :—

(1) Conceal, disdain—*do all things but forget.*"—*Ib*.

"Oh come! oh teach me nature to subdue,
Renounce my love, my life, myself—*and you.*"—*Ib*.

(2) "The strong-headed, manly, sharp-tempered, secular carpenter, with his energetic satisfaction

in work, his impatience of dreamers, and his early passion for Hetty's earthly loveliness" (then follows a long description of the principal characters in 'Adam Bede') "—*these, with the slighter*, but equally true outlines with which the picture is filled up, form one of the truest and most typical groups of English life I have ever seen delineated."—*Hutton.*

315 Brackets are used to mark the insertion of a Phrase or Sentence that is allowed to interrupt another sentence :—

"Yesterday, Thomas (*you know whom I mean*) assured me that you were no longer in England."

This kind of insertion is called a *Parenthesis, i.e.* a "side-insertion" (*para*, aside; *enthesis*, insertion).

Such expressions as "said he," "replied I," &c., are generally marked off, not by brackets, but by commas.

Inverted Commas, or Marks of Quotation, require no comment.

SCHEME OF PARSING.[1]

Owing to the confusion and ambiguity caused by the use of different abbreviations in Parsing Exercises, the following list is given below :—

ABBREVIATIONS.

Active	=	*Act.*	**Number**	=	**Nr.**
Adjective	=	**Adj.**[2]	**Object**	=	**O.**
Adverb	=	**Adv.**[2]	*Participle*	=	*Part.*
Antecedent	=	*Ant.*	*Passive*	=	*Pass.*
Apposition	=	*App.*	*Past Tense*	=	*P. T.*
Auxiliary	=	*Aux.*	*Person*	=	*Pers.*
Cognate	=	*Cogn.*	*Phrase*	=	*Phr.*
Comparative	=	*Compar.*	*Plural*	=	*Pl.*
Complement	=	*Complem.*	*Positive*	=	*Pos.*
Complete	=	*Compl.*	*Possessive*	=	*Poss.*
Conditional	=	*Cond.*	**Preposition**	=	**Prep.**
Conjunction	=	*Conj.*	*Present*	=	*Pres.*
Conjunctive	=	*Conj*ve.	*Pronoun*	=	*Pron.*
Direct Object	=	*D. O.*	*Relative*	=	*Rel.*
Future	=	*Fut.*	*Retained Object*	=	*Retd. O.*
Imperative	=	*Imper.*	*Singular*	=	*Sing.*
Impersonal	=	*Impers.*	**Subject**	=	**S.**
Incomplete	=	*Incompl.*	*Subjunctive*	=	*Subj.*
Indicative	=	*Indic.*	*Superlative*	=	*Superl.*
Indirect Object	=	*Ind. O.*	*Supplement*	=	*Suppl.*
Indefinite	=	*Indef.*	**Tense**	=	**T.**
Infinitive	=	*Inf.*	*Transitive*	=	*Tr.*
Interrogative	=	*Interr.*	**Verb**	=	**V.**
Intransitive	=	*Intr.*	*Verbal*	=	*Vl.*
Mood	=	**M.**	*Vocative*	=	*Voc.*
Noun	=	**N.**	*Voice*	=	*Vc.*[3]

[1] For explanation of all the technical terms in this "Scheme," the pupil is referred to the "Glossary of Grammatical Terms," page xvii, where will also be found references to the Paragraphs in the Grammar, giving fuller explanations.

[2] *Adjectival, Adverbial,* and other Adjectives. may be distinguished by adding *-l*, thus : *Adj*l., *Adv*l., &c. "Clause" may be written *Cl.*

[3] *Voice* need seldom be expressed, as it is implied by *Active* or *Passive*.

317   I. NOUNS.—Mention (i) FORM; (ii) USE.

  i. FORM: *Singular* or *Plural*.

  ii. USE: (1) *Subjective;* (2) *Possessive;* (3) *Vocative;* (4) *Objective*.

    iii. SUBDIVISIONS OF EACH USE:

      1. *Subjective.* (*a*) Subject, Partial or Complete, of a Verb; (*b*) in Apposition to some Subject; (*c*) Adverbial Subject, or Subject Absolute; (*d*) Supplement to a Verb.

      2. *Possessive.* (No Subdivision; always defines some Noun.)

      3. *Vocative.* (No subdivision.)

      4. *Objective.* (*a*) Object, Partial or Complete, or Cognate, or Indirect, or "Retained;" (*b*) in Apposition to some Object; (*c*) Adverbial Object; (*d*) Supplement to a Verb.

318   II. (*a*) PRONOUNS (ordinary).—i. ii. iii. same as Nouns; iv. stands for what Noun?

  II. (*b*) PRONOUNS RELATIVE.—i. ii. iii. same as Nouns; iv. has for *Antecedent* —?

  II. (*c*) PRONOUNS CONJUNCTIVE.—i. ii. iii. same as Nouns; iv. joins what sentences?

319   III. ADJECTIVES.—Mention (i) FORM; (ii) USE.

  i. FORM: Positive, Comparative or Superlative Degree.

  ii. USE: (i) joined to what Noun or Pronoun? (2) Supplementary to what Verb?

320   IV. VERBS.—(i) NATURE; (ii) FORM; iii. USE.

  i. NATURE: *Transitive* or *Intransitive*.

ii. FORM : Mention (1) *Voice ;* (2) *Mood.* (3) *Tense* and "*State*"; (4) *Person ;* (5) *Number.*

iii. USE : *A.* (*a*) has for Subject — ? (*unless Infin.*)

(*b*) has for Object — ? (*unless Intr. or Pass.*)[1]

(*c*) may have Subjective Supplement — (*if Intr. or Pass.*)

(*d*) may have Objective Supplement — ?

If in the Infinitive Mood, the Verb may be used as—

B. (*a*) *Noun ;* Subject or Object (Complementary or otherwise) of — ?

(*b*) *Adverb ;* modifying — ?

(*c*) *Adjective ;* qualifying — ?

321 V. PARTICIPLES.—(i) *Nature ;* (ii) *Form ;* (iii) *Use.*

i. NATURE : *Transitive* or *Intransitive.*

ii. FORM : (*a*) *Active* or *Passive.*

iii. USE : (*a*) joined to what Noun or Pronoun ?

(*b*) implies what Conjunctive word ?

A. If Active (see IV. above), may have Object, &c.

B. If Passive (see IV. above) may have Supplement.

322 VI. VERBAL NOUNS.—(i) *Nature ;* (ii) *Form ;* (iii) *Use.*

i. NATURE: *Transitive* or *Intransitive.*

ii. FORM : *Active*[2] or *Passive.*

---

[1] A Passive Verb may have a "Retained Object."
[2] The "State" of the action, whether "Complete" with *having,* or "Incomplete," without *having,* might also be mentioned. But these forms are often used indiscriminately.

iii. Use : *A. Noun-Uses.* See I. above.
   B. Verb-Uses. See IV. above.

323 VII. ADVERBS.—Modify what *Verb, Adjective, Adverb,* or *Sentence ?* [1]

Many Adverbs are used as Conjunctions, in which case call them Conjunctions or Conjunctive Adverbs, and parse them as Conjunctions.

Some Adverbs are used in three different ways : (1) *Interrogatively;* (2) in *dependent Interrogation,* or *Conjunctively;* (3) *Relatively.*

324 VIII. PREPOSITIONS.—Have what *Object?*
Prepositions are sometimes used as (1) *Adverbs;* (2) *parts of Compound Verbs,* and, when thus used, must not be parsed as Prepositions.

325 IX. CONJUNCTIONS.—Join what two sentences together?

---

[1] It is so seldom that a Noun is modified by an Adverb (and the ellipsis of an Adjective is so probable in such cases), that a Noun is not here included in list of words modified by the Adverb. See Par. 45. The Degree of Comparison of the Adverb is also omitted.

PART II.

DIFFICULTIES AND IRREGULARITIES IN MODERN ENGLISH.

CHAPTER I.

PROSE.

PARAGRAPHS 191—230 contained a few examples of Irregularities, shewing the method by which Irregularities must be explained. The present Chapter is intended to enumerate more fully and systematically the difficulties in Modern English Prose. The method of explanation will not be so fully given as before, in Part I.; but the pupil must bear in mind that in explaining these, and all other irregularities in English, and indeed in explaining any irregularity in any language, there is but one method :—

I. *Ascertain the Regular Construction.*

II. *Ascertain the cause of Irregularity.*

The following is a key to the arrangement adopted in this Chapter. But only those idioms are selected that present difficulty to an English student :—

327   **Syntax of Words and Sentences.**

SYNTAX OF WORDS; OR, THE SIMPLE SENTENCE.

1. *The Subject,* "It" (328—32). For the Infinitive used as Subject, *see* 3, *c*, below.
2. *Agreement of Verb with Subject* (334—9).
3. *Adverbs and Adverbial Phrases.*

    (*a*) Uses or Cases of Nouns (340—6).
    (*b*) Prepositions : "against" (349) ; "at" (350—5) ; "by" (353—7) ; "for" (358—64) ; "of" (365—372) ; "on" (373—5) ; "to" (377—9) ; "but" (380—1) ; used before Adverbs (382—3).
    (*c*) The Infinitive, used (1) as Subject or Object (386—9) ;   (2) Adverbially (390—402).
    (*d*) The Participle (404—12).
    (*e*) The Adverb (413—20).

5. *The Adjective,* "The" (421—6) "a" (427—9) ; the Possessive Objectively used (432—4) ; Noun with Preposition Adjectively used (436) ; Appositional use of "of" (437—9).

SYNTAX OF SENTENCES.

1. *Co-ordinate Sentences.* Co-ordinate Conjunctions (440—443).
2. *Subordinate Clauses.* Condensed Clauses (444—7); Subject and Object Clauses (448—54) ; Adverbial Clauses (455—8) ; Conditional Clauses (459—71); Concessional Clauses (472—7) ; Result, Purpose (478—82) ; Clauses of Comparison (483—97) ; Adjective Clauses (497—500).

For a full Alphabetical Index referring to each idiom explained in this and other Chapters, see page 327. Without the aid of this Index, the reader will not find it easy to refer to a particular idiom. For example, the Conjunctional use of "but" will not be found under "but" as a Preposition. But a reference to "but" in the Index will at once guide the reader to the right paragraph.

328   "It" Used as Subject.[1]

1. "It" is often used for (1) "the time, season," &c. ; (2) "matters, affairs" :—.

(1) "*It* will soon be November."

(2) "*It* will come to a quarrel."

This use has its origin in the earliest period of the language. It is explained not only by (I) desire of brevity, but also by the desire to express some unknown cause of inexplicable results : "*it* snows, *hails, thunders,*" &c. Hence also in Early English, even up to the Fifth Period, "*it repents, shames, yearns, pities,* me." The same tendency is observable in Latin to express feelings that are *not controlled by the person*, by means of *Impersonal Verbs*. A relic of the old usage is "methinks," *i.e.*, "it seems to me." Compare Shakespeare :—

"Where *it thinks* (seems) best unto your royal self."

A similar explanation applies to "if (it) you *please*," which is illustrated by Shakespeare's "So (it) *please* him (to) come."

329   "It" is also used to prepare the way for the Subject. (See Par. 151) :—

(3) "*It* is said that he will come."

(If the sentence ran "that he will come is said,"

---

[1] For the Infinitive used as Subject, *see* Par. 386.

an undue emphasis (III)[1] would be laid on "is said.")

(4) "*It* is necessary to make a choice."

More rarely "this" and "that" are used *after* the Subject for the purpose of recapitulation :—

(5) "To fail after a third attempt—*that* indeed would be disgraceful."

"It" is also used to prepare the way for the Object :—

(6) "I do not think *it* right to take this course."
(7) "I can make *it* clear that I am guiltless."

330 "It" often prepares the way for a clause introduced by the Conjunction *that* :—

(8) "*It* was then that the cavalry charged," *i.e.*, "the cavalry's charging was then."
(9) "When was *it* that they were in prison?"

(The redundance of *it* here is shewn by the fact that in the last example, which is modernised from Robert of Gloucester, the author omits the *it* :—

(10) "When was that they were in prison?")

Sometimes the Conjunction may be "whether":—

(11) "*It* is doubtful whether he will succeed."

331 *It* stands for "the person," and is the Antecedent of a Relative Pronoun in—

(12) "Who was *it* that said so?"
(13) "Thou art *it* that hath cut Rahab."

[1] The Roman numbers in brackets refer to the "Laws of Irregularity," Par. 198.

In the earliest English (Anglo-Saxon) version of the Gospel, "it," or rather the Saxon equivalent of "it," is not placed first, and we find St. John vi. 63 in this form :—

(14) "Spirit is *it* that giveth life."

But as early as Wickliffe the *it* had been separated from its Relative, and had been placed at the beginning of the sentence.

(15) "*It* is the Spirit that quickeneth."

332   In consequence of this change of position, the Verb agrees with the Preparatory Subject "it." Thus, instead of—

(16) "You were *it* that he laughed at,"

we say—

(17) "*It* was you that he laughed at."[1]

333   A Noun is sometimes used as the Subject or Object of some Verb understood, connected with another Verb by "and" :—

(1) (There were) "A few more struggles, and all was over."

(2) (We must walk) "A mile further, and we shall be at our journey's end."

---

[1] See Pars. 158—61. This construction is said not to be found in the earliest English, Mätzner, ii. page 25.

334 Agreement of Verb with Subject.

1. The Verb sometimes has the Plural Inflection to agree with an *implied* Plural Subject :—

(1) "Nor yew nor cypress *spread* their gloom,"[1] *i.e.*, "yews and cypresses do not spread."
(2) "Neither you nor your brother *were* mentioned," *i.e.*, "you and your brother were not mentioned."

It would be intolerably harsh to write, however correct it might be—

(3) "Neither you nor your brother *was* mentioned."

Evade the difficulty by writing :—

(4) "Neither your brother nor you were mentioned,"

so that the Verb may either agree with the Grammatical Subject "you," or with the *implicit* Subject "your brother *and* you."

335 2. A Subject is sometimes introduced without a Verb, in a parenthesis, the Verb having to be supplied by repetition—

(1) "His faults, not his recent *misfortune*, have alienated him from us."

where "has alienated" must be repeated after "misfortune."

[1] Campbell, quoted by Mätzner.

336 3. The Verb is in the Singular after a number of Nouns as Subject—

I. When the Nouns collectively express *one notion* :—

(1) "Much *blood and treasure was wasted* in these wars."

(2) "The *poetry and eloquence* of that age *deserves* our study."

In these cases the Nouns are often preceded by one Adjective, as above " much," " the."

II. When the *last Singular Noun* (coming at the end of a climax) is *prominently emphatic* :—

(3) "Honour, justice, *religion itself is* derided by such policy."

III. When the Verb *precedes* a number of Subject Nouns, the *first of which is singular.*

(4) " Blessed *is* the *womb* that bare thee and the *paps* which thou hast sucked."

IV. When the Verb is followed by *a Complementary Subject in the Singular Number* :—

(5) "To inferiors, gentleness, condescension, and affability *is* the only true *dignity.*"

337 4. A Collective Noun in the Singular may be used with a Plural Verb, where the notion of a number of *individuals* is more prominent than the notion of a collective *whole* :—

(1) "The crew *are* rushing to the boats."

(2) "The whole family *are* in tears."
(3) "The majority of the inhabitants *are* ready to petition against his return."
(4) "The army *are* anxious for a war."

But where the notion of *unity* predominates, the Singular of the Verb is used:—

(5) "The whole nation *rouses* itself like one man."
(6) "The army *is* mainly *composed* of raw recruits."

338 There is an apparent inconsistency in—

(7) "The army—which a month ago *was* pining for peace—*are* now, to a man, clamorous for war."
(8) "This people, who *knoweth* not the law, *are* cursed."

But this is explained (III)[1] by the harshness of using a Plural Verb after a *Relative* with a Singular Antecedent. Where the Plural Verb *closely* follows the Noun of Multitude, the meaning of multitude naturally affects the Verb, but the intervention of the Relative Pronoun [2] diminishes the effect of the Noun's Plural meaning.

339 The following examples (Mätzner, ii. 144) admirably illustrate the use of the Singular where the

---

[1] The Roman numbers in brackets refer to the Laws of Irregularity Par. 198.
[2] The effect of the intervention of the Relative is seen in the, strictly, ungrammatical passage of Pope, where the Third Person is used for the old Second:

"*Thou* great first Cause, least understood:
   Who all my sense *confin'd*
   To know but this, that Thou art good."

notion of unity, and of the Plural where the notion of plurality, is the more prominent :—

(9) "There *goes*" (unity) "a pair that only *spoil*" (mutual action necessarily implying plurality) "one another."

(10) "The stork-assembly *meets* " (unity) "for many a day.
Consulting deep and various" (notion of plurality introduced) " ere *they take*
Their arduous voyage through the liquid sky."

ADVERBIAL PHRASES.

I. The Uses of Nouns.

340 The Object is used (see Par. 129) to denote *extent, distance, duration,* or *point of time :*—[1]

(1) "A short *distance* from the town was a small stream."

(2) "One summer's *day* I was walking in the country."

(3) "I shall expect you this *day*" (point of time) "three *months*" (distance or interval of time.)[2]

(4) "I saw him five *days* ago."[3]

(5) "He bathes *summer* and *winter.*"

---

[1] Only a few unusual idioms are mentioned here. For the more ordinary idioms, the reader is referred to Par 127—131.
[2] In Old English (Layamon i. 344) a preposition "on" or "in" would be inserted before " months."
[3] In old English, "days" was sometimes made the Subject in a Parenthesis: "I saw him, *gone is five days*," "ago" being for "agone," the Passive Participle of "go."

341 In Early English this was expressed by what is now the Possessive Inflection, so that the last Example would have then run—

(6) "He bathes summer*es* and winter*es*."[1]

In the same way they used "night*es*," "day*es*," "year*es*," &c. In later times the Inflection was replaced by a Preposition "on," or "an," or "a-"; but sometimes we find the new Preposition introduced and the old Inflection retained, *e.g.* in "now-a-days." And this explains "in doors," "of late years," "o'nights." The old Inflection is retained, or has been introduced, in "always," "sometimes;" "sideways," "needs."

342 From a confusion (II) of "at three years of age" and "he was three years (Object) old" (see Par. 129), there has arisen the following irregularity :—

(7) "*At* three years, nine months, *old*."

Here "three-years-old," "nine-months-old," must be now regarded as Compound Nouns.

343 The Object is also used to denote *price* :—

(8) "Mutton is *eight-pence* a pound."

(Here "pence" is not the Subjective Supplement. "At" might be inserted before "eight.")
The distributive use of "a pound" in the last

[1] Morris's *Accidence*, page 194.

Example demands attention. It may be compared with—
(9) "I ride once *a day*."
(10) "He gave them five shillings *a-piece*, or *a man*."

In Early English (Morris's *Accidence*, page 195) this "a" is seen to be the old Preposition "on," "an," or "a." It is *not* (though it might seem to be) the Indefinite Adjective.

344 The Object is also used with Comparatives, to denote the *amount of excess or defect* :—
(11) "He is *a trifle* taller than my brother."
(12) "*The* sooner, *the* better."

In (12) "the" is not the Definite Adjective; it is a Use or Case of the old Relative or Demonstrative Pronoun (our "that"), and the meaning is "By *what* (in what degree) sooner, *by that* (in that degree) better."
(13) "*Thi*, (or *thy*) sooner, *thi* better."

345 A Prepositional force implied in the Adverbial Phrase "on this side" explains the use of the Object in :—
(14) "On this side (of) the *Tweed*."

346 The Object is irregularly used for the Subjective form in :—
(15) "*Whom* say ye that I am?"

P

The reason is, obviously, (II) *Confusion* with the regular construction :—

(16) "*Whom* say ye me to be?"

But, doubtless, euphony (the same feeling that makes the French say "c'est *moi*" and English children "it's *me*") is the reason for such irregularities as Shakespeare's :—

(17) "No mightier than thyself or *me*."
(18) "Is she as tall as *me*."
(19) "It is *thee* I fear."

Milton has "Than *whom*." Perhaps, "than" and "as" were regarded as quasi-Prepositions.

Pope (*Sat.* viii. 275) has—
"And lin'd with Giants deadlier *than 'em* all."

II. Prepositions.

347 The English Prepositions originally represented *local* meanings, *i.e.* they indicated rest or motion in *place*. For example, "of," "off," meant "motion from;" "by" meant "neighbourhood," and so did "with;" "for" meant "before."

By degrees the uses of the Prepositions were extended to denote the relations of *time* as well as of *space*. For example, "before" and "after" are used of both relations. But sometimes a Preposition assumed two forms, one to denote space, the other to denote time, *e.g.* " to " for space, " til " or " till " for time. See Par. 376.

348 Then the uses of the Prepositions were still further extended to denote other relations, *e.g. agency, instrumentality,* and the like. For example, we now say that a box is " made of (*i.e.* out of, motion from) wood." But there is no reason why we might not have used, instead of " of," some Preposition denoting " neighbourhood," *e.g.* " with " or " by." And here also (as with " to " and " till " above) the Preposition sometimes assumed two forms, one to denote the original local relation, *e.g.* " off," " the leaves are falling *off* the trees ; " another to denote the secondary relation, *e.g.* " the light *of* the sun."

Hence, in explaining the uses of Prepositions, the student should go back at once to the radical meaning of *rest* or *motion,* and thence should trace the derived meaning, whatever it may be.[1]

" A," " *a*-piece ; " see Par. 343 : " *a*-ground," " *a*-sleep," for " on ground," " on sleep ; " Par. 127.

349 1. " Against," now generally restricted to space, but still rarely (once commonly) used of time :—

(1) " We shall not be ready *against* the day of battle."

[1] Before the Pupil deals with Prepositions and their metaphorical meanings derived from their local meanings, he should thoroughly master the meaning of a Metaphor, and be able to expand a Metaphor into a Proportion or Simile. See *English Lessons for English People,* page 125.

It is more commonly used in modern vernacular English as a Conjunction (like "after," "before," used for "after that," "before that ") :—

(2) "We shall not be ready *against* (that) he comes."

350 2. "At," meaning "neighbourhood," was early used to denote "proximity of value," "equivalence," or "price" :—

(1) "The house is valued *at* a thousand pounds."
(2) "He lends money *at* a high rate of interest."
(3) "We are travelling *at* a great pace."

Hence it was used in Adverbial Phrases, where "estimated," "rated," can be supplied from the context :—

(4) "(Estimating your compensation) *At* (the) *least*, you will surely receive half the value of your loss" : so, "*at* most."

351 Hence it denotes (not "consequence," like "on," but) "*immediate* proximity, consequence, or dependence" :—

(5) "He fires up *at* a word" : "*At* the word he vanished."
(6) "The tiger cleared the avenue *at* a bound."
(7) "He lies *at* the king's mercy" : "He is removable *at* pleasure."

352 Hence "instrumentality," mostly of *games at* which one may be regarded as present :—

(8) "He plays *at* cricket, football, chess, draughts," &c. : "He is beaten *at* his own weapons."

353 Note that "at" is used with reference to *points*, while "on" and "in" are used with reference to *places*. Hence "at" is used for a *point* of time, but "on," "in," or "by" for a *space* of time :—

(9) "*On* Monday," "*at* dawn"; "*by* day," "*at* sunset"; "*in* the afternoon," "*at* noon."[1]

(10) "*At* first"; "*at* last"; "*at* length."

So also of place, "at" is used for small places regarded as points, "in" of large places regarded as spaces :—

(11) "*In* London"; "*at* Clifton."

Hence, metaphorically :—

(12) " Distinguished *in* war, literature, &c. ;" "Skilful *at* jumping, dancing, &c."

354 "In" denotes the *sphere* of action regarded as *influencing* the agent, e.g. "*in* wrath," "*in* anger," "*in* haste." "At" denotes the *point at* which one rests, without the notion of *influence*, e.g. "*at* ease," "*at* peace," "*at* liberty," "*at* large," "*at* rest," "*at* leisure" :—

(13) "He that marries *in* haste will repent *at* leisure."

355 3. "By," meaning originally "near the side of," *i.e.* neighbourhood, is used to denote "time" ("*by* four o'clock"), "instrumentality," and "agency."

---

[1] "*At* night" really means "*at* night-fall."

From the notion of "instrumentality," it came to express "manner," "number," &c. :—

(1) "They sell corn *by* the bushel, drink beer *by* the gallon," &c.
(2) "He is dying *by* inches, is wise *by* fits," &c.
(3) "The citizens streamed out *by* hundreds."

356 In Old English, the *repetition* of an action, e.g. "streamed" in the last Example, was sometimes expressed by *repeating* the Adverbial phrase "by hundreds," so that the sentence ran—

(4) "The citizens streamed out *by* hundreds, *by* hundreds : *by* one and *by* one ; *by* thousand and *by* thousand ; *by* little and little," &c.

So even Pope :—

(5) "Loth to enrich me with too quick replies, *By little and by little* drops his lies."

When some of these phrases were condensed for brevity's sake, the first " by " was omitted :—

(6) "They streamed out one *by* one."
(7) "The water oozed out drop *by* drop."
(8) "He is growing stronger year *by* year."
(9) "The army is diminishing little *by* little."

357 From false analogy, *i.e.* Confusion (II) with "They emigrated *by* hundreds," we say, even speaking of a single person—

(10) "He emigrated *by* himself."

But even in the Earliest English we find, not the Adjective " self " (*i.e. same*) and the Pronoun " he," "he-self," in Apposition to the Subject, but a kind of Adverb formed out of the Dative Case of "he." Consequently "by himself" is simply a Prepositional equivalent of the old Case-Adverb.

358 4. "For," radical meaning "before," "in front of;" hence (as a champion may fight *in front of*, or *in the place of*, the person he is championing) "instead of," *i.e.* in the stead or place of,[1] "as":—

(1) "She passed *for* his sister."
(2) "This was meant *for* a joke."

359 Hence, "for the purpose of," and hence, "considered for the purpose of," or "having regard to":—

(3) "Fit *for* food."
(4) "Small *for* his size."
(5) "These apples are too sour *for* eating," *i.e.* "for the purpose of eating, the apples are too sour."

Hence, "for the sake of," "because of":—

(6) "All kept away *for* fear of infection."
(7) "*For* shame," *i.e.* "(I cry alack) because of shame."

Some exclamation has to be supplied, and was often inserted in Old English.

360 It is easy to see how, after a negative, "for" may assume the meaning of "despite of":—

(8) "He was not liked *for* his good temper," or
(9) "He was disliked *for* all his good temper."

---

[1] Hence "I buy an apple *for*, *i.e.* in the place of, or sell it *for*, *i.e.* for the sake of, a penny."

Hence, even where there is no negative preceding, "for" might be thus used :—

> (10) "I shall succeed (*and you will not prevent me*) *for* all your tricks."

It is fair to say, however, that in Old English "for" is used in the sense of "prevention," without any negative preceding.[1]

361 From the notion of "purpose," "for" came to be used, even in Early English, with words denoting future *time* :—

> (11) "I have food stored up *for* (the purpose, or need, of) many years."
> (12) "I will repeat the Psalter daily *for* a year."

In the same way, "for" is used of *space*, with a notion of motion towards a *purposed* Object—

> (12a) "I am setting out *for* Paris."

362 Hence "for" came to be used of time and space, without any notion of purpose, but with the mere notion of *extension* :—

> (13) "We have loved one another *for* many years."
> (14) "*For* fifteen weary miles they plodded onward."
> (15) "*For* a short time."

Hence (II) by Confusion (where there is no notion of "extension") :—

---

[1] It has been suggested that "for" might derive a meaning of *opposition* from its radical meaning of "before," "in front of." See *Shakespearian Grammar*, page 103.

(16) "He is now sleeping, *for* the first time since last Monday."

(17) "Be sensible, *for* once."

363 The use of "for" after "but" is to be explained by reference to the radical meaning of "but," *i.e.* "except" (see Par. 381) :—

(18) "He would have died *but for* me," *i.e* "*except*, or *only*, (that it happened otherwise) *because of* me."

364 "For," in the sense of "in front of," *i.e.* "in behalf of," is often used *at the beginning* of a sentence, to call attention to that about which one is going to speak :—

(19) "*For* his part, he is indifferent."

Hence—

(20) "*As for* him, he is indifferent," *i.e.* "(So far) as (one may speak) *or*, *i.e.* in behalf of, about, him."

In the middle of the Sentence "for" is not now so common as it was once, *e.g.* in Bacon's time :

"(The counsel of Rehoboam) was young counsel *for* (*as regards*) the persons, and violent counsel *for* (*as regards*) the matter."

"For to," see Par. 402.

365 5. "**Of**," having originally the force of *off*, is still used with this meaning in—

(1) "Within ten miles *of* (*i.e.* from) the coast."

(2) "*Of* late." "*Of* old." "*Of* a child."—Mark ix. 21.

(3) "Upwards *of* (*i.e.* rising *from*) ten years."

From saying, logically, "ten *of* us," *i.e.* "ten *out of* our number," we have come to say, illogically—

(4) "All *of* us."

366 " Of " is also used with Verbs signifying " motion from " : (*a*) deprive, bereave, strip, rob, cheat, defraud ; (*b*) rid, deliver, acquit ; (*c*) cleanse, purge, cure ; (*d*) beware. Also with Adjectives signifying emptiness. This use explains—

(5) "Void *of* sense." "Clear *of* debt." "She was delivered *of* a child."

367 " Of," from meaning " motion from," comes to mean (6) " out of," (7) " belonging to," (8) " resulting from " :—

(6) "This box is made *of* wood." "He comes *of* good parentage." " Evil must come *of* evil."

(7) "The light *of* the sun," *i.e.* "the light *off* or *from* the sun."

(8) "The canal is full *of* water," *i.e.* "as the *result of*." " He did it *of* malice aforethought." "She died *of* a fever." "It smells *of* musk." "*Of* his own accord." "*Of* course," *i.e.* "as *the result of* the ordinary course of things."

Compare Bacon's—

(8*a*) "If Time, *of course* (*i.e. as the result of its ordinary course*) alter things to the worse."

368 From meaning "resulting from," "of" comes to mean (9) "on account of," (10) "because of":—

(9) "I accuse him *of* treason."
(10) "He is glad *of* success, afraid *of* death."

369 Hence, from meaning "that which comes from, has to do with, belongs to, or concerns," "of" has come to mean "concerning," "about":—

(11) "What *of* John? Tell me *of* his adventures."
(12) "I am going *of*[1] an errand."

Lastly, from meaning "about," it comes to mean "as regards":—

(13) "Light *of* foot." "Hard *of* heart."

370 Only in vernacular English is "of" now used for "during," a use that springs naturally from the meaning "coming from," "belonging to," *i.e.* "in," or "on":—

(14) "I can't get up *of* a morning."
(15) "*Of* a sudden."

But this was once more common. Compare Shakespeare's—

"My custom always *of* the afternoon."

371 Since the action *comes of*, or from, the agent, "of" may be, and once was, commonly used where we use "by":—

(16) "He was despised and rejected *of* men."

[1] This might be explained by (8) "as the result of."

(17) "That it might be fulfilled which was spoken *of* the Lord."
(18) "When he was demanded *of* the Pharisees."

372 The Partitive use of "of" without a preceding Noun, Pronoun, or Numeral Adjective, is now rare :

(19) "He gave us (*some*) *of* his best."
(20) "The dogs eat (*some*) *of* the crumbs that fall from their master's table."

"What sort *of*," "A rascal *of* a cabman," &c. See Par. 438.

373 6. "On," "Upon." Since one event can happen *on the top of* another, or can be *based upon* certain conditions it is easy to understand the use of the Preposition in—

(1) "*Upon* my arrival I will give you an interview."
(2) "He acted thus *on* your suggestion."
(3) "*On* hearing this, he rushed out of the house."
(4) "They surrendered the city *on* these conditions."
(5) "Pillage was prohibited *on* pain of death."

374 As we speak of being *supported* or *sustained* by bread, which we call the "staff of life," we naturally use "on" in the metaphorical expressions—

(6) "He lives *on* bread, feeds *on* success," &c.

Since an oath is taken "over" or "on" a Bible, sword, &c., it was natural to swear—

(7) "*On* the faith of a Christian." "*On* my honour."
"*Upon* my word."

Since an action may spring "out of" a feeling, or be based "on" a purpose, we can say—

(8) "He did it *of* malice," but "*on* purpose."

375 "On" is often abbreviated into "a-":—

(9) "A-board," "a-sleep," "a-live," "a-ground."

Shakespeare also has—

(10) "A-land," "a-sea," "an-end," *i.e.* "on end."[1]

376 7. "**Till**," which is now used only of *time*, was once used of *space* :—

(1) "They went *til* Snowdon."
(2) "*Tille* him came his son Richard."

377 8. "**To**," meaning "toward," is sometimes used, without a Verb of motion, to denote "neighbourhood" or "equivalence," where now "for" would be more commonly used :—

(1) "I call God *to* (*i.e.* as) witness."

In the last Example, motion may possibly be implied in "call;" but there is no motion implied in—

(2) "The seven had her *to* wife."

378 "To" seems to mean "up to," "as far as concerns," "as to" in—

(3) "*To* all appearance he is guilty."

---

[1] Even Pope has—
"A little house with trees *a*-row."

379 "To" was early used (in the sense of neighbourhood) for "toward" or "about" of *past* time, as well as of future, *e.g.* "*to*-eve" (yesterday evening). This explains the modern—

(4) "I saw him *to*-day."

"As to." See Pars. 487—489.

380 "But." See Alphabetical Index. When used as a Preposition, "but" should be followed by the Objective form; but, probably owing to *confusion* between the Prepositional and the Conjunctive usage, "but," even when a Preposition, is often followed by the Subjective form:—

"And was not this the Earl? 'Twas none but *he*."—
Philip Van Artevelde.

381 In explaining the many idiomatic usages of "but," two things should be borne in mind; (1) that the radical meaning of "but" is "leaving out," and that it was a Preposition; (2) that a negative is often omitted, for shortness, before it.

The transition from the Preposition to the Conjunction is well illustrated by the following modernised examples from Layamon:—

(1) "*Buten* læve," *i.e.* "*without* leave."—(*Preposition.*)
(2) "He saw that the Britons must fall *buten* heo red haveden," *i.e.* "*without*, or, *unless* they had counsel (rede)."—*Subordinate Conjunction.*
(3) "If you do this, well; *bute* (i.e. *otherwise*), he will never deliver Evelin to thee."—*Co-ordinate Conjunction.*

The omission of the negative was facilitated by the blending of the negative *ne* with the Verb, so that *nam* meant "am not."

(4) "Nabbe we *buten* the west end," *i.e.* we have *but* the west end."
(5) "*Nas* he there bute one night," *i.e.* "he was there *but* one night."

382 9. Prepositions are sometimes used with Adverbs (used as Nouns) for their Objects :—

(1) "What kind of country is it *between here* and Dover?"
(2) "The light comes *from behind*, not *from above*."
(3) "*Until* quite *recently*." "*Since then*." "*For once*." "*Of yore*."

The older and preferable forms "Whither?" "Whence?" seem in danger of being supplanted by the modern "Where-to?" "Where-from?"—

(4) "*Where* does this road lead *to*?"

383 Sometimes the Preposition precedes not an Adverb, but an Adverbial Phrase :—

(5) "The mountain trembles *from on-high*."
(6) "*From beneath-the-ground*." "*From beyond-the-seas*."
(7) "Not *till about-six-years-afterwards*." "*Till within-a-few-weeks-of-his-death*."
(8) "It was sold *for under-half-its-value*."

384 10. The Object of a Preposition is sometimes omitted, (1) when the Object is a Relative Pronoun, (2) when the Preposition completes a Verb in the Infinitive :—

(1) "The will (that) I told you *of* is lost."
(2) "He lent me his horse to escape *upon*."

Such sentences as (2) are found without the Relative Pronoun in Old English; it seems best to consider the Preposition in such cases as part of a Compound Verb—"escape on," like "ride on."

In Shakespeare we should often find "thereon" inserted—"to escape thereon."

385 "One another," "each other," have now come to be regarded as Compound Pronouns:—

(1) "They looked at *one another*, or, *each other*."

But the explanation of the construction is as follows: "They looked one at another, or, each at other"—"one" and "each" being in Apposition to "they," while "other" is the Object of "at." See Pars. 223, 531.

Preposition omitted; see Pars. 127—131.

The Infinitive.[1]

386 The "to" is omitted, not only after the Auxiliary Verbs, but also in a few very common idioms:—

(1) "Better (*to*)[2] wait a while."
(2) "You had better (*to*) be quiet."

Here "had" is Subjunctive, meaning "would have;" and the sentence would be in full—

---

[1] For convenience, the Infinitive, even when not Adverbial, is discussed here.
[2] This was the Infinitive, not the Imperative.

(2) "You would have (find) it better (*to*) be quiet."

(3) "I had rather (*to*) be a doorkeeper," *i.e.* "I sooner ('*rathe*' (Adj.) meant 'early,' 'soon') would have, *i.e.* "I prefer (*to*) be a doorkeeper."

"To" is also omitted after "have" in—

(4) "I must have you (*to*) attend."

(5) "You will have your father (*to*) blame you."

It is impossible to tell whether "Please help me" is for (1) "May it please you *to* help me," or for (2) "Help me, please," which is an abbreviation of "Help me, if you please, or, so please you."

"Do," O.E. *don*, originally meant "cause," *e.g.* "*do* me drenche,' "*cause* (some one) *to drench* me." About the thirteenth century it began to be used for simple emphasis, and in the fifteenth century, was regularly used thus.

In "How *do* you *do*," the first do is the ordinary one, O.E *don*, the second is O.E. *dugan* "to be good, or worth." (MORRIS).

387 The omission of "to" after such Verbs as *let, bid, make, dare, see, hear, feel*, may be explained (1) by the desire of brevity manifesting itself, specially in the use of words so common as these are; and (2) by the fact that old constructions (*i.e.* the Old Infinitive without "to") are to be looked for in common words. (See Par. 95, 96.)

388 But this explanation does not explain the omission of "to" after such uncommon words as "view," "behold," "mark," "watch," "observe," "perceive," &c. The explanation here is perhaps as follows: when the "to" form of the Infinitive came in, the construction would become—

(7) "I observed him *to come*."

Q

But, side by side with this, there would be the Old Participial or Verbal construction :—

(8) "I observed him *coming* or a-*coming*."

In (7) the Object of the Verb is a *fact*, viz. "the fact that he came." In (8) the Object of the Verb is a *person*.

But between these two constructions a compromise or confusion of thought was made, in which it was left uncertain whether the *fact* or the *person* was the more prominent; and, to represent this confusion of thought, there was made (II) a compromise or confusion of language, in which (I brevity) "to" was omitted as in (8), and "come" was substituted for "coming," as in (7), the result being—

(9) "I observed him *come*."[1]

The confusion between the Infinitive and the Participle or Verbal would be facilitated by the similarity of sound between the old Infinitive in -*en*, and the Participle in -*nd*, or the Verbal in -*ng*. See Pars. 585—6.

389 The "to" is often omitted after "than," where it can be supplied from some other clause in the sentence :—

(1) "Sooner than (I am prepared to) make this concession, I am prepared to go to law."
(2) "I will (*i.e.* wish ; Par. 93) (to) die sooner than (to) desist."

[1] This Infinitive would be rendered in Latin and Greek by a Participle.

III. Infinitive with "to."

390 (1) "I was given *to* understand by him."

The Active form is—

(2) "He gave me to understand,"

where "me" is the Indirect Object, and "to understand" the Direct Object, of "gave." Consequently the *correct* Passive form would be—

(3) "To understand was given me."

But "give to understand" being loosely treated as a Compound Verb, "me," in (2), has been taken as the Direct Object of the Active; and therefore the same Person, "I" in (1), has been made the Subject of the Passive.

391 This may be illustrated by—

(4) "So am I given in charge."[1]

The modern meaning of "I am given in charge" would be "I am placed in custody." But, in the foregoing example, "to give-in-charge" is treated as a Compound Verb meaning "to charge," "to commission," so that the sentence means, in Shakespeare, "I am charged, or instructed."

392 "To" follows naturally after "come," but expresses not a purpose, but a *result*, in—

(5) "How came you *to be left* behind?"
(6) "It came *to pass.*"

[1] *2 Henry VI.* ii. 4. 80.

After several Intransitive Verbs of the feelings, *e.g.* " wonder," " rejoice," " sorrow," " to " followed by a Verb is used, or " at " followed by a Verbal Noun :—

>   (7) " I wondered, rejoiced, laughed, &c., *to see* him there," *i.e.* " at seeing."
>   (8) " I blushed, was ashamed, angry, sorry, &c., *to hear* it."

393 After Adjectives, the Infinitive is sometimes used to limit the scope of the Adjective, " to " being used very much iike " in " :—

>   (9) " Sad *to relate*," *i.e.* " in relating,"[1] rather than " for the purpose of relating."
>   (10) " He was the first *to come*," *i.e.* " in coming."
>   (11) " You are unwise *to speak* so hastily," *i.e.* " for speaking."
>   (12) " This was strange *to hear*, after all his professions."

394 " To " is also used after many Nouns resembling or implying *Verbs that would naturally take " to " after them :—*

>   (13) " I have no wish, hope, ambition, desire, &c., *to succeed.*"
>   (14) " Give me your promise *to obey.*"

395 Somewhat different is the use of " to " after Nouns preceded by " the " :—

>   (15) " He had *the* sense *to perceive* his mistake," *i.e.* " the sense necessary, or enough, to perceive."

[1] Compare " mirabile dictu."

Some Adjectives, such as "necessary," "fit," have to be supplied in such cases :—

 (16) "I have *the* pleasure, honour, &c., *to inform you*," *i.e.* "the pleasure, honour, that goes so far as *to*," &c.[1]

396   In all the above Examples there are two causes for the use of "to" instead of "at," "for," "of," &c. (1) A Transitive Verb is often *implied* ; (2) "to" being constantly used with the Gerundive of purpose, came to be used with the Infinitive (used for the Gerundive) even where there is no sense of purpose. See Par. 94 ; also 585—6.

397   "So as to." "To" is often found after "so...as" :—

 (17) "Be so kind as *to* excuse me."

This might have been written without "so...as:" "Be kind to excuse me," *i.e.* "Be kind to the extent of excusing me ; " and this idiom is actually found, only with "enough" added :—

 (18) "Be kind enough *to* excuse me."

In Early English "so" was added in the sense of "to that extent :" "Be *so* kind *to* excuse me." Afterwards, to join together the two parts of the sentence, the Relative form of "so," viz. "as" (see Par. 203), was inserted.

---
[1] This Infinitive appears to describe the "honour," "pleasure," &c., and therefore rather to be Adjectival than Adverbial.

"To" in Questions and Relative Clauses.

398 There appears to have been an old Interrogative use of the Infinitive, of which we still retain remnants in such expressions as—

(1) "Where *to begin*? How (to) *excuse* myself?"[1]

In dependent questions this Infinitive was, and is, very common :—

(2) "I know not where *to begin*, nor how *to excuse myself*."

No doubt this idiom is facilitated by the analogy of "I know not the place *to begin*, nor the way *to excuse* myself," which may be compared with the Noun-use of "wherewith," *e.g.* "I have not the wherewith *to keep* a carriage," "I must know the *how* and the *why*." Add—

(3) "I know not whether *to term* it a fault or a misfortune."

(4) "The difficulty is *how to teach* him that he needs teaching."

399 The sentence "I have no money *to* buy food" is logically correct, but is felt to be unsatisfactorily incomplete. It has therefore been completed in different ways: (*a*) "I have no money *to buy* food *with*, or withal, or therewith;" (*b*) "I have no

---

[1] Although the words are not inserted, yet one *feels* that this is a short way of saying: "Where (am I) to begin? How (am I to) excuse myself?"

money *with which* I *may buy* food;" and the confusion between (*a*) and (*b*) has resulted in—
- (1) "I have no money with *which to buy* food."
- (2) "I have no object *for which to* strive."
- (3) "I want a place *in which to feel* at rest."

400   The Infinitive in Exclamations.

The Subject, not the Object,[1] is usually found before the Infinitive in exclamations :—
- (1) "*I to* be so happy!" "*He to* desert me!"

401   The Parenthetical Infinitive.

This is an Infinitive of purpose :—
- (1) "*To* tell you the truth, I was not up," *i.e.* "in order to tell you the truth (I must say that), I was not up."
- (2) "*To* be brief, or, not to be tedious, the expedition failed."
- (3) "*To be sure* he is not very clever, but he is very kind-hearted."
- (4) "Will you help me?" "*To be sure* I will."

The meaning of "to be sure" seems to be "certainly," but used in (3) *concessively*, in (4) *emphatically*. Compare "to wit," *i.e.* "to know (the truth.)"

[1] Compare the use of a Subject used absolutely with the Participle, where Latin and Greek usage would prepare one to expect some other form. Milton uses the Object with the Participle Absolute; but this is a Latinism. See Par. 408.

The Subject of the Infinitive, in "to be sure" and in "to wit," appears to be the *person addressed*, "that *you* may be sure," "that *you* may-wit."

402   The Infinitive with "for to."

In the Bible, the old Infinitive with "for to" is still found :—

(1) "What went ye out *for to see?*"

In Old English this Infinitive was used as Complement to a Noun, in the Object clause, just like the Infinitive with "to," *e.g.*—

(2) "A many of rude villains made him *for to* bleed."

(3) "If he will not suffer my people *for to pass.*"

We still, unconsciously, use this idiom, *e.g.*—

(4) "It is rare for a man to starve in this country."

Here the meaning is, not that "starvation is rare *for a man*" (for of course a man can only starve once), but that "*a man's being starved*, or, *that a man should be starved*, is rare." But, as this idiom is completely forgotten, we seldom use it, except where "for" *might take* for its Object the Noun preceding the following Infinitive, as in—

(5) "The night is too dark *for* us *to travel.*"

Here "us" *may be* called the Object of "for." But, in reality, the sentence owes its origin to the old use of "for to." It is impossible to treat "for" as governing a Noun Object in the first or third, and it is difficult in the second, of the two following Examples :—

> (6) "He was too much accustomed to deeds of violence *for* the agitation he had experienced *to be* of long continuance."—SCOTT.[1]
>
> (7) "The wind sits fair *for* news *to go* to Ireland."
>
> (8) "He belonged to a race that was too much detested—outside the cities—*for* him *to hope* anything from charity."—*Spectator*, 1874.

The Complete Infinitive.

403

Hopes and wishes about what is completed are necessarily reserved for cases where one has failed, and not fulfilled one's purpose. Hence with Verbs of *hoping, wishing, intending*, the old and correct use of Complete Infinitive (which it is most desirable to retain) expresses *an unfulfilled purpose* :—

> (1) "I hoped *to have succeeded*, but I failed."
>
> (2) But, on the other hand, "I hoped *to succeed*, and I succeeded."

So with some other Verbs :—

> (1) "I could *have repeated* all Homer by heart once," *i.e.* "if any one had challenged me, but no one did."

[1] Mätzner, Vol. iii. page 58.

(2) But, on the other hand, "I could *learn* a hundred lines in an hour once," *i.e.* "and I sometimes did."

404   IV. The Participle.

The Participle qualifying a Noun is sometimes incorrectly used, instead of a Verbal Noun qualified by a Possessive Adjective or Possessive form of the Noun, *e.g.* " In consequence of the *king saying* this" for " In consequence of the *king's saying* this." " Trusting to the certainty of the old *man* (for *man's*) *interrupting* him." This is rare, and not to be imitated. Putting " me " instead of " king " or " man " above, you see the incorrectness of the idiom. It is not now English to say " in consequence of me saying this " : " my " would be required in both cases.

405   The Passive Participle is perhaps allowable in this construction, *e.g.*—

(1) " He insisted on the *match being deferred*," instead of, " the *match's being deferred*."
(2) "In consequence of this *motion having been brought forward* without due notice."

These are not exactly Participles. For example, (1) does not mean " He insisted on the match when it was being deferred," or, "that was being deferred:" but " He insisted on *the-match-being-deferred*," *i.e.* "the deferring of the match." This (which may be called the *Noun-use* of the Participle)[1] is a Latin construction, alien to the genius of the English language; the native Verbal use should be retained, wherever euphony and clearness allow:—

(3) "He insisted on the *man's being reprimanded*."

The Participle with Conjunctions.

406 The Participle is ambiguous; see Par. 66. "Walking" may mean "*though* he walked," "*because* he walked," &c. Partly to prevent ambiguity, and partly by (II) Confusion of Construction, we blend together (*a*) "*Walking* on the ice I slipped," and (*b*) "*While*, or *when*, I *was walking* on the ice, I slipped;" and, combining the clearness of the latter with the brevity of the former, we say—

(1) "*While*, or *when*, walking on the ice, I slipped."
(2) "*Though* walking very carefully, I slipped."

407 It would be convenient to say "*because* walking;" but "*because*" and "*since*"[2] are not used with Participles. We sometimes, however, use "as" in

---

[1] It is sometimes called the *Gerundive* use of the Participle. *Gerundive* means "describing that which is to be done." The Latins had a special form for the *Gerundive*. See Glossary.
[2] "Since" is used, as a Preposition, with a Verbal Noun as its Object, but not with a Participle. "If" and "unless" are rarely used with Active Participles.

this way, generally with "being," more rarely with other Participles :—

(3) "He was exempted from serving on the jury, *as being* over sixty."

(4) "Our remaining horse was unfit for the road, *as* wanting an eye."

(5) "*If conquered*, I am at least not disgraced."

(6) "I should never have attempted it *unless* persuaded by you."

(7) "I always failed *till* helped by my brother."

The Participle used Absolutely with Subject.

In Early English the Objective form of the Pronoun was used, *e.g.* by Wyckliffe :—

(1) "*Him* speaking these things," *i.e.* "while he spoke."

Milton (probably imitating the classical usage) uses "him" and not "he" in—

(2) "*Him* destroyed . . . all this will soon follow."

The Participle used Absolutely.

Some Participles, through frequent use in certain expressions, have come to be used even where the Noun or Pronoun qualified by them has been dropped out, so that some of them have almost the force of Prepositions :—

Regular Construction. (1) "*Concerning*¹ you the decision is as follows."
Irregular ,, . . (1) "We talked for some time *concerning* the arrangements."
Regular ,, . . (2) "*Considering* the circumstances, I do not think him to blame."
Irregular ,, . . (2) "*Considering* the circumstances, it was thought that he was not to blame."

Respecting, regarding, and *touching* are thus used. More rarely we have—

(3) "*Talking* of books, here is a very rare book."
(4) "*Judging* from his own behaviour, he cannot be a desirable companion."
(5) "*Granting* that you are right, what do you infer from this?"
(6) "*Assuming* that he is guilty, what ought to be done?"

410 In most of such cases the Infinitive might be substituted for the Participle; and it is possible that the old sound of the Infinitive "talken" being like the sound of "talking," may have facilitated the introduction of the latter: but it is more probable that the direct cause of the construction is (*a*) the frequent use of the Participle regularly, and (*b*) its retention when the Pronoun is changed :—

(*a*) "*Talking* of books, I must tell you, &c."
(*b*) "*Talking* of books, there is a very fine copy of," &c.

¹ Here "concerning" may be said to qualify "decision."

"In talking," or "a-talking" (compare the French "en attendant"), might also naturally be contracted into "talking," and might then be confused with the Participle.

The Participle with Implied Noun.

411 It is scarcely correct, though not very uncommon, to say—

(1) "*Having* disposed of his first argument, his second argument remains to be considered," instead of "we have to consider."

(2) "My farm consisted of twenty acres of excellent land, (*I*) having given a hundred pounds for my predecessor's good will."—GOLDSMITH.[1]

412 Where a Possessive Adjective is used, *e.g.* "his," it may be sometimes said that "his" is the same as "of him," and that the Participle qualifies "him," which is implied in "his":—

(3) "*Having finished* his breakfast, *his* thoughts began to run on dinner."

(4) "*Repulsed* at all points, *their* courage grew cold."

Adjectives, as well as Participles, are thus used:—

(5) "Once *free* from debt, *his* best course is to emigrate."

Such an expression as the following is by no means to be imitated:—

[1] Mätzner, Vol. iii., page 80

(6) "He has a certain grandeur of soul, which cannot be contemplated *unmoved,*" *i.e.*, "by any-one unmoved."

V. Adverbs.

413 Some Adjectives appear to be used as Adverbs, *e.g.*—

"He ran *fast.*"

The explanation of these forms is as follows: In Early English an Adverb was often formed by adding *-e* to an Adjective, *e.g.* "bright" Adjective, "bright-*e*" Adverb. In Modern English the *-e* has been dropped (with many other Inflections), but several of the old Adverbs are retained, *e.g.* "quick,' "sweet," &c.

"**There**" redundant; see Par. 152.

414 "**So**" is used (1) for an Adjective, (2) for a Noun. The explanation of this is as follows: "So" means "in this way," and is a less emphatic form of "also," "all-so." Hence—

(1) "He is an Englishman, and *so* (also) are you," *i.e.*, "and you *also* are an Englishman."
(2) "I am sorry, and *so* (also) is he," *i.e.*, "he *also* is sorry."

In time this restricted use of "so" (restricted to indicate the repetition of a previous statement) was forgotten, and " so" was used in other constructions, e.g.—

(3) "The prince (for *so* he was) threw off his mask."
(4) "The blest to-day is as completely *so*
     As who began a thousand years ago."

In the two last Examples " so " must be parsed as put for " prince " and " blest " respectively.

In "I thought *so*, did *so*, said *so*," " so " may often be treated as an Adverb, and also in " It is so," i.e. " matters are *in that condition*."

415 *So* is sometimes used, not for the preceding Noun, but for something *like* (" in the same [1] way as ") the preceding Noun, *i.e. for a preceding Noun modified by some Adverb, such as " about," " nearly "* :—

(1) " I am going out for a minute or *so (about a minute.)* "

416 " Other " is used for " other-how " [2] (compare " other-wise ") in the expression—

(1) " I must help you some how or *other* "

417 " No " is often used with Comparatives, *e.g.* " *no* better," *i.e.* " in no degree better," and hence—

(1) " We saw him *no more*,"

where the Adverb " no " modifies the Adverb " more." " No," (" na," or " ne ") was used for

---
[1] See Par. 203.
[2] " How " is used as a Noun in " I must know the *how* and the *why*." See Par. 393.

"not" ("no-whit," "naught") in Old English, and is as correct as "not" in:—

(2) "Whether he comes or *no*, it matters little."

418 "Why" and "well" are used as expletives: (1) "Why?" appears to have been originally thus used as an exclamation of impatience or surprise, equivalent to "Why do you say this? Why are you surprised? Why are you acting thus?" (2) "Well" seems to mean "This having been well settled," and is used in the sense of "enough of this," "to pass on," &c., in order to prepare the way for a new point:—

(1) "Snakes! *Why*, there are no snakes in Ireland."
(2) "*Well*, now let us come to more practical matters."

419 Some Adverbs, especially those of place, are used with Nouns almost like Adjectives, except that they rarely come before the Noun:—

(1) "*God above* knows best."
(2) "What is the cause of your *arrival here?* I thought your *education abroad* would prevent your *return homeward*."

It is allowable to put the Adverb first in "The *above argument*." Byron also writes "The *then*[1] *world*," "My *almost drunkenness* of heart." Shake-

---

[1] This construction, sanctioned by Byron and Thackeray, is too convenient to be given up.

R

speare has " thy *here-approach*," " our *hence-going*," "till Harry's *back-return*."

420 Adverbs repeated.—Many Adverbs are repeated, sometimes to denote repetition, sometimes for emphasis. Thus we use "*again* and *again*," "*in* and *in*" (of horse-breeding), "*over* and *over*," logically; for the repetition of the action requires the repetition of the Adverb. But we also illogically use "through and through," "out and out," and Pope has :—

> "Know there are rhymes which *fresh* and *fresh*[1] applied."

This explains "*by* and *by*." "By" meant "near," either of space or time. Hence "*by* and *by*" meant "very near," either of space or of time. Chaucer uses it of space and speaks of "two knights sleeping *by and by, i.e. close by*." But we now use it only in the sense of "very soon." In early English (Layamon ii. 447) we find "*with* and *with*" for "*again* and *again*."[2]

---

[1] So a dinner is served up "*hot* and *hot*."
[2] The later text has one "with" only.

ADJECTIVES.

"The" and "A."

421 " **The** " is often used to denote "that which is known as," *e.g.*—

    (1) " *The* hero differs from *the* brute."

"*The* earth" means "the planet, *known* as earth," "the earth *known* as distinct from the sea,"[1] &c. "Earth" means "our Parent Earth" personified:—

    (2) " *The earth* is larger than *the moon.*"
    (3) "*Earth* smiles around, with boundless bounty blest."

We still use "the" before a Noun denoting a class, to *define* the individual selected out of that class—

    "*The* Prophet Daniel"; "*the* Astronomer Adams"; *i.e.*, "the astronomer *known* by the name of Adams."

Also, in the case of foreign titles, *e.g.*—

    "*The* Tycoon So-and-so"; "*the* Consul Appius"; "*the* Centurion Paullus."

422 But a familiar title is treated as a *part of the*

---

[1] Bacon says "*The* (*substance known as*) *matter* is in a perpetual flux."

proper name, and therefore dispenses with "the." Compare—

> "*The* Centurion Paullus," with "Captain Smith."
> "King Edward," with "*the* Emperor Napoleon."

In the earliest English, before this distinction was recognized, "the" was inserted before "king," "bishop," &c.; but Chaucer often omits "the."

423 Some epithets are *distinctive* of certain persons. For example, "Alfred" is *known* as "*the* Great;" Wellington as "*the* victorious;" "Minos" as "*the* inflexible." (1) In cases of great notoriety, "the" may come after its Noun; (2) in other cases before its Noun:—

> (1) "Alfred *the* Great is wrongly supposed to have established the form of trial by jury now existing among us."
> (2) "*The* classical Addison did not disdain to write a commentary on the ballad of 'Chevy Chase.'"

On the other hand, an epithet (like a title) is often treated as though it were part of the name, especially in Poetry, *e.g.* "*god-like* Turenne," and "the" is consequently omitted. See Par. 523.

424 Sometimes a proper name is used for a type of character; *e.g.* "Rupert" is used for "a dashing, impetuous leader." In such cases "the" may be prefixed, and we can say—

> (1) "Lord Derby was called *the* Rupert of debate."
> (2) "He was *the* Thersites (*i.e.*, wrangling reviler) of the assembly."

"The" is used before names that are regarded not so much as names as epithets, e.g.—

> "*The* Thames (river);" "*the* Atlantic (ocean);" "*the* Mediterranean (sea);" "*the* (range called) Chilterns;" "*the* (district known as) Crimea, Tyrol, Netherlands,[1] Levant, Palatinate."

"The" is omitted before names of towns, countries, and isolated mountains, all of which may be regarded as *individuals* requiring "proper names," e.g. "Paris," "England," "Snowdon," "Saddleback."

"The" in "*the* Rigi," "*the* Matterhorn," "*the* Schreckhorn," &c. is probably of foreign origin.

425 "The" is the old Demonstrative and Relative Pronoun "by how much" and "by so much" (See Par. 344) in—

> (1) "*The* sooner he leaves, *the* better for everybody."

426 There is no fixed rule as to repeating "the" between two Nouns, both of which are intended to be defined. Compare—

> "He arose and rebuked *the* winds and *the* sea," St. Matthew, viii. 26, with St. Luke viii. 25, "He commandeth even *the* winds and water."

"The" is perhaps more often omitted than inserted, provided the omission causes no ambiguity :—

> (1) "*The* prince and princess are expected;" "During *the* first and second centuries."

---

[1] "The Netherlands" = "The Low Lands."

427 " A " is used before "dozen," "hundred," "thousand," "million," "few," "great many;" all these words being half Nouns, inasmuch as they are preceded by "a," and half Adjectives, inasmuch as they are not followed by "of." See Par. 193.

Anomalous uses of "a," or rather of Numerals preceded by "a," arose very early:—

"A(n) 5 mile;" "a(n) 2 furlong;" "a(n) seven mile;" "a(n) twelve year."

Here, as in "a sennight (seven-night)", "a fortnight (fourteen-night)", (Shakespeare uses "one seven years"), the Numeral and the Noun seem to form a Singular Compound Noun. But we sometimes meet with "*a nine*, or *a ten*, of men," where the Numeral by itself is treated as a Noun.

428 "A" *appears to have (but has not)* the meaning of "one" in—

(1) "Five-pence *a* quart," "*a* year," "*a* man."

For in Early English the Preposition "on," "in," or "an" was used in such cases:—

(2) "Once *in* or *on* the year;" "I fast twice *in* the week;" "if he sin against thee *on day* seven times."

Hence "a" must here be regarded as an old Preposition.

429 " A " (like " the " above) is used before names, when the name represents a character, *e.g.* "*a* Crœsus," *i.e.* "a man of immense wealth."

"*A* little." See Par. 217.

With many Adjectives that from use or termination approach Adverbs, " a " is often placed after, instead of before, the Adjective, *e.g.* "many *a*,"[1] "what *a*," "such *a*," "half *a*." In Early English we also find " each *a*," " which *a*." Hence, though we cannot say "severe a man," we can say "*so* severe, *too* severe, *as* severe, *a* man."

" A " is for " one " in " all of *a* sort, *a* piece." Compare :—

"And surely, Heav'n and I are of *a* mind ?"—POPE.

Other Adjectives.

430 *Very* once meant " genuine " (Lat. *verus*). Hence it came to mean " itself," " themselves," &c. ; *e.g.*—

(1) " Your *very* looks betray you."

The Adjective *follows*, instead of dividing or preceding, "something," "anything," "everything," and other similar Compounds of "thing." The reason seems to be that in Early English these words were sometimes used Partitively and followed by "of," thus :—

(1) "Of Nazareth may *something of good* be ? "
WYCKLIFFE.

[1] See *Shakespearian Grammar*, Paragraph 81; See also Par. 218 above.

This has been shortened into—

(2) "I have heard *something good*."

431 The Superlative form of the Adjective is sometimes used as a Noun, *e.g.*—

(1) "He plunged into the *thickest, hottest,* of the fray."

This is easily explained by the confusion (II) with such expressions as "the *best* (*fish*) of your fish," "the *finest* (*streets*) of your streets." Here the Noun can logically be supplied, and the construction (owing to its convenient brevity (I)) has encroached, where, logically, it is unjustifiable.

A few Adjectives of French origin follow their Nouns, accordance with French usage, *e.g.* "heir *apparent,*" "blood *royal,*" "prince *regent.*" In poetry the transposition is common, for emphasis. See Par. 515.

Possessive Adjective, &c.

432 The following curious idiom requires explanation :—

(1) "That ugly face *of his* quite frightened the child."

The regular construction would have been "that ugly face *of him* ;" and, in the same way, instead of saying—

(2) "This news *of John's* is very strange."
(3) "A friend *of mine* is here."

—the regular construction would be "this news of John," "a friend of me."

433 In (3) it may be said that "mine" is put for "my friends;" but this explanation will scarcely apply to (2), and certainly not to (1): "that ugly face of his (faces)!"

The truth is that "of him" and "of me," used Possessively, are intolerably harsh; and ambiguity also might often result from the regular construction; for "this news *of John*" would naturally mean "*news about* John." Consequently, partly to avoid the *ambiguity* caused by the double meaning of "of" (viz. "belonging to" and "about"), and partly to avoid *harshness* of sound, we adopt the following illogical but serviceable device to make our meaning clear; we retain the Possessive "of," but we also add the Possessive '*s*. Thus we combine the *French Prepositional Idiom with the English Inflectional Idiom*.

434 A similar desire to avoid *harshness* (III) has made us add an illogical but euphonious '*s* to "your" and "our,' which are severally the Possessive Inflections of "you" and "we." "Your" sounds harshly at the end of a sentence, and requires some modification. Then steps in (II) confusion between "this is your" and "this is John's, William's, the man's," &c. "Your" has been treated as though it were a Noun, and has been changed into "your's" or "yours." But, *logically,* "*your's*" is as absurd as "*of of* you;" for "your" means "of you," and the addition of '*s* adds a superfluous "of."

435   "These forms were confined in the 13th and 14th centuries to the Northern Dialect, and are probably due to Scandinavian influences."—MORRIS.
The more ordinary form in the Southern Dialect omits the *s*.
"I wol be *your* in alle that ever I may."—CHAUCER.
The vulgar *yourn* is an old provincial form, and exemplifies the same tendency, viz., to emphasize an unemphatic termination, where emphasis is required.

(Prepositions in Adjective Phrases).

436   A Phrase consisting of a Preposition between two Nouns (especially when the former Noun is preceded by "the" or "a") often has the force of an Adjective, the Relative being implied, *e.g.*—

(1) "A bird (*that is*) in the hand is worth two (*that are*) in the bush."

Consequently, it is sometimes difficult to tell whether the Preposition is thus used to connect two Nouns, or to connect a Verb with an Adverbial phrase; *e.g.* "Send back the horse from the Red Dragon" may mean—

(1) "Send back *the-horse-from-the-Red-Dragon,*" *i.e.*, "the horse that has come from the Red Dragon," or:
(2) "*Send-back* the horse *from-the-Red-Dragon,*" *i.e.*, "send back from the Red Dragon my horse."

In the same way there is an ambiguity in—

(3) "Did you see my *agents at-Portsmouth?*"
(4) "*Did you see* my agents *at Portsmouth?*"

437 "**Of.**" When a name is given to a place, the name being regarded as the name of *a person*, and the town, land, castle, &c., as *belonging to* the person, the Preposition "of" was used in early times to denote the relation between the two :—

(1) "The city *of* London"; "the isle *of* Wight"; "river *of* Cydnus" (Shakespeare); "the lake *of* Gennesareth."

Hence, in the same way, "of" is used after other words denoting a *class*, to prepare the way for the particular name of the *individual* :—

(2) "The month *of* May"; "the hour *of* three"; "the feast *of* Tabernacles"; "the year *of* Jubilee"; "the name *of* George"; "the cry *of* 'breakers!'"; "the play *of* 'Hamlet'"; "the art *of* medicine"; "the element *of* fire"; "the virtue *of* resentment."

438 It is not so easy to explain—

(3) "He is a *jewel-of-a* man."
(4) "This *scamp-of-a* coachman."

Probably "of" is here partitive, as in "What sort, kind, *of* man is he?" The "man" is the *class;* the "sort" or "kind" is a *part* of the class, and therefore is naturally followed by the partitive "of." The answer to this question will necessarily be some *part* of the *class* "man :" he is "a good sort, bad sort, rascally sort, precious sort, *of* man ;" hence, for shortness, "He is a rascal, or jewel, *of* man."

But, owing to the Semi-Adverbial use of "What," "What sort," the Indefinite Adjective "a" is inserted before "man" (see Par. 219), so that the notion of *class* is lost, and "a man" appears to denote an individual, and "what sort of," "a jewel of," &c., come to be regarded as Compound Semi-Adverbial Adjectives.

439 The use of "of" after "whole," "all":—

(5) "The *whole-of* the day;" "all *of* us,"

—may be accounted for as a natural extension of, and (II) confusion with, similar expressions, *e.g.* "half, quarter, &c., *of* the day;" "ten, eleven, almost all, &c., *of* us."

SYNTAX OF SENTENCES.

Co-ordinate Clauses.

440 "And" sometimes joins a sentence to a previous sentence *implied but not expressed*. It is often used in passionate exclamations:—

(1) "(Is it true?) *And* will you then desert me?"

"And" sometimes comes between an Adverb repeated twice, the repetition having the force of emphasis:[1]—

(1) "More *and* more;" "worse *and* worse."

[1] See Par. 420.

441 Remembering that "by" means "near" of space, but also may mean "near" *of time*, we can understand—

> (2) "By *and* by," *i.e.* "near, very near (of time)," or, "very soon."[1]

An Adverb, when introduced emphatically, might be emphasized by the repetition of the Verb and Object with "and": "I must see him, and *see* him quickly." Instead of this, "that" was often in early times substituted for the previous phrase (just as "it" is a preparatory substitute for a sentence or phrase; see Par. 151):—

> (1) "I must see him, *and that* quickly."

Relatives used Co-ordinately.

442 "*What*" is sometimes used instead of "both" and "and":—

> (1) "*What* with his persuasive eloquence, and *wha* with the presence of his armed followers, he soon overcame all opposition."

This might naturally be explained as a condensation of "Reckoning *what* he effected with," &c.; but, more probably, "what" is to be treated

---

[1] Both "by and by" and "presently" (owing to the natural habit of exaggerating one's readiness) have come to mean much less than they once meant. "Presently" used to mean "at once."

as a kind of Noun meaning "part," and used Adverbially, like "partly." Compare "some-*what.*" "What" had come, very early, to be used as a Noun, so that men could say, not only "some-*what,*" but also "a little *what.*"[1]

443   "**Whether**" is sometimes used with "or," not to introduce an indirect question, but (like "what" above) as a Co-ordinate Conjunction, to mean "both ...and;" "either...or":—

(1) "The landlord reserves all game, *whether* birds *or* ground-game."

The full construction would be "whether it be;" but "whether" has so completely assimilated itself to "either" in such expressions that it seems best to parse "whether" as used for "either," and "birds" as Object, in Apposition to "game."

Subordinate Clauses.

Condensed Clauses.

444   1. Some Conjunctions are formed from Prepositions or Adverbs followed by "that," *e.g.* "after (that)," "before (*that*)," "now (that)." In such cases "that" is often omitted:[2]—

(1) "Now (*that*) we have arrived," But—

[1] *Shakespearian Grammar*, page 5. Compare in Latin "quum—tum," "qua—qua."
[2] In Shakespeare, "that" is used after "when," "while," "whether," "because," "if;" and also after the Prepositions *in, for.*

(2) "On the day *that* thou eatest thereof thou shalt surely die."

(3) "The instant (*that*) he saw me, he retired."

445   2. Conjunctions used with Participles: see Par. 406.

Conjunctions are also used with Adjectives and Nouns, the Verb being omitted :—

(1) "This news, *if* (it be) true, will alter our plans."
(2) "*Though* (he was) honest, he was not trusted."
(3) "*However* thoughtless (he may be), he is at least not deliberately mischievous."
(4) "*Although* (he is) a rascal, yet he's a very amusing rascal."

In parsing Conjunctions so used, the Verb should be supplied.

446   3. "**As**" is used with Nouns, (1) sometimes for as being," *i.e.* "since he is;" (2) sometimes it seems loosely used for "like," "in the character of" :—

(1) "*As* (being) a foreigner, he claims our special consideration."
(2) "*As* (in the character of) an author, he did not succeed."
(3) "They regarded him *as* (in the character of, like) an adventurer."

Such sentences can generally be reduced to their regular construction by bearing in mind the radical meaning of "as," viz. "in that way" or "in which way," or, as here, "in the way in which":—

(1) In full, "He claims our special consideration *in the way in which* a foreigner (would naturally claim it)."
(2) In full, "He did not succeed *in the way in which* an author (would be said to succeed)."
(3) In full, "They regarded him *in the way in which* (they would regard) an adventurer."

With "possible," after Conjunctions, ellipses are very common:—

(1) "Come as soon *as* (it is) possible."
(2) "Come *if* (it be) possible."

447 "That" sometimes implies a *principal* Verb before it in passionate exclamations:—

(1) "Oh, (I would) *that* I had wings like a dove!"
(2) "(To think) *That* it should come to this!"

Object Clauses.

448 "That" (the Conjunction) often introduces a Clause as the Object of a Compound Transitive Verb *implied*[1] in a previous sentence. For example, "I am sure," "I had no notion," "I have some hope," "I have evidence," all suggest the question

---

[1] Compare the use of the Infinitive after the implied Transitive Verb Par. 392.

"Of what?" after them. "That" is here equivalent to "of the fact that."

Distinguish the above use of "that" from its use when introducing a Clause in Apposition to a previous Noun, as in the following Examples :—

(1) "They made an agreement *that* they would share equally."

(2) "The axiom, *that* a whole is greater than its part, seems so true that its statement seems, at first sight, unnecessary."

449 On the other hand, "that" seems used for "for that," "in that," "because,"[1] after Verbs of rejoicing, sorrowing :—

(1) "I am sorry *that* (*i.e.* because) he failed."

Also, in parentheses after "not" :—

(2) "I must go now, not *that* (*i.e.* because) I want to go, but I have an engagement."

In—

(1) "Did you see John?" "Not *that* I recollect—"

"that" is a Relative Pronoun, and the Antecedent must be supplied from the previous sentence : "not (a seeing) *that* I recollect."

450 "But that," in its radical meaning, was "except that;" hence "barring," "to the contrary of." This explains—

(1) "I cannot be persuaded *but that* (to the contrary of the belief that) he meant mischief."

[1] Compare Latin "quod."

(2) "We did not know *but that* (to the contrary of the knowledge that) he might come."

Here "but" was originally a Preposition having for its Object the sentence following it.

451 Sometimes "what" is used for "that":—

(3) "Not *but what* he meant mischief," *i.e.* "I do not admit, however, anything to the contrary of his meaning to do mischief."

This may possibly be a confusion arising from the grammatical constructions :—

(4) "He says nothing *but what* is true."
(5) "Not a man (was there) *but what* cried shame."
(6) "Not a tree *but what* has suffered from the frost."

From these uses, "not but what" perhaps came to be used ungrammatically to mean "without any exception," "without any doubt;" but I have been unable to trace this construction. Yet it seems to be illustrated by the change from the *Relative* "that" in "For all *that* you did," to the *Conjunctive* "that" in "For all *that* you tried so hard." See Par. 475.

452 In time the "that" was omitted for brevity; and then "but" (though really a Preposition with the meaning of "prevention") appeared to be an ordinary Conjunction :—

(6) "Not *but* there are who merit other palms."—
POPE.

which originally would have meant, "I do not say anything *but* (*i.e.* to the contrary) that there are," &c., but it gradually came to mean "I deny it not; *but*, so far from denying, I admit that there are," &c.

(7) "Never dream *but* (*i.e.* anything *but*, *except*, or *to prevent* that) ill must come of ill."[1]—SHELLEY.

(8) "Who knows, *but* (anything *but*, *except*, or *to prevent* that) he'll come yet?"

453 Hence, after "doubt not," "but" came to be used regularly with its ordinary adversative force, so that there is no difference between—

{ (9) "Doubt not *that* God will help you," and
{ (10) "Doubt not, *but* God will help you."

(11) "It cannot be denied *but*, or *that*, he is a rascal."

The curious inconsistencies of idiom are illustrated by comparing—

(1) "He is all *but* perfect," and
(2) "He is anything *but* wise."

In (1) the meaning is "He is altogether (perfect)," "all except (being absolutely) perfect;"[2] in (2) the meaning is "He is anything *except* wise."

454 The Prepositions "of" and "about" are (rarely) used before Object-sentences :—

(1) "He tells us a good deal *about* why he travelled, but nothing *of* how he travelled."

The Adverb "where" is not only used as a Noun

[1] Mätzner.   [2] Compare ὅσον οὐ

s 2

(Par. 398), but also as a Noun and Relative Adverb together :—

    (1) "He lives about ten miles from *here*." "From *where?*"

    (2) "He lives ten miles from *where* I am living," *i.e.* "from the *place in which* or *where* I am living."

ADVERBIAL CLAUSES.

455 "**That.**" Instead of "when" used Relatively, sometimes the Relative Pronoun "that" is used (Par. 444) :—

    (1) "He never (at no time) sees me *that* (at which time) he does not mock me."

Compare, in Early English—

    (2) "Scarcely was this speech finished *that* (*i.e.* when) they saw Hengist approach."[1]

456 "**But**" being used after negatives to intensify an affirmative, *e.g.* "This is *nothing but* the truth," came to be irregularly used, in Shakespeare's time, after Negative *Comparatives*, *e.g.* "This is *no* more but the truth."

This seems to be a (II) confusion between "nothing but" and "no more than."

Hence (in colloquial English), after "not," "no sooner," "scarcely," and other words *implying* a

[1] Layamon, ii. 202.

negative, "but" is used, partly as an Adversative Conjunction, and partly with a Relative force:—

(1) "No sooner did he hear her *but* he burst into a passion."

(2) "I had scarcely gone a mile *but* I met him again."

In the last Example the negative is *implied:* "I had not gone a mile." In Modern English it will be advisable to treat "but," when thus used, as an Adversative Conjunction, as though the sentence ran, "He had not fully heard her; *but* (before fully hearing her) he burst into a passion."

457   "Since" once meant "later-than," hence "after," hence "because;" (Early English, *sith than, i.e.* "later than.")

"Until" is the same as "unto;" "til" being often used for "to" in Early English. Par. 376.

"That," used for "because:" see Par. 449.

"That" is used for "so that" in impassioned questions:—

(1) "Is he an oracle, (so) *that* we are to regard him as infallible?"

(2) "What were you doing, (so) *that* you were not in time to-day?"

458   "Forasmuch as" and "Inasmuch as" = "for that," "in that," *i.e.* "because."

"As," in virtue of its radical meaning, is often interchanged with "that:" Par. 205. The "as much" appears intended to emphasize, and give importance to, the cause.

"Seeing," like "concerning," "considering" (see Par. 409), has come to be used as a Conjunction, meaning "since." The Regular Construction would be—

(1) "*Seeing* that you are a foreigner, I will strain a point for you."

Hence comes the Irregular Construction, by confusion :—

(2) "*Seeing* that you are a foreigner, you are entitled to special consideration."

Conditional Clauses.

459 "If" is sometimes used of a supposition made for the sake of argument; hence of a concession; hence (190) of an *admitted fact* :—

(1) "*If* I *am* poor, yet I am honest."

"If" (like other Conjunctions; Par. 445) is often used with Nouns, Adjectives, and Adverbs, the Verb being omitted :—

(1) "*If* somewhat *slowly*, he at least did his work thoroughly."
(2) "*If* not *to-morrow*, we shall at all events arrive next day."

"On condition," "in case," "provided," "supposing," are often used as Conjunctions, "that" being omitted after them :—

 (1) "*In case* (that) you come early, we will have a long walk."

 (2) "*Provided* (that) you agree, it matters little who disagrees."

"In case (that)" and "provided (that)" may be treated as Conjunctions; or, in the last Example, "you agree" may be regarded as a Subject-clause used absolutely, and qualified by the Participle "provided."

460 "**So that**" is sometimes used to express *condition* :—

 (3) "You may go where you like, *so that* you are back by five."

In Elizabethan and earlier English the Subjunctive would here be used :—

 (4) "It is a pleasure to see the errors of others, *so* always *that* this prospect *be* with pity," *i.e.* "yet *in such a way in which way* the prospect may be with pity."

461 "**So as**" is less common in the sense of *condition*, and is now restricted to vernacular English. But Shakespeare has—

 (5) "*So as* thou livest in peace, die free from strife."

Sometimes neither "that" nor "as" is inserted in Elizabethan English (the Verb being in the Subjunctive):—

(6) "*So* it *be* new, there's no respect how vile."

This brief idiom is still used colloquially, with the Indicative for the Subjunctive.

462 The Imperatives "suppose," "admit," "grant," "say," are used to introduce conditional clauses:—

(1) "*Say* I fail at first, I have another chance."

463 A question may be used to introduce a Condition, thus:—

(1) "Did you not know his intention? Then, of course you were surprised."

It is an easy transition from this to the use of the Conditional Mood (Indicative form in Antecedent, the "shall-form" in Consequent), *retaining the Interrogative arrangement of the words:*—

(2) "*Did I not know* his intention, I should of course be surprised."

This also explains the Interrogative arrangement of the "shall-form" in the Antecedent:—

(3) "*Should you see* him, you would find him much changed."

The original use of Interrogatives to express Condition may explain the following:—

(1) " *Whether* he said it or denied it, the facts remain the same," *i.e.*, "Whether said he it, or denied it ? In either case the facts remain the same."

(2) "*Whoever* said this, it was a mistake," *i.e.*, " Who in the world said this? It was at all events a mistake."

(3) "*However* hard it may be, you must try," *i.e.* " *In whatever degree*[1] it may be hard (*in that degree, i.e.* none the less) you must try."

In Early English this use was more common :—
"*Knew I her name*, I were happy."

464   "As" seems used for "though" in—

(1) "Young *as* I am I cannot be deceived by this."

The fuller construction is "As young as I am," and this appears to be an abbreviation of "(Be I) as young as I am," *i.e.* "though I be."

465   "Should" and "would" are often used where a Condition is implied though not expressed :—

(1) "I wish summer *would* come."

This is a confusion between "I *should* be glad if summer *would come*" and "I wish summer *to come*."

(2) "I am willing that he *should* receive the money."

Confusion of (1) "*I am willing* that he *shall*" and (2) "I *should be willing*, if, or that, he *should*."

[1] "How" and "why" are old cases of "who."

(3) "It is shameful that he *should* be treated thus."

Confusion of (1) "It *is shameful* that he *has been*" and (2) "It *would be shameful,* if, or that, he *should be.*"

(4) "It is not strange that he *should* have succeeded."

Confusion of (1) "It *is* not *strange* that he *has succeeded*" and (2) "It *would not have been* strange, if, or that, he *should have succeeded.*"[1]

(5) "It will be better that I *should* withdraw."

Confusion of (1) "It *will be better* that I (*shall*) *withdraw*" and (2) "It *would be better,* if or that, I *should withdraw.*"

466 "Unless" was once "on less," and followed by "than," *e.g.*—

(1) "This cannot be, *on less than* (*i.e.* on a less condition than this, viz. that) we gain the battle."

The notion of comparison falling out of sight, the Conjunctive "that" was substituted for "than," and lastly "that" was omitted for brevity.

467 "But," meaning radically "except," was very early used for "if not," with the Subjunctive. We still retain this use in—

(1) "It never rains *but* it pours."
(2) "Ten to one *but* he comes."

[1] See Par 236, note.

This last sentence is a confusion of "I lay ten to one *that* he comes" and "I'll pay you ten to one *if* he does *not* come," *i.e.* "*except* or *but* he comes":—

(3) "Beshrew my soul *but* I do love," &c., *i.e.* "if I do not love;" compare our "I'll be hanged *but*" &c.

"**But that**" is to be explained as "except because":—

(1) "*But that* he has a family, he would have left England long ago."

Just as "as" (Par. 205) is used for the Relative Pronoun "that," so "but" is used for "that not":—

(2) "There is no one *but* hates me," *i.e.* "*that* hates me *not*."

"**But**" ("except," "unless," "if not"), used without a Verb, generally in connection with some Preposition, *e.g.* "but for," "but to," &c., may be explained either as a Preposition governing an Adverbial phrase, or as a Conjunction with the Verb omitted:—

(1) "*But* for you, we should have failed," *i.e.* "*if* it had *not* been (otherwise) for (because of) you, we should have failed."

(2) "To whom can he be referring *but* (*i.e. if* he is *not* referring) to his brother?"

470 "Without" is sometimes used for "unless":—

(1) "He will not come *without* he's compelled."

But this is not to be imitated.

471 "Save" seems originally to have been used as a Passive Participle, like "except," "provided," &c., with a Noun used as a Subject absolutely.[1] But now (like "except") it is used as a Preposition, and is followed by an Object.

Concessional Clauses.

472 A Concessional Clause is sometimes expressed by the old Subjunctive used interrogatively (Par. 463) without any Conjunction:—

(1) "*Be* it a trifle, it should be well done."
(2) "Which refuseth to hear the voice of the charmer, *charm* he never so wisely,"

i.e. "(though) he (should) charm so wisely (as) never (he charmed before)."

(3) "He will never equal his brother in singing, *sing* he ever so well."

473 The last Example, which is the modern idiom, appears to have arisen from a misunderstanding of the old negative. We say, colloquially, "He was *ever* so ill;" but the correct (though old-fashioned)

---

[1] "All the conspirators *save* only he."—*Julius Cæsar.*

idiom would be "He was *never* (before) so ill (as then)," or "he was so ill as (he was) never before":[1]—

(4) "*Were* you a millionaire, you could not afford such expense as this."

(5) "*Come* who may, I am not afraid," *i.e.*, "(though there may) come who(soever) may (come)."

474 Here the Antecedent "understood" is the Subject of "come;" but sometimes the Subject of the Verb is omitted, as in the following :—

(6) "*Do* (I) what I may, I cannot persuade him of my innocence."

(7) "*Say* (you) what you will, you will fail."

In such sentences as the last it is not easy to tell whether the Verb is Subjunctive or, as in Par. 462, Imperative.

"However," as a Co-ordinate Conjunction, is a contraction of "however it be," sometimes found in the form "how-be." Compare "howbeit," "albeit."

475 "For all that," in the Antecedent part of a sentence, naturally acquires the meaning of "although," when there is a negative in the Consequent. The transition can easily be traced :—

(1) "He will not change his mind *for* (*i.e.*, because of, to oblige) you."

(2) "He will not change his mind *for all* your efforts, or, *for all* that you can do."

[1] The full idiom is found in Layamon, vol. iii. page 4, where it is said that soldiers assembled, "swa muchel swa þer nevere ærer,," *i.e.* "so many as *never* before."

In the last Example "that" is a Relative Pronoun, having for its Antecedent "all;" but it is an easy transition (the "all" being irregularly retained for emphasis) to the use of "for all that" as a Conjunction, where "that" is Conjunctional (as in "after that," "before that;" see Par. 444: and compare the change of "not but *what*" into a Conjunction; Par. 451) :—

(3) "He will not change his mind *for all that you tried* so hard to persuade him."

476 This emphatic use of "all" in Concession Clauses may be illustrated by its use in "although," *i.e.* "all-though," which is sometimes written "though-all" in Early English. Compare also "al(l) be it," *i.e.* "(though) *it be all*, *i.e.* altogether true that." In Early English we sometimes find "all-if" used like "all-though."

477 "Notwithstanding" is rarely used as a Conjunction :—

(1) "*Notwithstanding* (that) he is so rich, he is excluded from respectable society."

This Conjunction is, by derivation, a Participle used absolutely with a Subject sentence: "The fact that he is so rich *not withstanding*, *i.e.* being no obstacle, he is still excluded," &c.

Result ; Purpose.

478 A result following an action is naturally expressed by stating that "the action was done *so* (*i.e.* in such a way) *that* (in which way) the result followed." Hence "that" and "as" (both of which mean "in which way") are Conjunctions naturally used to introduce sentences expressing result.

"**That**" was once used for "so that," and is found so used in Shakespeare :—

(1) " A sheet of paper
Writ on both sides the leaf, margent and all,
(So) *That* he was fain to seal on Cupid's name."

This irregularity (of which (I) "brevity" is a sufficient explanation) was common in Early English, and might perhaps explain—

(2) "He never sees me *that* he doesn't mock me."

But "that" here is more probably "when." See Par. 455.

479 "As" is used after "so," to denote, not exactly resultant *facts*, but results regarded as *possible* or *future*; hence "as" is used before Infinitives :—

(1) "He was so kind *as* to promise."

This is nearly the same as " he was so kind that he promised," but not quite so strong.[1]

---

[1] Compare the use of ὥστε with the Infinitive to denote *possible consequence*, and with the Indicative to denote *fact*. See Par. 204.

480 In Elizabethan English "as" is used, where we use "that," before an Indicative :—

> (2) "Thou hast given the house of York such head *as* thou shalt reign but by their sufferance."
> (3) "Such signs of rage they bear *as* it seemed they would debate with angry swords."
> (4) "If a man have that penetration of judgment *as* he can discern what things are to be laid open."

This use of "as" is now a vulgarism.

481 "So that" (= "in that way, in which way") naturally expresses purpose with the Mood of Purpose :—

> (1) "Work *so* (in that way) *that* (in which way) you may earn your bread."

482 "Lest" is a contraction for "by which the *least* or *less*" (compare the Latin "quominus"). "Be careful *lest* you may make a mistake, *i.e. by which* (care) you may *the less* (probably) make a mistake."

Clauses of Comparison.

483 "As" is a contraction of "all-so," "alse," and means sometimes "in which way," sometimes (like "so") "in that way." Consequently "as" is, by derivation, an emphatic form of "so." Hence the words are sometimes very similarly used :—

> (1) "He is not *so* clever as you."
> (2) "He is *as* clever as you."

The reason for altering "so" into "as" (except after negatives) is, perhaps, that the notion of *similarity* favours the repetition of the *same* word. But the "not," introducing the notion of *dissimilarity*, favours the retention of the old *dissimilar* forms.

Sometimes both forms are retained :—

(1) " *So*, or *as*, far as I know."

484 Any Relative Adverb (compare Latin "quum... tum," "qua...qua," and the use of "what with... what with," Par. 442) may naturally be used with its correlative to express "both...and." Hence the following idiom :—

(1) "*As* (*in the way in which*) he was first in the field, *so* (*in that way*) was he preeminent in the council-hall."

485 "As" (Par. 205), being often used to express Relative Adverbs, came sometimes to be used for the Relative Pronoun :—

(1) "Tears such *as* (*i.e.*, which) angels weep."

(Shakespeare uses "which"[1] and "that" thus, after "such") :—

(2) "He is the same *as* or *that* he always was."
(3) "Bring such books *as* you have."

486 "As," in a Conditional Sentence, often has a Consequent implied after it :—

(1) "He looks *as* (he would have looked) if he had seen a ghost."

Even Pope has :—
"Let *such* teach others *who* themselves excel."

T

The "if" was sometimes omitted, the Condition being expressed by the old Subjunctive; and this omission is still sometimes found in modern poetry, *e.g.* in Byron's :—

(2) "And half I felt *as* (*if*) they were come
To tear me from a second home."

"*As*" = "in the character of:" see Par. 446.

487 "As" is used with "yet," to remind the hearer that the statement *is limited* to a certain time, and does not extend beyond it. Compare—

(1) {"I have never been beaten *yet*."
"I have never been beaten *as yet*," *i.e.*, "*so far as concerns* past time, but not the future."

This use of the word was common in Early English with dates :—

(2) "He died *as* in twelve hundred year and eight *and no more*."

Here the "as" and "no more" seem to have the same force, viz. that of *limitation*. Compare—

(3) "He wished to chastise him discreetly *as* (*i.e.*, so far as he could, only) by word and not by deed."

(4) "You must be very secret *as* in this case," *i.e.*, "so far as concerns this case."

In the last Example and many others, "as" is equivalent to our "just." Compare—

(5) "Though in mysterious terms judg'd, *as* then, best," (MILTON) *i.e*, "just then," "at that precise time."

488   There seems to be a different use of "as," still current in some parts of England, *e.g.*, Derbyshire, where the word implies that a time mentioned is not vouched as accurate by the speaker, but is merely mentioned by another :—

>   (6) "He says he will come *as* to-morrow."

489   "As" is generally used in the sense of *limitation* before "for" and "to" :—

>   (7) "*As to* your affairs, you must decide ; but *as for* myself, I shall remain neutral."

490   "The" is not the ordinary Adjective, but a form of the Demonstrative and Relative Pronoun, meaning "by how much," "by so much," in—

>   (1) "*The* sooner he comes, *the* better it will be," *i.e.*, "*by how much* the sooner he comes, *by so much* the better it will be."

"The" is to be parsed in the same way in "*the* more," "*the* less," &c.   See Pars. 344, 571.

491   "More than," from its ordinary use in "more than man," came to be used as part of a Compound Verb in—

>   (1) "He *more-than-hesitated*, he refused."

Beware of supposing that you can supply a Verb before "more than," *e.g.* "He refused more than hesitated ;" that is not the meaning here : the meaning is "He did *something-more-than-hesitate.*" In the same way, "more than" is part of a Compound Adjective in—

>   (2) "This is *more than ridiculous*, it is immoral."

T 2

Compare Byron's use of "less than woman" as a Compound Noun in—

(3) "Go! let thy *less-than-woman's* hand assume the distaff."[1]

492 "Than," when followed by a Noun or Pronoun, requires care; for, as the sentence following "than" is generally abridged, it is impossible to tell whether the Noun or Pronoun is Subject or Object, till we have supplied the implied Verb or Preposition:—

(1) "I like you better *than* (I like) Thomas," Object.
(2) "I like you better *than* Thomas (likes you)," Subject.
(3) "There is no one respects you more *than* { Thomas (*respects you*)," Subject. (*he respects*) Thomas," Object.

493 "Than," meaning "in which degree," "whereas," may loosely be used like "whereas," and join together two sentences in which the *principal Verb is not the same*, e.g. "Whereas John *has given* good counsel, there *is* no counsel better;" i.e.—

(1) "There *is* no counsel better *than* John *has given*."[2]

It would seem easy to explain the above Example (and many others of the same kind) by supposing the Relative Pronoun "that" to have dropped out

---
[1] Mätzner, iii. 410.
[2] See Layamon, iii. 275 for a precisely similar example.

after "than," *i.e.* "than (is the counsel that) John has given;" but the use of "than" without the Relative Pronoun in Early English is so common that this easy explanation does not seem to be correct. Compare :—

> (2) "This is as fine a horse *as* I have ever seen," *i.e.* "*As* (in what degree, whereas I have ever seen (a fine horse), this is as fine a horse."

After "than" the Conjunction "that" is sometimes omitted, perhaps for euphony as well as for brevity :—

> (3) "Rather *than* (that) he should be punished I would make any sacrifice."

"Other," conveying a notion of comparison, is followed by "than" :—

> (1) "This boy is no *other than* my long-lost son."

But here it is difficult to supply the Verb omitted after "than." It seems as though it would logically be "*Whereas* my long-lost son (is of a certain nature) John is no *other, i.e.* in no way different." But more probably the sentence is formed by Confusion, on the analogy of "no taller *than*, shorter *than*, &c. ;" "other" being felt, *by its termination, to have a comparative force.*

"Than" in this phrase (and sometimes in others)

has occasionally assumed the force of a Preposition, *e.g.* in Shakespeare :—

(2) "Elect no other king *than him*."
(3) "And lin'd with giants deadlier *than 'em* all."—
POPE.

Hence sometimes "other *but*" or "other *from*" is used for "other *than*." "Who *else than*," though supported by Byron's authority, (and though "else" is, by derivation, an Adverb meaning "otherwise,") is scarcely to be imitated; it is more customary to say "who *else but*."

Adjective Clauses : Relative Pronouns.

497 The use of "the...that," with a Superlative between them, seems to require explanation. Compare—

(1) "He is *the* old man *that* I saw yesterday."
(2) "He is *the oldest* man *that* I know."

In (1) the Antecedent of "that" is "old man," and you can substitute "old man" for "that" thus : "He is the old man which old man I saw yesterday." But substitute similarly in (2), and what is the result? "He is the oldest man which oldest man I know." This is at once felt not to be the meaning : the meaning is "He is the oldest man *of the men that* I know."

How then account for (2)? The explanation appears to be as follows : It was usual (and logical) to say (a) "He is the oldest man in England *among my friends, acquaintances*, &c." But "a man among my acquaintances" is the same thing as "a man that I know." Hence came (b) "He is the oldest *man-that-I-know*." But "man that I know" is a sort of Compound Noun, and the Antecedent of "that" is not "oldest man" but "man."

An Antecedent is rarely implied in a Possessive Adjective :—

"*Theirs* is the fault, *who* began the quarrel."

But this is common in Shakespeare : see *Shakespearian Grammar*, Par. 218.

498 " But " when used for the Relative and "not," is generally Subject. It is rare to find :—

"Who ne'er knew joy *but* friendship might divide."—
POPE.

499 "That" is (rarely) used for "for which," "why," in—

(1) "This is the reason *that* I sent for you (for)."

In early English the different uses of "that" were more numerous ; the word represented (2) "where ;" (3) "when ;" (4) "with which : "—

(2) "In the place *that* they were."
(3) "At the first sight *that* (*i.e.* when) men see the souldan."
(4) "With the loudest voice *that* (*i.e.* with which) they could."

500 "That" in "It is you that... :" see Par. 159. From the Relative use of "that" in "It is you that," we must distinguish the Conjunctive use in—

> (1) "It was then *that* the Danes first came to England."

Here the words "that the Danes...England" are equivalent to "The Danes' invasion of England;" "it" is redundant (see Par. 162), and the sentence is "The Danes' invasion was, *i.e.* took place, then."

But "that" seems not a Conjunction but a Relative Pronoun in—

> (1) "It was of you *that* I spoke."

This is the same as—

> (2) "It was you *that* I spoke of, or mentioned," where "that" is clearly Relative.

Hence it would seem that "It was of you that I spoke" is a transposition of "It that I spoke of was you." On the other hand, in "It was owing to you *that* I failed," the meaning is "My failure was owing to you," and "that" would appear to be a Conjunction.

CHAPTER II.

POETICAL CONSTRUCTIONS.

501 The object of ordinary Prose is to give information, but the object of Poetry is to give pleasure.

Hence Poetry is (1) archaic; (2) irregular; (3) terse.

I. Poetry is archaic, because pleasing associations are often connected with many old-fashioned words and forms that may have fallen into disuse in Prose, as not being the fittest to give information.

II. Poetry is irregular, because it is more "passionate"[1] than Prose. Hence it readily breaks the rules that bind Prose, wherever these rules hamper the expression of passion.

III. Poetry, disliking lengthiness, abridges *grammatical* constructions (though it expands, and dwells on, ornament, *e.g.* preferring the expanded form of the Simile to the compressed form of the Metaphor).

Pope speaks of:
"Prose swell'd to verse; verse *loit'ring into prose.*"

[1] Poetry, according to Milton, ought to be "simple," "sensuous,' *i.e.* appealing to the senses, "and passionate."

The reader should commit to memory the following description of the Thames (as it was) by Denham, a model of terse yet varied clearness, repeatedly imitated by Pope :—

"Though deep, yet clear ; though gentle, yet not dull ;
Strong without rage, without o'er-flowing full."

I. Poetical Archaisms.

502 Archaisms may be (1) of *words;* (2) of *constructions*.

Archaic *words* are such as "hallowed," "sojourn," "woe," "ire," "wrath," "a-weary," "ken," &c. "Thou" for "you" Singular, and "ye" for "you" Plural, are also archaic.

503 Instances of Archaic *Construction* are—

(1) "Meseems," "methinks," *i.e.* "it seems, thinks,[r] to me."

504 The use of the Subjunctive to express a wish :—

(1) "*Perish* the man whose heart is backward now."
(2) "Ruin *seize* thee, ruthless king."
(3) "To White's a bull *be* led."
(4) "'And *rest we* here' Matilda said."—Scott.

505 The use of the Subjunctive to express a Conditional Antecedent, and of other old Conditional forms :—

(1) "His spear, to equal which the tallest pine *Were* but a wand."—*Paradise Lost*, i. 294.
(2) "Else I often *had* (should have) been miserable."

[r] "To think" once meant "to seem :" see Par. 328.

(3) "I am content, *so* (*i.e.* "so that," "provided that," Par. 460) thou wilt have it so."
(4) "And into strange vagaries flew, "*As* (if) they would dance."—*Ib.* vi. 615.

506 More rarely the Subjunctive is used with Conjunctions of *time* :—

(5) "*Ere* thou *go.*"
(6) "Ridotta sips and dances till she *see.*"—POPE.

507 The old Interrogative (without "do") is used for the modern lengthy form. This is both archaic and terse:—

"Gives not the hawthorn-bush a sweeter shade?"
"Breathes there a man with soul so dead?"

508 "Him," "them," are used for "himself," "themselves." This again is terse as well as archaic :—

"The poor contents *him* with the care of heaven."—
POPE.

509 The old use of the Interrogative, or semi-Interrogative Pronoun, where the moderns use the Relative and Antecedent :—

"*Who* builds a church to God, and not to fame
Will never mark the marble with his name."—
POPE.

This use, being (III) terse, is a favourite use with Pope (though his style is by no means archaic) and is extended to sentences that cannot be resolved into question and answer. In Pope it is perhaps an imitation of Latin usage :—

> "To help *who* want, to forward *who* excel."
> "In *who* (*i.e.* those that) obtain defence, or *who* defend."

510 The Relative, in Milton, often precedes the Antecedent, according to Latin usage :—

> "*Whom* they hit, none on their feet might stand."—
> *Paradise Lost*, vi. 592.

511 The old demonstrative use of "he" combines archaism and "sensuousness," *i.e.* picturesqueness, in—

> "*He of Tusculum*" for Cicero ; "*He of Marengo's field*" for Napoleon I., &c.

"The demonstrative character of this Pronoun is seen in such expressions as '*He* of the bottomless pit.'"—MORRIS.

512 "Or" is used for "either":—

> "But they *or* underground, or circuit wide
> With serpent error wandering."—
> *Paradise Lost*, vii. 301.

II. Poetical Irregularities.

513 The Subject is sometimes put first, because it is uppermost in the Poet's mind ; then, after a pause, a Pronoun is introduced, as the legitimate subject of the Verb. It is as though the Poet were half in doubt whether to speak *of* a thing as *Subject*, or *to* it *Vocatively* :—

(1) "*The Pope he* was saying the high, high mass."—
SCOTT.

(2) "*The smith*, a mighty man is he."

514 The Verb is sometimes (*a*) placed after the Object, sometimes (*b*) before the Subject. The arrangement is subordinated to emphasis. In the following Example the Subject "stalk" seems to gain emphasis from its position, and so does the Verb "breathes" :—

(1) "So from the root
Springs (*b*) lighter the green *stalk*, from thence the leaves
More aery; last, the bright consummate flower
Spirits odorous (*a*) *breathes*."—
Paradise Lost, v. 480.

The Object is sometimes placed before the Verb, and the Subject after the Verb, the whole sentence being reversed :—

(1) "*Such resting found the sole*
Of unblest feet. *Him followed* his next *Mate*."—
Ib. i. 238.

515 The Epithet is often placed after the Noun. Indeed, great license is assumed by Poetry as to the position of the Epithet; for this reason, that the Epithet is used as a substitute for Participles, Verbs, Conjunctions, &c. (see Par. 525), so that it has a larger and more varied use than in Prose :—

 (1) "They ended parle, and both addressed for fight *Unspeakable.*"—*Ib.* vi. 297.

 (2) "A stream of nectarous humour issuing flowed *Sanguine.*"—*Ib.* vi. 333.

 (3) "Nor from the Holy One of Heav'n Refrained his tongue *blasphémous.*"—*Ib.* vi. 360

Even a Noun in Apposition may be placed before the Noun with which it is in Apposition :—

 (1) "*Two broad suns*, their shields Blazed opposite."—*Ib.* vi. 305.

 (2) "*All heart* they live, all head, all eye, all ear."— *Ib.* vi. 350.

516   The irregularities of Poetry, though very numerous and manifold, can generally be readily explained by reference to the meaning, which ought to be rather made more clear than less clear by the irregularity. The following is a good instance of "passionate" irregularity. Satan is speaking, under the influence of strong "passion," pouring forth "words interwove with sighs," and, though his meaning is clear, his sentence cannot be grammatically analysed :—

 "Thrice he assayed, and thrice, in spite of scorn,
 Tears such as Angels weep burst forth : at last
 Words interwove with sighs found out their way.
 'O Myriads of immortal Spirits, O Powers

> Matchless, but with th' Almighty—and that strife
> Was not inglorious, though th' event was dire,
> As this place testifies, and this dire change
> Hateful to utter: but,' " &c.—*Ib.* i. 622.

Here the speaker is led away by "passion" into a Parenthesis, which prevents him from continuing the address he had begun to the "immortal Spirits."

Many of the Irregularities of Poetry will find their place under head III., "terseness;" see Pars. 517—532.

517   III. Poetical Abridgments.

Poetry chooses short forms of words, *e.g.* "questionless" for "unquestionably;" "altern," "marge," "scarce," "vale," for "alternately," "margin," &c.

518 The Verb "is," or "was," is sometimes omitted:—

(1) "Dagon (*was*) his name." "Cruel (*was*) his eye."

519 Sometimes the Subjunctive "be" is omitted:—

(1) "Woe (*be*) to the man." "Peace (*be*) to his bones"

520 The Relative Pronoun is omitted, even when it would be the *Subject*, if it had been expressed:—

(1) "'Tis distance (*that*) lends enchantment to the view."

(2) "What is this (*that*) absorbs me quite,
   Steals my senses, shuts my sight?"

521 The Conjunction "that" is used for "so that":—

> "With high woods the hills were crowned
> With borders long the rivers: (so) *that* earth now
> Seem'd like to heav'n."—*Paradise Lost*, vii. 329.

522 The Adjective is used for the Adverb, partly to avoid the lengthy Adverbial form, partly because Poetry dwells rather on *distinguishing marks* than on *methods*, and therefore prefers *Adjectives* to *Adverbs*:—

> (1) "While the billow *mournful* rolls."
> (2) "My wedding bell rings *merry* in my ear."
> (3) "Hope springs *eternal* in the human breast."
> (4) "Less *winning* soft, less amiably mild."

In the last Example certainly, and probably in the others, the Adjectives should be parsed not as Adjectives, but as Adverbs. In Old English it was common to form an Adverb by adding *-e* to the Adjective, *e.g.* "bright," Adjective; "brighte, Adverb." See Par. 413.

523 "The" is often omitted before an epithet, the epithet being treated as part of the name:—

> (1) "See *god-like Turenne* prostrate on the dust."
> (2) "On such a stool *immortal Alfred* sat."

Also before names of rivers, which, in Poetry, are often *personified*:—

> (3) "Firm reedy Simois:" "The flies and gnats of Nile."

524 " Neither " is omitted preceding " nor " :—
  (1) "Helm nor hauberk's twisted mail."
  (2) "Sigh, nor word, nor struggling breath."

525 Poetry dispenses, as far as possible, with dependent[1] Conjunctional sentences and Relative Pronouns, avoiding them by means of (*a*) Apposition, (*b*) Adjectives and Participles, (*c*) Parentheses, or co-ordinate sentences :—

  (*a*) "Next Chemos (who was) *th' obscene dread* of Moab's sons."—*Paradise Lost*, i. 406.
  (*a*)   "The fiend,
  Mere serpent in appearance, . . where he might find
  The whole included race, his *purposed prey*."
        Ib. viii. 416.
  (*a*) "(He) each perturbation smooth'd with outward calm
  Artificer (*i.e.*, since he was an *a*.) of fraud."
        Ib. iv. 121.

526 (*b*) "See that your *polish'd* arms be primed with care," that is, "be polished *and* primed."
        COWPER.
  (*b*) "Lely on *animated* canvas stole
  The sleepy eye which spoke the melting soul."
        POPE

That is, "the canvas *that* assumed animation under his pencil."

  (*b*) "And reck'nest thou thyself with spirits of Heav'n,
  Hell-doom'd ?"—*Paradise Lost*, ii. 167.

That is, "*whereas*, or *though*, thou art hell-doomed."

---

[1] This is in accordance with Milton's dictum that Poetry must be "simple."

(b) "(while) *Alive*, ridiculous; and (when) *dead*, forgot(ten)."—POPE.

527 (c) "Hell
Grew darker at their frown, *so matched they stood.*"—*Paradise Lost*, ii. 719.

(c) "Eve separate he spies,
Veil'd in a cloud of fragrance where she stood,
*Half-spied—so thick the roses blushing round
About her glowed.*"—*Ib.* ix. 426.

That is, "*or rather* only half spied, *because* the roses," &c.

(c) "Down he fell . . .
Reluctant, but in vain . . . . *a greater power
Now ruled him.*"—*Ib.* ix. 576.

528 Hence Poetry prefers the Participle Absolute to a Conjunctional sentence, and occasionally even places the Participle before its Noun :—

"An Iris sits . . . . and, *unworn
Its steady dyes*, while all around is torn
By the distracted waters, bears severe
Its brilliant hues."—*Childe Harold.*

529 The *Epithet* is substituted for the thing denoted. Thus Milton uses "the dank" for "water;" "the dry" for "land." This is both terse and "sensuous" :—

(1) "Below the chestnuts, when their buds
Were glistening to the breezy *blue.*"
                                TENNYSON.

(2) "Neither *keen*
Nor *solid* might resist that edge."
                        Paradise Lost, vi. 323.

530 The principal Verb is omitted, and the question is expressed by the Infinitive (possibly an old form; Par. 398) :—

> (1) " Why longer dwell on horrors ? "   " Why still delay ? "

The desire to be terse produces countless irregularities in Poetry, even in a polished and fastidious Poet such as Pope. His meaning is transparent, but his grammar is (pardonably) most irregular :—

> (1) "O'er the pale marble shall they join their heads
> And drink the falling tears *each other* sheds."
> POPE.
>
> (2) "Though there's a difference in each other's loving."—*Hamlet*, First Quarto.

531 We are accustomed, in Prose, to the condensed expression (see Par. 223)—" they loved *each other;* " but this is a condensation of " and drink the falling tears—*each* (shall drink the tears that the) other sheds." Practically, no doubt Pope regards " each other " as a Compound Pronoun.

> (3) "Who has the vanity to call you friend
> But wants the honour, *injur'd*, to defend."—*Ib.*

That is, "to defend *you* when you are injured."

> (4) "Who first taught souls enslav'd, and realms undone,
> Th' enormous *faith of many made for one ?* "—*Ib.*

That is, "the abnormal belief that the governed are made for the governor."

(5) "And on the washy ooze (the waters) deep channels wore;
Easy (*i.e.*, an easy task), ere God had bid the ground be dry."—*Paradise Lost*, vii. 304.

(6) " 'Gainst Pallas, Mars; (*'gainst*) Latona, Hermes arms."—POPE.

532 Terseness is aided by the license of making (*a*) Verbs out of Nouns, (*b*) Transitive Verbs out of Intransitive :—

(*a*) "And as they please
They *Limb* themselves."—*P.L.* vi. 352.
That is, "endow themselves with limbs."

(*a*) "Hell saw
Heav'n *ruining* from Heaven."—*Ib.* vi. 868.
"Part, huge of bulk,
Wallowing unwieldy, enormous in their gait,
Tempest the ocean."—*Ib.* vii. 412.

(*b*) "The terms we sent were terms of weight
And *stumbled* many."—*Ib.* vi. 624.

(*b*) "*That be assured*," *i.e.*, "know that for certain."
Ib. ii. 685.

APPENDIX I.

ON THE GROWTH OF THE ENGLISH LANGUAGE.

Chronological Summary.

533 A.D. 450—547. The English language was brought into Britain. It adopted a very few Celtic terms, and one or two Roman local names.

A.D. 596. Christianity was introduced, and with it several Latin ecclesiastical terms.

A.D. 878. Cession of Northumbria, East Anglia, &c., to the Danes, and—

534 A.D. 1017—'42. A Danish dynasty reigns in England. Hence the introduction of several Scandinavian terms and a general unsettling of Inflections in the Northern Dialect.[1] Hence (in part at least)—

A.D. 1100. The "Period of Confusion" begins, first affecting the *orthography* of Inflections, and afterwards *dispensing with* the Inflections.

---

[1] It has been asserted that, even in parts of the North where no traces of Danish influence can be suspected, the inflections were becoming unsettled. But there is difficulty in proving the *absence* of Danish influence.

535 A.D. —.[1] The Norman Conquest introduced, *in course of time*, some terms belonging to the church, chivalry, the law, the chase, and cookery. Norman-French was established as the language to be used in the law-courts and the records of state. For some time the nobility retained French as their language, and hence the English was little influenced by the French; but, by degrees, the coalition between the nobles and commons in King John's time, the loss of Normandy in the same reign A.D. 1204, and the French wars of Edward III. A.D. 1339, brought about a degradation of the French from "French of Paris" to the French after the school of "Stratford atte Bowe" (Chaucer, *Prologue*, l. 125), and, still lower, to the French "of the ferthest ende of Norfolke" (*Piers the Plowman*, Passus v. 238, Ed. Skeat). By degrees, French was not only debased but disused. Hence, not to conciliate the lower class, but to suit the higher—

536 A.D. 1362. An Act of Parliament directed that all pleadings in the law courts should be conducted in English and not French, inasmuch as French had become "much unknown in the realm."

Naturally, when the higher classes adopted English as their native tongue, there came at once an influx of Norman-French words, and an increased degradation of the English Inflections.

[1] The date is purposely omitted lest the reader should be led to suppose that any sudden change took place in A.D. 1066. The Norman Conquest *was very slow in its results on English.*

537 A.D. 1500. The revival of the study of Latin Literature introduced a vast number of Latin words direct from the Latin. The English Inflections were now lost, but the *sense of Inflections*, and the consequent license, remained.

538 A.D. 1600. A reaction set in against the excessive Latinisms and licenses of the sixteenth century. This reaction was aided by—

539 A.D. 1660. The Restoration, which brought French influence to bear on the language, partly in words, but more by favouring a lighter structure of sentences, and increased regularity in grammatical construction.

540 A.D. 1800. The study of chemistry, geology, zoology, &c., has introduced a vast number of scientific terms, mostly compounded from the Greek.

The Vocabulary.

541 Celtic.—The Celtic words introduced into our language directly are very few. They mostly relate to (1) coarse dress and rough household work or agriculture ; (2) to wild scenery :—

> (1) Breeches, darn, clout, mop, pillow, cradle, crock, mattock, kiln, basket.
> (2) Crag, glen, pool.

542 The Norman-French introduced some of these words borrowed from the old Gallic ; most of these are of Class (1), but some relate to (3) petty trade:—

(1) Bonnet, bucket, button, chemise, mitten, gown, ribbon, bag, basin, barrel, pot, varlet, vassal, rogue, car, cart, gravel, marl, bran.

(3) Bargain, barter.

543 Danish.—Several words in common use, *e.g.* "scold," "shy," "sly," "fellow," "cake," "call," "cast," are of Scandinavian origin; as also is *-by* in "Der*by*," "Apple*by*," &c., meaning "town." "Are," the 3rd Pers. Plur. Pres. of "be" is also Danish.

544 French.—French words came into the language in small numbers until the thirteenth and fourteenth centuries; then they were plentifully introduced, *e.g.* in Chaucer's time. The earlier importations were mostly terms of war, religion, and literature. But in the fourteenth century there was an influx of the technical terms of law, art, commerce, medicine, astrology, and the other sciences; and these technical terms (compare the history of Latin technical terms, such as "influence," "triumph") when incorporated in the language often assumed metaphorical and wider meanings.[1]

545 Latin (First Period), A.D. 43—426.—From the Roman occupation we have borrowed *-cester* ("camp"),

---

[1] See *English Lessons for English People*, Paragraph 37, page 51.

e.g. in "Glou-*cester,*" "*Chester,*" "Dor-*chester,*" &c.; also the words "street" and "wall"[1] (*vallum*).

546 (Second Period), A.D. 596—1200.—The introduction of Christianity introduced (*a*) a number of religious technical terms, *e.g.* " preach"[2] (*prædicare*), "mass" (*missa*), &c., together with a few names of (*b*) food, *e.g.* " butter ;" (*c*) trees, *e.g.* " fig ;" (*d*) animals, *e.g.* " camel ;" (*e*) weights and measures, *e.g.* " pound," " ounce," " inch."

547 (Third Period), A.D. 1200—1400. — Indirectly through the French ; see above.

French words were not *freely* admitted into the language till the upper classes began to adopt English as their native tongue, *i.e.* till A.D. 1300—1350. In the earlier text of Layamon's " Brut" (A.D. 1205) there are only about 112 Norman-French words throughout the whole of the poem. See the lists of Norman-French words in Morris's *Historical Outlines*.

548 (Fourth Period), A.D. 1500—1660.—Direct importation of Latin words, through the revival of the study of Latin Literature. Many of these words have changed their meaning, either (1) *narrowing* their meaning (*e.g.* " extravagant " no longer means " wandering outside,"[3] but simply " wandering beyond the due bounds of expense "), or (2) *extending*

---

[1] I have Mr. Skeat's authority for inserting this word, as probably borrowed from the Latin; cf. Welsh *gwal*, "a rampart."
[2] " Preach" has come to us through the French; but it is also found in A.-S. " predician "—both from the Latin " predicare."
[3] "The *extravagant* and erring spirit."—*Shakespeare*.

their meaning (*e.g.* "influence" no longer means "the power that *flowed* from the stars *on* to men," but "any modifying power"), from a narrow technicality to a broader and metaphorical meaning.

549 A few French "words of society" and military terms were introduced during the eighteenth century. Later introductions have been for the most part technical terms of philosophy and science, formed from the Greek.

Inflections.

550 Six Periods may be marked out in the growth of the English language : I. A.D. 450—1100 ; II. A.D. 1100—1250 ; III. A.D. 1250—1350 ; IV. A.D. 1350 —1500 ; V. A.D. 1500—1600 ; VI. A.D. 1600 to present time.

551 First or "**Synthetical Period,**" A.D. 450— 1100.—This may be called the "Inflectional or *Synthetical* Period;" for during this period the language shewed a power of *construction* (*syn*, con ; *thetical*, structional) so as to represent Tense, Person, Number, Gender, Case, &c , by Inflections. In particular, the distinction was carefully observed between—

To Love.

Noun Infinitive.	Gerund, or Infinitive of Purpose.	Active Participle.
lufi-an	(*to*) **lufi-anne**	**lufig-ende.**

552   But already, towards the end of this period, there seems to have arisen, partly perhaps owing to the influence of the Danish invaders, some confusion among the Inflections, and a tendency to simplify them by assimilation. See the extract from the Gospel of St. Mark in Par. 558.

It has been asserted (but see Par. 534, note) that, apart from Danish influence, there was a tendency (*a*) in the North to discard Inflections while retaining old forms; (*b*) in the South to cling to Inflections while freely modifying forms.

553   Second Period, or "Period of Confusion," A.D. 1100—1250.—This may be called the "Period of Confusion;" for during this period (perhaps partly in consequence of political confusion) the language began to assimilate forms by *confusing* sounds and Inflections. In particular, the vowel sounds of Inflections were assimilated so that *a*, *o*, and *u* frequently became indistinguishable by being all changed into *e*.[1]

---

[1] The same confusion of vowels and diphthongs is found in the Greek MS. of the New Testament.

554 The following changes are some of those mentioned as occurring in this period by Dr. Morris (*Historical Outlines*, p. 52), to which the reader is referred for fuller information on this subject :—

1. Dative *him* used for Accusative.
2. The *n* in *min, thin,* dropped before Consonants, but retained in the Plural and Oblique Cases.
3. The Infinitive (even in the South) often drops final *-n. To* is sometimes used before ordinary, as well as before Gerundial Infinitives.
4. The Gerundial or Dative Infinitive often ends in *-en* or *-e* (the ordinary Infinitive ending) instead of *-enne* (*-anne*).
5. The Present Participle (Southern) ends in *-inde* (instead of *-ende*), and is frequently used for the Gerundial Infinitive, *e.g.* "to swiminde" used for "to swimene." The Participle Passive often drops *-n*.
6. Nominative Plural Inflections in *a* or *u*, and Dative Plurals in *-um*, were supplanted by *-e* or *-en*. Genders began to be confused.
7. *Shall* and *will* began to be used as Future Auxiliaries.

555 A specimen of the tendency to drop Inflections is given in the two following extracts from the earlier and later texts of Layamon, the earlier written about A.D. 1200, the later about A.D. 1250 :—

1. Early	...	"Up	heo	duden	heora	castles	gaten."
2. Later	...	"Up	hii	dude	hire	castles	geate."
3. Modern	...	"Up	they	did	their	castle's	gates."

Note also the approximation to modern usage in the dropping of the *o* in "heo," "heora." A similar approximation may be noted in the following Example (in which observe "alse," the later form of "al-swa") :—

1. Early ... "And ferden ut *swa* stille *swa heo* stelen wolden."
2. Later ... "And werde ut *so* stille *alse he* (?*hi*) stele wolde."
3. Modern... "And they marched out as still as (if) they would steal."

556 Third, or "Analytical Period," A.D. 1250—1350.—As the First Period was called *Synthetical*, so the Third may be called *Analytical*, the tendency being developed to *take the language as it were to pieces*, dropping Inflections and using existing words, *e.g.* Prepositions and Auxiliary Verbs, to replace them. The Present Participle in *-inge* appears about A.D. 1300, and the ordinary Infinitive takes " to " before it.

French words now became so common as to be estimated at 4 per cent. of the Vocabulary.

557 Fourth, or " National Period," A.L. 1350—1500.—This period witnessed the decay of the last refuge of many Inflections, viz. final *-e*. During the earlier part of the period, *-e* was used according to rule, and represented—

(1) The mark of (*a*) the Plural Adjective; (*b*) the Definite Adjective :—

(*a*) " smalë " fowles ; " (*b*) " the gretë see."

(2) The mark of the Adverb, *e.g.* " brightë " (brightly).

(3) The mark of the Infinitive, and of the Past Tense :— [1]

" Him thoughtë that his hertë woldë brekë." [2]

558 But, towards the end of this period, the use of final *-e* became uncertain. Also the Present

---

[1] It represented the Plural of Past Tense of Strong Verbs, the Singular and Plural of the Past Tense of Weak Verbs, also some Cases of Nouns, &c.

[2] Chaucer, quoted by Morris, *Historical Outlines of English Accidence*.

Participle in -*ing* (*inge*) had now become the usual form.

Before this period many Passive Participles of Strong Verbs dropped the final -*n;* and it is curious to observe that the anti-inflectional tendency reached lengths from which it has retrograded in modern English. Thus the -*n* or -*en* was dropped not only in *fought, bound, shrunk, sunk,* but also in *spoke, broke*—curtailed forms that are found even in Milton and Shakespeare, but are not accepted in modern English. Chaucer (who drops -*n* as a rule) even uses "be" for "been."

Note that we retain some of these old Participial forms as *Adjectives:* "a *molten* image;" "our *bounden* duty;" "a *foughten* field;" "a *drunken* man;" "a *sunken* ship."

It may be useful to compare the early part of this period, when English had been just recognized by royal edict as the language of the realm, with the language of the First or "Synthetical Period."[1]

---

[1] Mr. Skeat suggests the following alternative names for the six Periods. They may conveniently be set by the side of the names suggested above.

1. *Anglo-Saxon,* or *Oldest English.*   1. Inflectional.
2. *Late Anglo-Saxon.*   2. Period of "Confusion."
3. *Early English.*   3. Analytical.
4. *Middle English.*   4. National.
5. *Tudor English.*   5. Period of "License."
6. *Modern English.*   6. Modern English.

St. Mark i. 6, 7 ; 34.

WYCKLIFFE, A.D. 1380.	A.D. 1000.[1]	About A.D. 1150.
And John was clothid with heeris (a) of camelis, and a girdil of (a) skyn abowte his leendis; and he eet locustus, and hony of (a) the wode, and prechide, seyinge A strengere than I schal (c) come aftir me, of whom (b) I knelinge (d) am not worthi for to undo the thong of (a) his schoon.	And Iohannes wæs gescryd mid oluendes hær-um (a) & fellen (a) gyrdel wæs ymbe his lend-enu. & gærstapan & wudu (a) hunig he æt. & he bodude & cwæth. stiengra (c) cymth[2] æfter me thæs (b) ne eom ic wyrthe that ic his sceona (a) thwanga bugende (d) uncnytte.	And Iohannes wæs ge-scryd mid olfer.des hære, (a) & fellen (a) gyrdel waes embe his lendene & garstapen & wude (a) hunig he æt. & he bodede & cwæth. strengre (c) kymth æfter me. thas (b) ne æm ich wurthe that ic his scone (a) thwange bugende (d) un-cnette.
....	....	....
And he suffride hem nat for to (e) speke	& hi sprecan (e) ne let	& hyo sprecen (e) ne leten.

Here we find (a) the old cases in -*um*, -*en*, -*a*, dropped and replaced by Prepositions ; (b) the Interrogative "of whom" has supplanted the Possessive Case of the old Relative "thæs ; " (c) the Auxiliary "schal" has stepped in to form a Future ;

---

[1] The Gospel according to St. Mark in Anglo-Saxon and Northumbrian Versions. Edited by the Rev. Walter W. Skeat, Cambridge, 1871.
Of the A.D. 1150 Version, Mr. Skeat says, in his Preface, page x. "It is interesting as shewing how the language began to lose strength in its Inflectional forms, as is at once apparent by comparing it with the older text here printed beside it."

[2] Here, it is true, the original has the Present; but in v. 8, "he shall baptize you," the same difference is apparent.

(*d*) instead of the Present Participle in *-ende* (bugende), we have the form in *-inge* (kneelinge); notice also (*e*) the change from "sprec-*an*" to "spre*cen*," and thence to "*for to* speke."

560 As English was recognized as the language of the whole nation soon after the beginning of this period, and was so far settled that the *Vocabulary* (as distinct from the Orthography and Inflections) of Wyckliffe differs little (except in scantiness) from our own Vocabulary, we may call this period "the National Period." A glance at the three columns above will suffice to show the great difference between "the National Period" and "the Inflectional Period," in point of *Vocabulary*.

561 Fifth, or "**Period of License,**" A.D 1500— 1600.—Before the end of this period the use of *-e* (which fell into disuse or abuse soon after Chaucer's time) became quite forgotten. Indeed, there was in this period a tendency to carry the disuse of Inflections even to a greater degree than has been sanctioned by modern English, *e.g* "spoke"[1] for "spoken;" so "chose(n)," "rode" (for "ridden)," "drove," "took," &c. "To" as the sign of the Infinitive was used irregularly, "I saw him *to* walk," but "You ought not walk." This therefore (like Period II.) was to some extent a "Period of Confusion." In Shakespeare we find "I have *swam, spake, fell, droven, strucken, splitted, beated.*"

[1] The *n* had been dropped as early as the thirteenth century.

The -y that is historically an Adv.[1] prefix in "y-wis" (i.e. Germ. "gewiss," *certainly*) was, by misunderstanding, changed into "I" in "I wis." The "of" that is regularly and intelligibly used after a Verbal Noun, e.g. "the shepherd is a-blowing, i.e. (in-blowing) *of* his nails," was retained even when the Verbal had been completely confused with the Participle : "The shepherd is *blowing of* his nails."

562 The old power of forming Adverbs from Adjectives by adding -e (once sonant) was extended to the license of using any Adjective as an Adverb, and this even with Latin words, so that "honourable," "excellent," could be used as Adverbs. Even Latin Inflections (where they fell in with the Old English Inflections) were experimented upon, so that Shakespeare uses "deject" for "dejected," "infect" for "infected."

563 Generally it may be said that in this period the *Inflections had departed, but the sense of Inflections still remained,* causing many curious irregularities and licenses, and adding to the obscurity and to the vigour of the sixteenth-century English. Hence this may be called the "Period of License."

564 It may be added that this period witnessed (1)

---

[1] See Mr. Skeat's Index to *Piers the Plowman:* "*y-,* prefix; answering to G. and A.-S. *ge-,* which is etymologically the same as Lat. *con-, cum.:* usually pref. to Past Participles, but also to Past Tenses, Infinitives, and Adjectives." The word was commonly written "I wis" even in the fourteenth century. The "I" in "I wis" is the same prefix as the "a" in "aware."

x

a great influx of Latin words, (2) an introduction of the periodic structure, involving a freer use of Conjunctions and of the Subjunctive Mood.

565 Sixth Period, or "Period of Settlement," A.D. 1600 to the Present Time.—This was a period of reaction from the "Period of License." The use of "shall" and "will," variable toward the end of the "Period of License," was defined in the seventeenth century. Many old licenses (*e.g.* the use of "of" after (what are now) Participles) were discarded as vulgarisms, or as unjustifiable irregularities.[1] The periodic structure wa simplified by the easy vigour of Dryden and the incisive French style. Several

566 superfluous words of Latin importation were rejected. Many Elizabethan usages, theoretically accurate, had become practically inconvenient. For example, "so" being by derivation connected with "as" ("al-so," "alse," "als"), had been, in Elizabethan times, freely interchanged with "as;" "which" being the original co-relative to "such," had been used where we use "as," *e.g.* "such *which*" for "such *as;*" "as" retaining its original force of "in which way," had been used as the natural sequel to "so" ("so...*as*," where we use "so *that*") —all theoretically legitimate usages, and based on ancient derivations: but, as the derivations were

---

[1] Pope even discards the use of *mine* and *thine* before a vowel, preferring "my eye," "thy eye." In revising a Concordance to Pope, I have noticed *thine* twice, *mine* (as an Adjective before a Noun) never.

forgotten, and greater clearness was required to make up for the disuse of Inflections, it had become necessary that the province of each particle should be narrowed and defined; *e.g.* that " as " should no longer bear the burden of " that " so as to denote

567 consequence and purpose. Thus, in many respects the language of Pope is less ambiguous than that of Bacon or Shakespeare. But unfortunately, in sweeping away monopolies, the old distinction, generally observed by Shakespeare, between the Relative Pronouns " that " and " who," fell into oblivion; and, in the course of a reaction against the excessive use of " that," " who " was allowed unduly to encroach.[1] This is the most serious blot in Modern English.

568 More recently, the Inflections of the Participles (after a long-continued fluctuation) have been settled so as to prevent ambiguity, *e.g.* we have rejected the Participle " chose," " spoke," though sanctioned by Pope, and the Past Tenses " sung," " rung," though sanctioned by Milton.[2]

569 Some specimens of the Accidence of the First or

---

[1] *Who* introduces a new fact about the Antecedent: *that* completes the Antecedent. This is the general rule subject to a few exceptions arising from the desire of euphony. See *How to Write Clearly,* page 17.

Addison, in his *Humble Petition of Who and Which,* allows the petitioners to say, "We are descended of ancient families, and kept up our dignity and honour many years, till the Jack-sprat *That* supplanted us." But *That* was the legitimate sovereign and *Who* and *Which* were the *Jack-sprats.*

However, Pope, perhaps in consequence of Addison's mistake, often uses "who" for "that."

[2] The forms *sung, rung, in the Plural,* are sanctioned by the usage in Early English. See Morris's *Outlines,* page 159.

"Synthetical Period" are given below, to show the extremely complex nature of the language before it was simplified in the "Period of Confusion."

NOUNS.

Singular Number.

	Fem. (tongue)	Neut. (word)	Fem. (hand)	Masc. (son)	Masc. (shep-herd)
Nom.	tung-e	word	hand	sun-u	hird-e
Gen.	tung-an	word-es	hand-a	sun-a	hird-es
Dat.	tung-an	word-e	hand-a	sun-a	hird-e
Acc.	tung-an	word-e	hand	sun-u	hird-e

Plural.

Nom.	tung-an	word	hand-a	sun-a	hird-as
Gen.	tung-ena	word-a	hand-a	sun-a	hird-a
Dat.	tung-um	word-um	hand-um	sun-um	hird-um
Acc.	tung-an	word	hand a	sun-a	hird-as

Self.

In O.E., Pronouns were often used reflexively without "self," which merely added emphasis. "Self" was an Adjective meaning "same," so that "he killed *himself*" meant emphatically "He killed the *same* or the *above-mentioned him.*" Gradually this Adjective ceased to be inflected, and came to be regarded as a Noun. The following were the changes:—

(1) "I came *me* (Dat.) *silf-um* (Dat. Adj.)."
(2) "I came *me* (Dat.) *silf* (Nom. Adj.)."
(3) "I came *mi* (Gen.) *silf* (Indeclinable Adj. or Noun)."
(4) "I came myself."

Hence the modern "our *selves*," "his better *self*."

PRONOUNS.

SINGULAR.

	(I)	(Thou)	(He)	(She)	(It)
Nom.	Ic	thu [5]	he	heo [1]	hit
Gen.	min [2]	thin [2]	his [2]	hire [2]	his
Dat.	me	the	him [2]	hire [2]	him
Acc.	mec,[3] me	thec,[3] the	hine	hi	hit

PLURAL.

			hi
Nom.	we	ge	hi
Gen.	user, ûre [2]	eower [2]	hira (heora)
Dat.	ûs	eow	hem [4] (heom)
Acc.	ûsic,[3] ûs	eowic,[3] eow	hi

[1] **She** is an altered form of the Old Feminine Definite Adjective, **Seo,** or **sio.**

[2] Hence we see the origin of the Possessive Adjectives "mine (my)," "thine (thy)," "her," "our," &c. Also we see the Dative origin of "hi-m," "he-r."
Note also that **he, heo, hit** was really a Demonstrative Adjective. Cf. the Latin **is, ea, id. He** means "that man"; **heo** means "that woman."

[3] Chiefly Northumbrian forms. The substitution of *they* (= *thai, thâ*) for *hi* is due to Northumbrian influence.

[4] In the Elizabethan dramatists, and even in Pope, we often find *'em* printed with an Apostrophe, as though it were a contraction for *them.* But this is not so: it represents the Old English *hem.* See Dr. Morris's *Accidence,* Par. 160.

[5] *Thou* was discarded as being discourteous, and was replaced by *you.* See *Shakespearian Grammar,* Pars. 231—35.

570 To explain the modern forms "she," "that," "they," "them," we must have recourse to the old declinable Definite Adjective :—

DEFINITE ADJECTIVE, Modern "THE."				
	Singular.			Plural.
	Masc.	Fem.	Neut.	
Nom.	se	seo	thæ-t	thâ
Gen.	thæ-s	thæ-re	thæ-s	thâ-ra
Dat.	tha-m	thae-re	tha-m	thâ-m
Acc.	tha-ne	thâ	thæt	thâ
Instrumental Case	thî, thê		thi, thê	

Relative Pronoun, Modern "That."

"The" (Indeclinable).

571 Origin of "she," "they," "them," &c.

Just as in Latin *is* and *ille* differ so little that they may be easily interchanged, so in English "he" and "se," both meaning "that man," were interchanged, *e.g.*—

"Ich am *the* (*he*) that spec (spake)." [1]

The interchange of the Feminine forms "heo" and "seo" became so common that "seo" (possibly as being less similar to "he," and therefore less

[1] Morris.

liable to confusion with "he" than "heo") supplanted "heo" in the North, and subsequently also in the South. Hence our "she."

In the same way "thâ" supplanted "hi," and made our "they;" "thâ-m" supplanted "hem," and made our "them;" "thâra" supplanted "hira," and made our "their."

Note also the Instrumental form "thê," which still exists in our "*The* sooner *the* better." See Par. 344.

572   Changes in the Relative Pronoun.

In the First Period "se" was the Definite Adjective, and "the" the Relative. Later,[1] the form "the" came to be used as the Definite Adjective, and consequently ceased to be used as the Relative, being supplanted by the heavier form "that" (the Neuter), which had become the ordinary Relative in the fourteenth century. When the need of a *Possessive and Objective Case* for the Relative was felt, the Possessive and Objective Cases of the Interrogative, "whose" and "whom," were used as early as the thirteenth century; but "*who*" was not common as a Relative till three centuries later. As to the way in which the Interrogative came to be used Relatively, see Par. 27.

[1] In the North, "the" appears early as the Definite Adjective, even in the tenth century.

573 VERBS.

THE VERB "BE."

It is curious to note the multiplicity of *forms*, as compared with the barrenness of *Tenses*, in the old Verb "be." Our modern Verb contains remnants of three distinct roots :—

I. AS (IS).   II. BE.   III. (WAS).

INDICATIVE MOOD.

Presen Tense.

	Singular Number.		Plural Number.	
	I. Root ("as.")	II. Root ("be.")	I. Root ("as.")	II. Root ("be.")
1.	eo-m, ea-m[1]	beo-m, beo	ar-on, sind[2]	beo-th
2.	ear-t	bi-st	ar-on, sind	beo-th
3.	is	bi-th	ar-on, sind	beo-th

Past Tense.

	Singular Number.	Plural Number.
	III. Root "was."	III. Root "was."
1.	waes	waêr-on
2.	waer-e	waêr-on
3.	waes	waêr-on

[1] Our "a-m" is a contraction from "ar-m," or "as-m," where the "as" is the same root as in the Greek "eimi" or "esmi," I "am." The terminations *-m, -t, -s,* are Personal Inflections; so that the Relations between the Original Root "as" and the Modern Verb, are represented in the following column :—

ROOT.	MODERN.
as-m	a-m
as-t	ar-t
as-th	i-s

[2] "Sind" is said to be for *as-ant.* Cf. Latin *s-unt,* also the Subjunctive *si, sin,* below.

Par. 574--576] *"IS," "BE," "WAS."* 313

574

SUBJUNCTIVE MOOD.

Present Tense.

	Singular Number.			Plural Number.		
	Root I. ("as.")	Root II. ("be.")	Root III. ("was.")	Root I. ("as.")	Root II. ("be.")	Root III. ("was.")
1. 2. 3.	sí	beo	wes-e	sí-n	beo-n	wes-e-n

Past Tense.

	Singular Number. Root III. ("was.")	Plural Number. Root III. ("was.")
1. 2. 3.	waer-e	waer-e-n

575

IMPERATIVE MOOD.

	Root I. ("as.")	Root II. ("be.")	Root III. ("was.")
Sing. 2	seo or si	beo	wes
Plur. 2	—	beo-th or beth	wes-ath

576

INFINITIVE MOOD.

Root I. ("as.")	Root II. ("be.")	Root III. ("was.")
—	beo-n or ben	wes-an

Anomalous forms of "Be."

577 *Are.*—Our "are" represents the old Northern "aron," and is therefore a lasting monument of the influence of the Northern dialect.

578 *Be.*—The Southern "be" is now banished from the Indicative (except in vulgarisms), but it is retained in the rare Conditional "if it *be* true."

The retention of *be* in the Subjunctive may be explained by the fact that the Verb *beon* in A.S. from the earliest times had a future force.

Even in Shakespeare and Milton we find a kind of transitional use of "beest" in hypothetical sentences, the *form* "be" being used to denote *hypothesis*, and the *Indicative Inflection* to denote the *truth* of the hypothesis:—

"If thou *beest* he."[1]—*Paradise Lost*, i. 84.
"If thou *beest* Stephano."—*Tempest*, ii. 2, 104.

579 The Indicative "be" in the Plural and in the 1st Person Singular remained in use long after the extermination of the 2nd and 3rd Persons Singular; seemingly because the absence of Inflection assimilated these forms to the Subjunctive (which was spared for the present), and thus

---

[1] Perhaps this use may be in part accounted for by the feeling that "thou," having a Verbal inflection of its own, and a very marked one, ought not to be deprived of it even when the Verb is in the Subjunctive. Compare "wert" below.

allowed them as it were to exist under this disguise.

"Be" in Modern English, as Indicative, is an archaism.

580 *Bi-n*, used by Shakespeare as the 3rd Person Plural of "be," is the Midland form. There are—

(1) *Bes*, Northern.

(2) *Ben*, Midland.

(3) *Beth*, Southern.

581 *Was-t.*—In Early English the 2nd Person Singular Past Indicative of a Strong Verb had *e-* for its Inflection, *e.g.* "thou heold-*e*," and, above, "thou waer-*e*." But in the fourteenth century the Inflection in Strong Verbs was varied with, and finally assimilated to, that of Weak Verbs, *i.e. -est*. Hence "thou heold-*e*" became "thou held-*est*;" and in the same way "thou **were**" became "thou **wast**."

582 *Wert* is even more anomalous than the Conditional "be-est" above. The old Subjunctive form is "were." But, apparently, a sense that the marked Verbal Inflection usually following "thou" ought not to be dispensed with, even when the Verb is in the Subjunctive, led to the construction of a new word, similar to the modern Subjunctive in *form*, and to the modern Indicative in *Inflection*. From this confusion resulted **wert**, which is now established English, so that no one but a pedant would venture to write "if thou *were.*"

The Regular Verb.

It may be useful to compare the scanty Tenses of the Verb in the First Period with the developed Verb as we now have it:—

FIRST PERIOD.

583   Luf-*i*-an = "to love."

INFINITIVE.

Noun Form.   *Form of Purpose (Gerund.)*
lufi-**an**   lufi-**anne**

PARTICIPLES.

Active.   *Passive.*
lufig-**ende**   luf-o-d

INDICATIVE MOOD.

Present and Future Tense.		*Past Tense.*	
Sing.	Plural.	Sing.	Plural.
1. lufig-**e**	lufi-**ath**	1. luf-*o*-de	luf-*o*-den
2. luf-**ast**	lufi-**ath**	2. luf-*o*-dest	luf-*o*-den
3. luf-**ath**	lufi-**ath**	3. luf-*o*-de	luf-*o*-den

SUBJUNCTIVE MOOD.

Present.

Sing. Plural.
1.
2. } lufig-e } lufig-**on**
3.

Past.

Sing. Plural.
1.
2. } luf-*o*-**de** } luf-*o*-**don**
3.

IMPERATIVE MOOD.

Sing. Plural.
2. luf-**a** 2. lufi-**ath**

584 "TO

ACTIVE

		Simple or Indefinite.	Incomplete or Continuous.
			INFINITIVE
		(to) help	(to **be**) helping
			PARTI
		helping	helping
			INDICATIVE
Present Past Future		(he) helps (he) helped (he) **will** (I) **shall** } help	(he) **is** helping (he) **was** helping (he) **will** (I) **shall** } be helping
			OBSOLESCENT SUB
Present		(he) help	(he) **be** helping
			ANTECEDENT CON
Present Past	(if he)	helps helped ² **should** help **were to** help	(if he) { **is** helping **were** helping **should** be helping **were to** be helping

¹ This Verb has been chosen because (if it is to be learned by heart, may oblige the pupil to pronounce distinctly.
² Same as Indicative.
³ Several of these forms are not used. And there is not the least symmetry with which Tenses *might* be constructed with the aid of

HELP."[1]

VOICE.

	Complete.	Complete, Post-Continuous.
MOOD.	(to) **have** helped	(to) **have been** helping
CIPLES.	**having** helped	**having been** helping
MOOD.	(he) **has** helped (he) **had** helped (he) **will** } **have** helped (I) **shall** }	(he) **has been** helping (he) **had been** helping (he) **will** } **have been** helping (I) **shall** }
JUNCTIVE MOOD.	(he) **have** helped	(he) **have been** helping
DITIONAL MOOD.	(if he) { **has** helped **had** helped[2] **should have** helped[2] **were to have** helped	(if he) { **has been** helping **had been** helping[2] **should have been** helping **were to have been** helping[3]

which is quite unnecessary) the difficulty of pronouncing "helped"

use in committing them to memory. But it is useful to see the logical the Auxiliary Verbs.

ACTIVE

	Simple or Indefinite.	Incomplete or Continuous.
		CONSEQUENT CON
Present[1]	(he) **will** / (I) **shall** } help	(he) **will** / (I) **shall** } be helping
Past	(he) **would** / (I) **should** } help	(he) **would** / (I) **should** } be helping
		MOOD OF
Present	(that he) { **may** help	(that he) { **may** be helping
Past	(that he) { **might** help	(that he) { **might** be helping
		IMPERA
	help	be helping

[1] Same as

The Passive Voice is easily formed from the Verb "to be," by placing after it the Passive Participle "helped."

It has no pretensions to be called a Passive "Voice," and would not have been called so but for a desire to ape the terms of Latin Grammar. The Latin Passive Voice has distinctive Inflections, and deserves its name. The English "Voice" is a mere imposture.

VOICE.

Complete.	Complete, Post-Conditional.
DITIONAL MOOD.	
(he) **will** (I) **shall** } **have** helped (he) **would** (I) **should** } **have** helped	(he) **will** (I) **shall** } **have been** helping (he) **would** (I) **should** } **have been** helping
PURPOSE.	
(that he) { **may have** helped **might have** helped	(that he) { **may have been** helping **might have been** helping
TIVE MOOD.	
have helped	—

Future Indicative.

The Infinitive.

The results of the confusion between the Noun Infinitive, the Gerundial Infinitive, the Active Participle, and the Verbal Noun, are so important in their influence on modern English that they deserve special mention. The old forms of the Infinitive mentioned in Par. 551 had been modified as follows :—

Y

322   INFINITIVE, GERUND.   [Par. 586, 587

A.D.	NOUN INFINITIVE.	GERUND, OR INFINITIVE OF PURPOSE.	ACTIVE PARTICIPLE.	VERBAL NOUN.
—1100	-an	(to), anne (-enne)	-ende	-ung
—1250	-en, -e	(to), -ene, -en, -e	-inde	-yng
—1350	(to), -e	(to), -en, -e	-inde. rarely -inge	-yng, -ing
—1500	(to), -e sometimes omitted		usually -ing(e)	-yng, -ing
—1600	(to)		-ing	

586   The law of these changes is not difficult to perceive. (1) The Noun Infinitive has become confused with the Gerundial Infinitive; (2) the Active Participle with the Verbal Noun. In both cases there has been a compromise: (1) the Noun Infinitive has dragged down the Verbal to its own Inflectionless state, but it has also accepted the " to " from the Gerund; (2) the Active Participle has accepted the *termination* of the Verbal Noun, but has communicated to the Verbal Noun, as will be seen below, some of its own *syntactical* peculiarities.

587   While these processes of assimilation were going on, various experimental confusions were introduced and rejected :—

1. The Participle (1) in the twelfth century, in the form *-nde*, (2) in the fourteenth century, in the form *-inge*, invaded the province of the Gerundive; and we find "for *to* witi*ende*," *i.e.* "to guard;" "to wit*inge*," *i.c.* "to wit;" "the night that is to com*yng*," *i.e.* "to come;" "to ber*inge*," *i.e.* (ready) to bear."[1] But in the fifteenth and following centuries these forms died out.

2. In the latter part of the fifteenth century we find an attempt, on the part of the form in *-ing*, to appropriate the province of the Noun Infinitive : "Our lord will yeu*yng* (= yev*en*) hym pardon." But this is both late and exceptional.[1]

But the great and important change was the assimilation of the *syntax* of the Verbal Noun to the *syntax* of the Participle. At first the uses were distinct :—

PARTICIPLE.	VERBAL.
"He *is* hunt*inde*."[2]	"He *went on* hunt*inge*."[2]
"*Lesende* ane finger."	"Up peyn of *losing of* a finger."

While this distinction was preserved, the Verbal Noun was not used (according to Dr. Morris) after "is" or "was," except in *Passive* signification :—

"The churche was *in* byld*ynge*;" "As this was *a* (i.e. *in*, *on*, or *an*) doyng."

---

[1] Morris's *Historical Outlines*, page 177.
[2] So also "He fell on sleep*inge*," but not "he *was* on hunt*inge*," *ib.* p. 177. "Was" and "is" were followed by the Active Participle. But the Active Participle is said to be very rare between 1150—1250 A.D., only occurring twenty-two times in the whole of the earlier text of Layamon, and only eleven times in the later. See Par. 24, *Dissertation on the English Verb*, by Emil Schwerdtfeger, Holt and Co., New York.

But in course of time the two usages became confused.

590 1. Hence, Ben Jonson, *while carefully selecting the (then) archaic termination in -and, with the intention of representing the old Participle, places "of" after it, just as though it were a Verbal Noun:*—

> " With all the *barkand* parish-tikes set at her,'
> While I sat *whyrland of* my brazen spindle."
> *Sad Shepherdess*, i. 2 *ad fin.*

591 2. On the other hand, Shakespeare, while inserting -*a*, as though he were using the Verbal Noun *nevertheless omits "of," using the Verbal just like the Active Participle*, even after "is" and "was" in *Active* signification :—

> " He's *a-birding ;*" " When green geese *are a-breeding.*"
> " The slave that *was a-hanging thee.*" [1]

592 3. Again, sometimes the "of" is inserted, but the *a-* omitted :—

> " The shepherd *blowing of* his nails."

593 4. Again, sometimes both -*a* and "of" are

---

[1] See Schmidt's admirable *Shakespeare Lexicon* for these and many other instances.

omitted, but "the" is inserted, indicating the Noun nature of the word :—

"Nothing in his life
Became him like *the leaving* it."

594 5. Further, to such an extent had the Verbal Noun encroached under the Participial mask, that we not only have the legitimate uses "a *riding*-whip," "a *walking*-stick," but also in Shakespeare and Bacon :—

"A *trembling* contribution," *i.e.* "a contribution that has to do with trembling."
"The *loading* side," *i.e.* "the side that has to do with loading."

These and other idioms give the impression that the Active Participle may be Passively used, *e.g.* that "loading" is put for "laden;" and perhaps this in part explains the apparent use of "seeing" for "it being seen;" "providing" for "it being provided;" "considering" for "it being considered."

595 The modern result of all these confusions is this : our modern Participle often represents a *latent Verbal Noun and an omitted Preposition*, and is therefore used where, in strictness, a Participle could not be used :—

(1) "I shall go (a-) fishing."
(2) "The kettle is (a-) boiling."
(3) (Perhaps) "I saw him (a-) *walking*."

(4) "*Speaking* roughly, there were about a hundred." "In speaking," or "it being spoken," or "to speak."

(5) "(On) *walking* on, you will see the river."

It is not at all unlikely that in (3) and (4) there are also traces of some confusion with the Infinitive, such as is mentioned in Pars. 67, 68, Note 388.

Dr. Morris gives instances of "he fell *to, of, on, a* fighting," which shew the diversity of the Prepositions that may be supplied before the Verbal.

INDEX.

(*For an Explanation of Grammatical Terms, see the Glossary, page* xvii.)

A.

A (adj.), "*a* ten furlongs," 213, 427.
"*a* dozen sheep," "*a* little pudding," &c., 193.
"many *a*," "what *a*," 218.
"a jewel of *a*, what sort of *a*, man," 438.
"*a* Crœsus," 429.
"we are all of *a* mind," 429.
A-, Prefix to Verbal Nouns, 591.
from "on," 375.
"*a*-fishing," "*a*-foot," &c., 127.
"*a*-year," 428.
"*a*-row" for "in a row," 375, note.
"eightpence *a*-pound," "*a*-piece," 343.
Ablative (Absolute), imitated by Milton, 408.
-able, Suffix, 285.
About, "he tells us nothing *about* how he travelled," 454.
Absolute, Subject used absolutely, 135.

Accuse, "I *accuse* him *of* treason," 368.
Active (Form), 59—62.
Addison, his mistake about "who" and "that," 567, Note.
Adjectives, uses and Inflections of, 41—44.
sometimes used as Supplements," 149.
inflected in Chaucer's time, 43, 557.
degrees of comparison, 43.
used for Adverb, 113, note, 522.
used Participially after Nouns, 149.
after Nouns in poetry, 515.
with implied Nouns, 412.
(Clauses) with Relative Pronouns, 497—500.
(Phrases) with Infinitive, 98.
"the *thickest* of the fray," 431.
"heir *apparent*," 431.
Adverbs, 413—20.
uses and Inflections of, 45—54.
Interrogative, how used, 49.

☞ The references are in all cases to the **Paragraphs**, and not to the pages.

Adverbs, repeated, 420.
 used as Nouns, 382, 454.
 in *-e*, old form, 413, 522.
 used like Adjectives with Nouns, 419.
 in *-e*, 557.
 Adjectives used as, 562.
Adverbial Clauses, 455—8.
 Phrases, 340—420.
 Phrases, omit Prepositions, 131.
 Phrases, containing Infinitive, 98.
Against, a Conjunction, 349.
Ago, "five days *ago*," 340.
Agreement of Verb with Noun, 78, 79.
 not true of the Imperative Mood, 91.
 apparently violated, 86.
 violated after "nor," 228, 334.
 violated in use of "none," 227
A-ground, 348, 375.
Albeit, 476.
Almost, "my *almost* drunkenness of heart," 419.
All, "*all of* us," 199, 215, 365.
 "for *all* that," = "though," 475.
All, "*all*-if," like "*although*," 476.
Analysis, scheme of, 265.
 of Sentences, 239—265.
 meaning of, 253.
 Analytical structure of language, 556.
And, "*and* will you leave me?" 440.
 "*and* that, quickly," 441.
 "by *and* by," 441.
-ant and *-ent*, 288.

Antecedent, in Conditional sentence, 167.
Antecedent (of Relative), omitted, 25.
 implied in Possessive Adj., 497.
Apostrophe, when inserted and omitted, 37.
 in '*em*, 569, Note 4.
Apposition, 137—143.
 with implied Noun, 143.
Apposition, with Ind. Obj. and Possess.-Case, rare, 141, 142.
Appositional verbs, 147—150.
Archaisms, Poetical, 502—512.
Are, origin of, 577.
As, radical meaning of, 203.
 used for Rel. Pron., 205.
 vulgar use of, 207.
 parenthetical use of, 208.
 redundant, 209.
 for "that" (Conj.), 480.
 in condensed clauses, 446.
 "so *as*" = "provided that," 461.
 in Early English, 487.
 "*as* far *as* I know," 483.
 "*as*—*so*" = "both—and," 484.
 "*as* good as" but "not *so* good as," 483.
 for "as if," 486.
 "*as* yet;" "*as* then," 487.
 "*as* for;" "*as* to," 364, 489.
 "this will serve *as* ink," 209.
 "*as* if," "*as* though," 211.
 "This is *as* fine a horse *as* I have seen," 493.

☞ The references are in all cases to the **Paragraphs**, and not to the pages.

As, "he was so kind *as* to promise," 479.
provincial, "he says he'll come *as* to-morrow," 438.
"inasmuch *as*," 458.
"*as* far *as*," &c., 53.
"young *as* I am," 464.
"*as* being," 407.
Ascendant, used by Pope as Adj., 228.
Ask, "he *asked* me a question," 119.
"I *was asked* three questions," 122.
"he was *asked* to explain," 103, 105.
Asleep, 348.
At, 350—353.
difference between *at* and "in," 353, 354.
"*at* three years old," 342.
Auxiliary (Verbs) take the old Infinitive, 93—96.
used Conditionally, 170.
used Indirectly, 174.
used in Past Tense after a Past Tense, 180, 181.

B

Be, an Appositional Verb, or Verb of Identity, 147—150.
takes a "Supplement," 148.
old form of, conjugated, 573—576.
in the Indicative, 578—579.
Subjunctive modern, 168, note.
omitted "woe to the man," 519.

Beest, "if thou *beest*," 578.
Ben Jonson used Participle in—*and* before "of," 590.
Better, origin of, 43.
"you had *better*," 386.
"*better* wait a while," 386.
Bin, origin of, 580.
Blue, "the breezy *blue*," 529.
Brackets, when used, 315.
But (Preposition), 380—1.
Radical meaning and uses of, 381.
"'twas none but *he*," 380.
transition to *adversative* use, 452.
But, (Conjunction) put for "that not," 202.
"*but* for," 469.
= "*that* not," rarely as object, 498.
"we did not know *but* that," 450.
"not *but what*," 451.
"*not but* there are, &c," 452.
"it cannot be denied *but*," 453.
"it never rains *but* it pours," 467.
"I'll be hanged *but*," &c. 467.
"there is no one *but* hates me," 468.
"No sooner—*but*," 456.
"I had scarcely gone a mile, *but*," 456.
"he is all *but* perfect,"
"anything *but*," 453.
"*but* for me," 363.
But that, "*but that* he has a family," 468.
"I cannot be persuaded *but that*," 450.

☞ The references are in all cases to the **Paragraphs**, and not to the pages.

By, 355—357.
 "little *by* little," 356.
 "*by* himself," 357.
 "*By and by*," 420.
By and by, change in meaning of, 441, Note.

C

Came, "It *came* to pass," 392.
Cardinal (Numbers), see Glossary.
Cases, 32.
 meaning of term, 33.
Causative (Verbs), "lay," "fell," "raise," "set," &c., 76.
Caxton, his remarks on the English of his time, 82.
 —*ce*, *se*, "licence," "license," 290.
Charge, "I am given in charge," 391.
Celtic terms, 533, 541, 542.
Clause, defined, 239.
Clauses, Subordinate, 444—500.
 Condensed, 444—447.
 Object, 448—454.
 Adverbial, 455—458.
 Conditional, 459—471.
 Concessional, 472—482.
 Comparative, 483.
 (Adjective) with Relative Pronouns, 497—500.
Clear, "*Clear of* debt," 366.
Collective (Noun) with Plur. and Sing. Verb, 337, 338.
Cognate (object), 125.
Colon, 309.
Come, "he *is come*," 62.

Comma, 294.
 general rules for, 294—308.
Complementary (Infinitive), 97
 (Infinitive) as Subject, 106, 107.
Complete the *Complete* "State" of an action, 72.
Complex (Sentence), 250.
Compound (Sentence), 247.
Concessional (Clauses), 472—482.
Condensed (Clauses), 444—447.
Conditional (Mood), 163—180.
 anomalies of, explained, 231—238.
 difference between Mood in Antecedent and Consequent, why, 231—233.
 with "should," 236.
 (Clauses), 459—471.
Conjunctions, 52.
 used with Participles, 407.
 Co-ordinate, 246. note.
 Sub-ordinate, 249.
Considering, Participial Preposition, 409.
Could, "I *could* have," 403.
Course, "*Of course*," 367.
Courtesy, discards "thou," 569.
 substitutes "will" for "shall," 87.

D.

Danish influence on Inflections, 534, 543, 552.
Dare, with and without "to," 96, note.
Dash, used as stop, 314.

☞ The references are in all cases to the **Paragraphs**, and not to the pages.

INDEX. 331

Dative, Early English, 126, 128.
" him " used for Accusative, 554.
Plural in *-um* supplanted, 554.
Dependent, and *dependant*, 288.
Do, original meaning of, 386.
" how *do* you *do*," 386.
"*do* what I may," 474.
Done, "this *done*, they departed," 135.
Doors, " in *doors*," 196, 341.
Doubt, "doubt *not but*," or "*not that*," 453.
Dozen, " a *dozen* sheep," 193.
Distance, " it was a short *distance* off," 340.
Drier, spelling of, 268.

E.

-e final dropped and retained before affixes, 270.
what it represented, 557.
used for *-en*, *e.g.* "broke(*n*)," 558
Each, not with Plural Verb, 224.
"They hated *each* other," 223.
Each other, "*each other* sheds," 530.
-ede, *-eed*, spelling of, explained, 283.
Either, "*either a* or *b was*," not "*were*," 228.
- ive, affix spelling of, 283.
-el, Verbs ending in *-el*, double *l* in Pres. Participle.
Ellipses, see *As, Than, That*, &c.

'em, represents not *them* but *hem*, 569, note 4.
-en, Participial Adjectives in, 558.
Infinitive termination, 94 —96, 585, 586.
-ene, *enne*, Gerundive termination, 585, 586.
Enlargement, of Subject or Object, 263.
English, Periods of, 533—595.
recognized as the National language, 536.
Caxton's remarks on, 82.
Enough, 216.
" kind *enough* to," 397.
Epithet, used for thing denoted, 529.
-er, suffix for Comparative, 43.
Verbs ending in *-er* accented, double *r* in Pres. Part., 277.
Ever, " he was *ever* so ill," 473.
Every, "*every* hundred years," 225.
Exclamation, note of, 313.
Extension (of Predicate), 263.
Extent, Adverbial Phrases of, 340.

F.

Feel, followed by Passive Participle, 260, Note.
Few, " a *few* men," 217.
Foot, " bound hand and *foot*," 128.
For, 358—364.
"*for* a year," "*for* once," 362.
"*for* my part," 364
"*for* shame ! " 359.

☞ The references are in all cases to the **Paragraphs**, and not to the pages.

INDEX.

For, "*for* all," &c. 360.
  "*for* all that"="though," 475.
For to, with Infinitive, 402.
  "'what went ye out *for to* see?'" 402.
Fortnight, derivation of, 214.
Free, "I had rather starve *free*," 113, Note.
French, influence of on position of Adjectives, 431.
  terms, 535, 556.,
  debased, 535.
  later influence of, 539, 549, 565.
  idiom combined with English, 433.
Fresh and fresh, 420.

G

Genders, none in Modern English, 37, Note.
  confused, 554.
Genitive, see *Possessive*, also the Glossary, p. xxii.
Give, "I was *given* to understand," 390.
Gerundial Infinitive, changes in, 554, 585, 586.
"*Governing*" an Object, 84.
Grow, "I *grew* tall," 260, Note.

H

Had, "you *had* better," 386.
Half, "*half* the country," 213.
Hand, "bound *hand* and foot," 128.

Have, "I *have* caught," a Present Tense, 73.
  "I hoped to *have*, could *have*, succeeded," 403.
  "You might *have* helped me," 177.
  "I must *have* you attend," 386.
He, "*He* of Tusculum," 511.
Hear, "I *heard* her sing," 94—96.
Help, "More than I can *help*," 104, Note.
Her, old form of, 569.
Him, old form of, 569.
  for "himself," *i.e.* "the same *him*," 508, 569.
Himself, "by himself," 357, 569.
Home, "go *home:*" sometimes Adverb in E.E., 127.
Honour, or "hon*or*," 284.
  "I have the honour *to* inform you," 395.
Hope, "I *hoped* to have succeeded," 403.
How, "I know not *how* to begin," 398.
  derivation of, 463, Note.
However, derivation of, 474.

I

I, old form of, 569.
  "*I* wis," 561.
-ible, suffix, 285.
Identity, Verbs of, 147—150.
-ieve, affix, spelling of, 282.
If, influence of on Conditional forms, 233.

☞ The references are in all cases to the **Paragraphs**, and not to the pages.

INDEX. 333

If, of admitted facts, 459.
"*if* true," 445.
Imperative (Mood), defined, 70.
  always in Second Person, 88.
  Passive, 89.
  generally omits Subject, 90.
  or Subjunctive, doubtful, 474.
  used to express condition, 462.
Impersonal (Verbs), 328.
In and "at," difference between, 353, 354.
Inasmuch as, 458.
Incomplete, State of action, 72.
Indefinite (Article), see Glossary, *Article* and *Indefinite*.
  state of action, 72.
Indicative (Mood) defined, 70.
  used illogically, 80.
  even after "hope," "fear," &c. 184, Note.
  after "if," illogical, 189.
Indirect Object, 117—120.
  after Passive Verb, 122.
  "retained," 123.
  rarely admits "apposition," 141.
Infinitive (Mood), 92—113, 386—403.
  defined, 70.
  Tenses of, 92.
  preceded by "to," 390—401.
  without "to," 93—96.
  ordinary, in -*ing*, very rare, 587.
  after Adjectives, 108, 393.
  Adjectival use of, explained, 109.

Infinitive, changes in Inflection, 551—559.
  changes table of, 585—586.
  "Complete" after Verbs of hoping, &c., 403.
  as Noun, Adverb, Adjective, 98—100.
  after Nouns, 394, 395.
  Exclamatory, 111.
  in exclamations, 400.
  Parenthetical, 110, 401.
  See "to" for examples.
Inflections, see *Noun, Verb*, &c.
  confused, 553.
  -*ing* represents -*ung*, -*inde*, -*enne*, and perhaps -*en*, 585—588.
Intend, "I *intended* to have come," 403.
Interrogation, note of, 312.
Interrogative, the old, without "do," 507.
  used to express condition, 463.
  (Adverbs) used Relatively, &c., 49.
  (Subjunctive), 472—474.
  "*Do* what I may," 474.
  (Pronoun) supplants Relative, 559, 567.
Intransitive (Verbs), 55—58.
  Verbs followed by "Supplements," 147—149.
Irregularities, how explained, 191—199.
  bred by custom, 213, Note.
  of words, 195—197.
  in poetry, 513—516.
  -*ise* or -*ize*, 289.
It, old form of, 569.
  as Antecedent, 331.
  as Antecedent, "who was *it* that you saw?" 158.

☞ The references are in all cases to the **Paragraphs**, and not to the pages.

It, as Antecedent, "*it* is you that say so," 160.
preparatory, 329.
"*it* was then that," &c., 162, 330.
"*it* is said that he is coming," 151.
"*it* will soon be November," 328.
"*it* pities me," 328.
"*it thinks*" for "*it seems*," 328.
-ize or *-ise*, 289.
-it, Verbs in *-it* accented double *t* in Pres. Part., 277.

K.

Know, "he is *known* to be honest," 107.

L.

Latin, words derived from, 533—548.
Lay, principal parts of, 76.
causative of "lie," 76.
Layamon, texts compared, 555.
Present Participle rare in, 588, Note.
Less than, "thy *less-than* woman's hand," 491.
Lest, derivation of, 482.
followed by "should" instead of "might," 166.
Let, "*let* me see," 88.
"a house to *let*," 109.
Lie, principal parts of, 76.
connected with "lay," 76.
Like, "I *like* a rascal to be punished," 97.
Little, "by *little* and *little*," 191, Note, 356.

-ll, modified before affixes, 275.
Lose, "this will *lose* you your friends," 117.

M.

Make, "they *made* him king," 148.
Many, "*many* a," 218.
May, double meaning of, 170, 175—6.
Methinks, 328.
Might, after "that;" "should," after "lest," 166.
"he *might* have helped me," 172.
"a king, who *might* keep us in order," 185, Note.
different meanings of, 175—6.
Milton, his *dictum* on poetry, 501, Note.
anomalies in, 568.
"than *whom*," 346.
use of Ablative Absolute, 408.
Mine, 197, 569.
Moods, see *Indicative*, &c., 70.
More, used as a Noun.
"he *more than* hesitated," 491.
"some *more* pudding," 219.
"asking for *more*," 221.
My, old form of, 554, 569.

N.

-n final, dropped in Passive Participles, 554, 558.

☞ The references are in all cases to the **Paragraphs**, and not to the pages.

-*n*, dropped in *min* and *thin*, 554, 569.
dropped in Infinitives, 544.
Nam, for "am not," 381.
Nathless, 230.
Naught, 417.
National, the "National" Period of the English Language, 535.
-*ne*, the old -*ne* retained for emphasis in "none," "mine," &c., 197.
Near, derivation of, 197.
Needs, "I must *needs* come," 341.
Negative, before "but," 381.
Neither—nor, followed by Plural Verb for Singular, 33, 228.
Never, "though you were *never* so ill," 473.
"he *never* sees me *that* he does not laugh," 455.
No, Adverbial, 230.
"you are *no* soldier," 230.
"whether he comes or no," 417.
"he slept *no* more," 220.
and "none," difference of use," 229—30.
Nominative Plurals, changes in, 554.
See also *Subject*, and Glossary.
None, for "no," 197, 229.
Singular, 227.
used as Plural, 227.
Adverbial, 229.
Nor, "*nor* yew nor cypress *spread*," for "spreads," 334, also 33, 228.
Norman-French terms, 535, 544.

Northern Dialect, 533—583.
Not, a contraction for "naught," 417.
"*not* but what," 451.
"*not* but," 452.
Notwithstanding, 477.
Nouns, Uses and Inflections of, 30—37.
Plural Inflections of, 34—36.
of the Synthetical Period, 569.
Noun-object, 81.
Noun-phrases, containing Infinitive, 98.
Noun-subject, 81.
Now, "*now* (that) we've come," 444.
Now-a-days, 196, 341.
Numeral (Adjectives), why Irregular, 193—212.
Number, "agreeing *in number*," 78.

O.

Object, 12—20.
meaning of, 13.
different forms of, 15.
"governing an *Object*," 84.
with Verb omitted before "and," 333.
(Indirect), see *Indirect*.
Cognate, 125.
Adverbial, 127—131.
used Absolutely by Milton and Wyckliffe, 408.
(Clauses), 448—454.
before Verb in Poetry, 514.
Of, 365—372.

☞ The references are in all cases to the **Paragraphs**, and not to the pages.

Of, after Participial Verbals, 561, 590.
"all *of* us," 199.
"he is a jewel *of* a man," 438.
"he tells us nothing *of* how he travelled," 454.
"that ugly face *of* his," 432.
"the city *of* London;"
"the cry *of* 'breakers,'" 437.
"*of* a child," 365.
"*of* course," 367.
"light *of* foot," 369.
"to eat *of* the crumbs," 372.
"blowing *of* his nails," 592.
Off, emphatic form of "of," 348.
Old, "ten years *old*," 129.
"at three years *old*," 342.
Olden, 43.
On, 373, 375.
"*on* my honour;" "*on* purpose," 374.
abbreviated to "a," 375.
Once, derivation of, 196.
"at *once*," 196.
One, various uses of, 226.
"their young *ones*," 226.
One, "*one* ... another," 385.
Only, anomalous use of, 45.
Or, "*either* A *or* B *was*," not "*were*," 228.
-or, -our, spelling of, 284.
Other, "no *other* than," 495.
"somehow or *other*," 416.
"they hated each *other*," 223, 385, 530.
Ought, "you *ought* not (to) walk," 561, 93.

Our, old form of, 569.
Ours, 435.
Ourselves, derivation of, 569.
Over, "*over* and *over*," 420.

P.

Paint, "I *painted* my house white," 149.
Parsing, scheme of, 316—325.
Participles, 63—69.
have no tenses, 261.
imply (1) Adverbial, (2) Adjectival Phrases, 261.
Participle Active, table of changes in, 585, 586.
followed by "of," 590.
modern results of old confusions, 595.
confused with Gerundial Infinitive, 554.
in *inge*, 587, 556, 558.
rare in Layamon, 588.
"in consequence o. the king *saying* this," 404.
Participle Passive, 65, 404, 412.
in *-en, -e*, 558.
used as Gerundive, 405.
with implied Noun, 411—412.
with Adverbial Subject, 135.
with Conjunctions, 406—407.
used Absolutely with Subject, 408.
as Preposition, 409.
404, 412.
Passive (Form), 59—62.
(Voice), an imposture, 584.
Verbs, followed by Objects and "Supplements," 147—149.

☞ The references are in all cases to the **Paragraphs**, and not to the pages.

INDEX. 337

Periods, of the English language, 533—595.
Person, explanation of term, 79.
  agreement "in Person," 78.
  Personal endings in Past Tense of Strong Verbs, 581.
  Personal Pronouns, 38, 569.
  see *him, her*, &c.
Phrase, defined, 239.
  Noun Phrases, 240.
  Adjective Phrases, 241.
  Adverbial Phrases, 242.
  Relative, 255.
Pity, "it *pitied* me," 328.
Play, "he *played* me a trick," 119.
Please, "*please* help me," 386.
  "if you *please*," 328.
Pleasure, "I have the pleasure *to* inform you," 395.
Plural, Inflections of Nouns, 34—36.
  (Verbs) with Singular Nouns, 86, 336, 338, 339.
Poetry and Prose, difference between, 500.
  archaic, irregular, terse, 500.
Pope, ungrammatical, 530, 338, Note.
  "*than 'em* all," 346.
Position (of words) irregular in poetry, 513—516.
Possessive Inflection, 37.
  rarely admits Apposition; "William the *Conqueror's* character," 142.

Possessive (Adjective) irregularly used, 432—435.
  "that ugly face of *his*," 433.
  implies Antecedent of Relative, 497.
Predicate, 263.
Prefixes, see *a-* above.
  alter spelling, 275.
Prepositions, 50—51, 349—383.
  original meanings of, 347.
  derived meanings of, 348.
  omitted, 127—131.
  in Adjective Phrases, ambiguous, 436.
  with Adverbs as Objects, 382—383.
  Objects omitted, 384.
  parts of Compound Verbs, 384.
  followed by "that," become Conjunctions, 444.
Present, used for Future, 189.
  used indifferently with Future by Pope, 191.
Presently, change in meaning of the word, 441, Note.
Price, expressed by Adverbial Object, 343.
Pronouns, uses and Inflections of, 38.
  See *Personal, Reflexive, Relative*, &c.
  of the Synthetical Period, 569—572.
Prose and Poetry, difference between, 501.
Punctuation, hints on, 292—315.
Purpose, conjunctions of, 478—482.

☞ The references are in all cases to the **Paragraphs**, and not to the pages.

R.

Rather, " I had *rather*," 386.
Reduplication, of Inflections, 196—197.
Reflexive (Pronoun), 569.
   omitted in Poetry, 508.
Rejoice, "I *rejoiced to* see him," 392.
Relative Pronoun, old form of, 570.
   changes in, 572.
   how to parse, 21—24.
   omitted, 26.
   Antecedent omitted, 25.
   Antecedent implied, 497.
   once Interrogative, 27.
   before Prepositions, 51.
   omitted, as Subject, in poetry, 520.
   implied before Prepositions in Adjective phrases, 436.
   supplanted by Interrogative, 559, 567.
   "the oldest man *that I* know," 497.
   "there *goes a pair that* only *spoil* one another," 338.
   difference between "who" and "that," 567, Note.
   Phrases, 255.
Retained (object), 123.
Result, conjunctions of, 478—482.
Rivers, "the" inserted before, 424.
   omitted before, 523.
Royal, "blood *royal*," 431.
Rung for "rang," 76, 568.

S.

-s in "unawares," "now-a-days," 196.
   in "yours," 197, 434.
Sang and "sung," 76, 568.
Save, "*save* only *he*," 471, Note.
Say, "*say* I fail at first," 462.
   "he is *said* to be coming," 98.
   "*whom say* ye that I am?" 346.
-se, -ce, "license," "licence," 290.
Scotch, use of "will" for "shall," 170, Note.
   "it is *some* late," 222.
See, "I *saw* him *shot down*," 68.
   "I *saw* him *come*," 96.
Seeing, irregular use of, 458.
Self, Selves, 569.
   omitted in poetry, 508.
Semi-colon, 310, 311.
Sentence, defined, 239.
   Simple, 245.
   Co-ordinate, 246.
   Compound, 247.
   Principal, 248.
   Subordinate, 249.
   Complex, 250.
   Contracted, 252.
   see *Clause*.
Shakespeare, anomalies in, 561, 562.
Shall and *will*, distinction between, 87.
   introduced as Auxiliaries, 551.
   originally meant "I owe," "I am bound," 177.
   "John says he *shall* help us," 177.
   "if he *shall* come," 236, 237.

☞ The references are in all cases to the **Paragraphs**, and not to the pages.

INDEX. 339

She, origin of, 569—571.
Should, confused use of, 465.
  after "lest;" "might" after "that," 167.
  used in Antecedent, "would" in consequent, 237.
  different meanings of, 177, 178.
  "John said he *should* help me," 178.
  "It is a shame that I *should* be insulted," 188.
  "*should* I see him," 233, Note.
  "he ordered that no frog *should* croak," 187, Note.
  "if you *should have* taken vengeance," 236, Note.
Short, "they *shouted* applause," 125.
Side, "on this *side* the Tweed," 345.
  "he stood this *side* of me," 131.
Sideways, explanation of, 341.
Since, derivation of, 457.
Singular (Nouns) with Plural Verbs (see *Agreement*), 86, 337, 338.
Smell, "it *smells* of musk," 367.
So, why changed into 'as,' 484.
  "*so as*" = "provided that," 461.
  "he is *so*," 203.
  "*so* as to," 397—204.
  "the prince (for *so* he was)," 414.
  "a minute or *so*," 415.
Some, "*some* more pudding," 219.
  "*some* twenty men," 222.
  "it is *some* late," 222.

Something, "*something* good," 430.
Sometimes, explanation of, 341.
Songster, 197, Note.
Sorry, "I was *sorry* to see it," 393.
Sort, "what *sort* of a man," 438.
Spelling, hints on, 266—291.
  influenced by pronunciation, 267, 271, 273.
  influenced by earlier or later introduction of words, 36, 283, 284.
-ster, old Feminine termination, 37, Note, 197.
Stops, 292, 293.
Strong Verbs, assimilated to Weak Verbs, 581.
Subject, 1—11.
  omitted, 6.
  position of, 8—10.
  different forms of, 11.
  with Verb, omitted before "and," 333.
  Adverbially used with Participle, 135.
  used with the Infinitive, 400.
  repeated, 513.
  placed after Verb, 514.
  in Parenthesis, 335.
Subjunctive (Mood), 163—190.
  defined, 70.
  used Indefinitely, 188.
  quasi-Interrogatively, 472.
  Tenses of, 189.
  Anomalies of, explained, 231—238.
  of "be," 579.
  of Purpose, after "pray," "beseech," 167.

☞ The references are in all cases to the **Paragraphs**, and not to the pages.

Subjunctive (Mood) in Poetry,
to express a wish, 504.
old form of, 505.
in Poetry, after "ere,"
till, 506.
"*Do* what I may," 472.
"*Come* who may," 473.
Subordinate Clauses (see *Sentence*), 444—500.
Such, "*such* a," 218.
"let *such* teach others *who* themselves excel," 486.
Suffixes, see *-ster, -ible, -en*, &c.
Sung and *sang*, 76, 568.
Superlatives, how formed, 43.
"the oldest man *that* I know," 497.
Supplement, follows "be," "seem," "appear," "appoint," "make," &c., 147—148.
sometimes Adjective, 149.
Sure, "*to* be sure," 110, 401.
Sword, "*sword* in hand," 136.
Synthesis, meaning of, 253.

T.

Talking, "*talking* of books, here is a book," 410.
Teach, Object after, 117.
Tell, "to *tell* you the truth," 110, 401.
Tenses (see *Present*), 71—75.
Than, explained, 252, 493.
"who else *than*," 496.
"he *more than* hesitated," 491.
"no other *than*," 495.
"thy less *than* woman's hand," 491.

Than, "*than* me" for "*than* I," "*than* whom," 346.
"There is no counsel better *than* John has given," 493.
That (Rel. Pron.), supplanted by "who," 559, 567.
Early English use of, 499.
for "as," 206.
for "so that," 521.
omitted as Subject, 201.
omitted after "than," 494.
= "on account of which," 499.
"the oldest man *that* I know, 497.
"not *that* I recollect," 449.
That (Conj.) for "so *that*," 478.
omitted after "in case," &c., 459.
"so *that*" = provided that, 460.
omitted, meaning "when," 444.
"on the day *that* thou eatest thereof," 444.
"He never sees me *that* he does not mock me," 455.
"the axiom *that*," &c., 448.
"I am sorry *that*," 449.
"*That* it should come to this!" 447.
"What were you doing *that* you were late?" 457.
"I cannot be persuaded but *that*," &c., 450.
"But *that* he has a family," 468.
old form of, 570.

☞ The references are in all cases to the **Paragraphs**, and not to the pages.

INDEX. 341

That (Conj.) omitted in Poetry, 523.
The, 421—429.
"*the* sooner *the* better," 344, 490, 571.
"*the* leaving it," 593.
"during *the* first and second centuries," 426.
"*the* earth," "*the* astronomer Adams," 421.
"*the* classical Addison," 423.
"*the* Rupert of debate," 424.
"*the* Thames, Chilterns, Levant, Rigi," 424.
Thee, "it is *thee* I fear," 346.
Their, old form of, 569.
Them, old form of, 569, 570.
origin of, 571.
spelt '*em*, 569, Note 4.
Then, "the *then* world," 419.
There, preparatory, "*there* was once a boy," 151.
They, old form of, 569, 570.
origin of, 571.
Thi, a Case of "the" in "*the* sooner *the* better," 571.
Think, "we *thought* her foolish," 149.
"where it *thinks* best," 32.
Thine, 569.
This, "*this* day three months," 340.
Thou, old form of, 569.
followed by Verbal Inflection in -*e*, 581.
replaced by "you," 569, Note 5.
Though, "*though conquered*," 407.
"as *though*," 211.
Thy, 569.

Till, once used of space, 376
Time, Adverbial Phrases of, 340.
To, 377—379.
used before Infinitives, 554, 556.
used irregularly, 561.
omitted or inserted, 93—96, 386—389.
after Intr. Verbs of feelings, 392.
after Verbs of the senses, 388.
after Verbs of asking, 105.
after "than," 389.
"pleasant *to* see," 108.
"he was ordered *to* come," 107.
"water *to* drink," 110.
"willing *to* help," 104, Note.
"*to* think that he should say so," 111.
"*to* tell you the truth;"
"*to* be sure," 110, 401.
"I know not *how to, whether to*," &c., 398.
"I have no object for which *to* strive," 399.
"he was the first *to* come," 393.
"give me your promise *to* obey," 394.
"be kind enough *to* excuse me," 397.
"Where *to* begin!" 398.
"I call God *to* witness," 377.
"I have the pleasure *to* inform you," 395.
"*to* all appearance," 378.
"he is said *to* be coming," 98.
"nothing *to* do," 109.

☞ The references are in all cases to the **Paragraphs**, and not to the pages.

To-day, 379.
Transitive (Verbs), 55, 58.

U.

—*um*, Early Dative Inflection, 126, 128.
Unawares, 196.
Understand, "I was given to understand, 390.
—*ung*, for -*ang* in Milton and Pope, *e.g.* "sung," 76, 568.
Unless, derivation of, 466.
Upon, 373—5.
"*upon* my word," 374.
Upwards, "*upwards* of ten years," 365.
Use, "we *used* to walk," 104, Note.
Utopia, More's spelling in, 267.

V.

Verbs, see *Transitive*, *Strong*, *Weak*, &c.
  old, conjugated, 573, 583.
  modern, conjugated, 584.
  agreement of, see *Agreement*.
  Negative and Interrogative form of, 77, 381.
  emphatic form of, 77.
  of seeing, feeling, hearing, &c., 68.
  of Motion, used Passively, 62.
  of asking, commanding, &c., followed by "to," 105.
  made from Nouns, 532.
  Plural for Singular, 22 88, 334—339.

Verbs, omitted after "if," "though," &c., 445.
  omitted in poetry, 518, 519.
Verbal Noun, 54.
  confused with Participle, 585—94.
  counterfeits a Passive Participle, 594.
  preceded by "a" 591.
  preceded by "the," 593.
  used after "went," "fell," &c., but not after "is," "was," except in Passive signification, 588, 589.
Very, "your *very* looks betray you," 430.
Void, "*void* of," 366.
Vowels, assimilated, 553.
  changed in Plurals of Nouns, 36—553.
  changed in Strong Verbs. *See* Glossary, "Strong."

W.

Wait, he "waited an hour," 131.
Was, "If I *was* you," 168, Note.
Wast, 581.
Way, "he came the shortest *way*," 131.
Weak Verbs, *see* Glossary, and 581.
Week, *month*, &c., "this day *week*," 340.
Well, as Conjunctional Adverb, 418.
Were, Subjunctive, 168, note. "if he *were* to," 189.
Were, for "wast," 581.
Wert, anomalous, but now correct, 582.

☞ The references are in all cases to the **Paragraphs**, and not to the pages.

INDEX. 343

What, how used Relatively, 27—8.
    used in dependent questions, 28.
    "*what* with—*what* with," 442.
    "not but *what* he meant mischief," 451.
    "*what a*," 218.
When, "*when* walking," 406.
Whence, supplanted by "where from," 383.
Where, "from *where ?*" 454.
    "I know not *where* to begin," 398.
Where-to, for whither, 382.
Whether, once Interrogative, 463.
    used as Co-ord. Conjunction, 443.
Which, for modern "as" in Shakespeare, 206.
    "I have no money with *which* to buy food," 398.
    "*which a*," 218.
While, "*while* walking," 406.
Whither, supplanted by "where-to," 384.
Who, how used Relatively, 27.
    used in dependent questions, 28.
    three centuries later than "whose" as a Relative, 572.
    for "he that," 509.
Whom, "*whom* say ye that I am?" 346.
Why, as Conjunctional Adverb, 418.
    derivation of, 463, Note.
Will and *shall*, distinction between, 87.
    "I *will*"="I shall willingly," 173.

Willing, "*willing to* wound and yet afraid *to* strike," 104, note.
Wis, "I *wis*," 561.
Wit, "to *wit*" 401.
With and with, 420.
Without, for "unless," 470.
Worth, followed by Object, 129.
Would, different meanings of, 177—8.
    used in Consequent "should" in Antecedent, 237.
    ="used to," 179.
    "O that he *would*," 185, Note.
    after "prayed," "besought," &c., 167, 185, Note.
    "I wish he *would* come," 465.
    "He thought he *would* take a walk," 173.
    Scotch use of for "should," 170, Note.
Wyckliffe, 408, 558.

Y.

—*y*, changed in passing from Sing. to Plur., 267.
Ye, old form of, 569.
    once only used as Subject, 38.
You, substituted for *thou*, 569, note 5.
    substituted for *ye*, 38.
Your, old form of, 569.
    old use for "yours," 435.
    "this of *yours*," 434.
Yourn, origin of, 435.
Yourselves, derivation of, 569.

☞ The references are in all cases to the **Paragraphs**, and not to the pages.

WORKS BY THE SAME AUTHOR.

Seventeenth Thousand.　Small 8vo.　2s.
HOW TO TELL THE PARTS OF SPEECH.
AN INTRODUCTION TO ENGLISH GRAMMAR.

Fourteenth Thousand.　Crown 8vo.　4s. 6d.
ENGLISH LESSONS FOR ENGLISH PEOPLE.
By the Rev. E. A. ABBOTT, D.D., and Prof. SEELEY, M.A.

Twenty-Ninth Thousand.　Small 8vo.　1s. 6d.
HOW TO WRITE CLEARLY.
A GUIDE TO ENGLISH COMPOSITION.

Twenty-Second Thousand.　16mo.　2s. 6d.
LATIN PROSE THROUGH ENGLISH IDIOM.
WITH SYLLABUS OF THE NEW LATIN PRONUNCIATION.

SEELEY, JACKSON, AND HALLIDAY, 54, Fleet Street, E.C.

Eleventh Thousand.　Extra fcap. 8vo.　6s.
A SHAKESPEARIAN GRAMMAR.
LONDON: MACMILLAN AND CO.

www.ingramcontent.com/pod-product-compliance
Lightning Source LLC
Chambersburg PA
CBHW020302240426
43673CB00039B/676